THAT DAY'S STRUGGLE

EDITED BY CAITRIONA LAWLOR

Seán MacBride

That Day's Struggle

A Memoir 1904-1951

CURRACH
PRESS

First published in 2005 by
CURRACH PRESS
55A Spruce Avenue, Stillorgan Industrial Park, Blackrock, Co. Dublin

www.currach.ie

1 3 5 4 2

Cover by Anú Design
Index by Therese Carrick
Origination by Currach Press
Printed by ColourBooks Ltd, Dublin

The editor has asserted her moral rights.

ISBN 1-85607-929-5

CONTENTS

LIST OF ILLUSTRATIONS

PREFACE

Seán MacBride wrote this memoir in the 1970s, first recording his recollections in chronological order and then carefully checking and editing the transcript. The text was prepared by 1976. When I worked with him he returned to the manuscript finalising and checking.

As editor I have taken care to respect the integrity of the memoir in style and substance. My work has been to check the text, supplying factual information where this was implied by the author and remove duplication. This involved checking details against the archival collection, providing additional factual information, providing some dates, full names, or other references mentioned *en passant*.

The aim of editing the text in this way was to allow the memoir to speak to the reader, much as its author intended. Seán MacBride had both a clear memory for recall and one disciplined from the earliest by a liberal education and studies in law, practising at the Bar through to the 1980s. His sense of chronology, his recall of detail and the information he brought have all contributed to make this memoir unusual in providing a picture of events and people, as he saw them at the time, rather than with the benefit of hindsight.

Mindful of the growing interest in Seán MacBride's role during the first half of the twentieth century, I decided to release for publication his memoir, which, though incomplete, covers this period of MacBride's life. My decision to do so at this time is for the following reasons:

a) There has been no accurate in-depth chronological account of MacBride's contribution to the development of this nation;

b) The centenary of his birth signalled renewed curiosity about this remarkable Irishman, whose first independent action was to join the movement to free his country from oppression by force, and who later became an outstanding advocate of the Rule of Law.

That Day's Struggle presents a first-hand account of Seán MacBride's early life in Paris, his return to Ireland, and his friends in the republican movement. His experiences either in jail or 'on the run' are recounted, and we are treated to his reminiscences concerning incidents in which he was involved. This is the story of a life spent as a republican, a prisoner, a journalist, lawyer, and a politician.

Following upon his career in domestic politics, Seán MacBride played an important role globally; he was a founder-member of Amnesty International and Chairman of the International Executive from 1961 until 1974. He was appointed Secretary General of the International Commission of Jurists, Geneva, and remained in the post from 1963 until 1970. Very close to his heart was the work of the International Peace Bureau, also in Geneva; he became Chairman from 1968 until 1974, and President of the Executive from 1974 until his death. He also chaired the Special NGO Committee on Human Rights from 1968 to 1974, he was a Vice-President of the World Federation of United Nations Associations (WFUNA), and in 1973 he was elected by the General Assembly of the UN to the post of United Nations Commissioner for Namibia.

In 1974, Seán MacBride was awarded the Nobel Peace Prize in Oslo. He used his share of the award to translate, print and distribute the *Bradford Peace Proposals* which were published by the International Peace Bureau (IPB) in all the languages of the United Nations. MacBride returned to Ireland late in 1976, but suffered a personal blow in November that year when his wife, Catalina (Bulfin), died.

The Director General of UNESCO appointed MacBride Chairman of the prestigious International Commission for the Study of Communication Problems in 1977 at the age of 73. This involved a punishing workload, a lot of travelling, and the publication in 1980 of *Many Voices, One World*. Throughout this period Seán MacBride maintained his contacts with an array of Irish organisations and undertook many engagements at home and abroad. His love of trees, the inland waterways, the railway network, his appreciation of indigenous industry, his love of country, coupled with his abhorrence of partition and misrule, all combined to make MacBride probably the most unusual Irishmen of his era.

His father, John MacBride, a native of Westport, was educated in St Malachy's College, Belfast, and was shadowed by detectives for years prior to his emigration in May 1896, as 'a dangerous nationalist'. On his arrival in South Africa, MacBride Senior immediately organised the Irishmen of Johannesburg and Pretoria into National Associations. His main achievement was the establishment of the Transvaal Irish Brigade on the outbreak of the Boer War. On 1 October 1899, in Von Brandis Square, Johannesburg, the same day that thousands of Irish supporters met in Beresford Square, Dublin, the Brigade enlisted and selected their officers. The Transvaal Irish Brigade 'took part in twenty battles and nearly three times that number of skirmishes', according to Major MacBride, and lost about 80 men until it finally disbanded at Komati Poort. The Irish Brigade neither received nor expected payment – Major MacBride holding that the mercenaries were all on the other side.

Two years before they married, John MacBride and Maud Gonne embarked together on a lecture tour of America which lasted for several months, during which they spoke in 48 cities. Much media coverage was given to the anti-recruitment element of their talks, which I am sure was not forgotten when Major MacBride was court-martialled and executed for his role in the Easter Rising of 1916. His son was 12.

By the time Seán MacBride was 17, he was already immersed in the defence of prisoners, and his experiences confirmed his impression that military courts, juntas, and indeed ordinary civilian courts in the judicial process were very unreliable, capital punishment was most fallible, and the death sentence should never be carried out. For seven decades he concerned himself with the situation surrounding those in prison and the circumstances of their detention, no matter what jurisdiction they were in. On one occasion, I arranged to meet him in Paris, only to find that he had been secretly dispatched to Iran in an attempt to negotiate for the release of the fifty-three American hostages taken in November 1979. The sense of responsibility which gave rise to this initiative showed itself again and again, not least during those terrible days of the

Maze hunger strike in 1981, the first time I saw him cry.

One of the most appealing aspects of Seán MacBride's personality was, I always felt, his ability to treat people equally, and to give of his best to his audience, be it a high-powered international gathering, or a school meeting. With him at Presentation College, Athenry in springtime 1984, I was particularly conscious of this – the intensity of his contribution, the youthfulness of his audience, the calibre of their questions, the respect in which he held them, and the stillness as they listened to every word.

To some, he appeared arrogant; that was never my impression. The MacBride I knew developed an even keener sense of humour as time passed by; coupled with this was a steely determination to see things through. And so, there follows the partly told story of a driven man – focussed and intense, who managed to make a difference.

Caitriona Lawlor
March 2005

CHAPTER I

Formative Years • *Paris*
London • *Ireland*

At the time of my father's execution and of the 1916 Rising, I was at school in Paris. I had started school at the Ecole St Louis de Gonzague in 1911 and the Rector, who because of the war had been making daily announcements as to casualties related to the schoolboys, also announced the death of my father 'who had been executed by the British for fighting for the freedom of his country'. Communication with my father was mostly by way of a written correspondence during those years. Our household consisted of Mother, Iseult, myself, and our governess, M. Barry O'Delaney, poet and writer. Our holidays were spent in Colleville-sur-Mer and Evian. We also had a trip to Frascati and Rome during Easter 1911 where we had an audience with Pope Pius X. We attended Mass, celebrated by the Pontiff early next morning, with some first communicants and the Vatican household. My visit to Rome on this occasion was the start of a lifelong affection for the city.

From the time of my father's execution, Mother was making constant efforts, as she had made at the beginning of the war, to get back to Ireland. However, she was refused a passport by the British. She used to haunt the British Embassy in Paris to try and get a passport and finally she was given one as far as London on condition that she would not come to Ireland. There were no separate passports for Ireland at the time; they were all British. When we got to London — I would say it was the end of 1916 or the beginning of 1917 — we took a house in

King's Road, Chelsea. Chelsea in those days was not as fashionable a place as it is now. The house was a redbrick house over a shop. As far as I remember, the name of the shop was King, and it always struck me as odd that there should be a King living on King's Road. It was between the Chelsea Town Hall and a cinema which was farther down King's Road towards Battersea.

We lived a type of double-life most of the time in London. On the one hand, Mother kept contact with her family, particularly an uncle called Arthur Gonne and also Miss Chotie Gonne, a nice old lady who was fond of me. Arthur was much stiffer. I can't remember whether Mother's sister was still alive then or not. Certainly, if she was alive, she was not in London. Probably she was in Switzerland as she suffered from TB and spent a lot of her life in Davos. She had been staying with Mother before that at the beginning of the war. The other side of our lives were the contacts which Mother had developed with Patricia Lynch, who was a great friend of Helena Malony's — Mother and Helena Malony were bosom friends. Patricia Lynch was just beginning to write children's stories, usually about donkeys. Later she married Dick Fox, who was a journalist and a writer and who wrote a number of books on socialism. At that stage Patricia was not married and was working very closely with the Pankhursts, Sylvia in particular. Sylvia Pankhurst had a journal, I've forgotten whether it was weekly, fortnightly or monthly. Mother became involved in writing for it on Irish politics and things happening in Ireland.

During that whole time, Mother was trying to think of ways and means for getting back to Ireland. Since the first day of our arrival in London, indeed on our arrival at Waterloo Station, we were escorted by a number of detectives. There were two Scotland Yard men stationed day and night outside the house in King's Road, which caused great concern indeed to our Mr King, the landlord. He did not know whether to approve or disapprove of tenants who were under full police surveillance in London in those war days; war, remember, was still at its full height. There were air raids almost every night. I remember seeing a Zeppelin over London and going out often to watch the fireworks, the shootings and the bombings. Mother suffered from rheumatism and indeed used to go to Dax for treatment. In

London she gradually developed the habit of going to the Turkish baths at regular hours, on regular days, in the evenings I think on two or three nights a week. She then conceived the scheme that she would go to the Turkish baths and then leave very shortly afterwards. So she built up absolute regularity about her Turkish bath hours and I was given the job of following the two detectives. I watched what the detectives were doing while Mother was having a Turkish bath. Naturally I enjoyed doing this a great deal; it was a very thrilling game and I found within a short space of time that after Mother went into the Turkish baths, which lasted roughly two and a half hours, the Scotland Yard men went into a public house and stayed there for a couple of hours. When it was time for her to leave, they came out to pick up the trail again. I verified this on a number of occasions.

When the day was fixed for leaving London, elaborate plans were made. The plan was that Mother would be dressed up as a very old woman. Mother had acted a good deal, Sylvia Pankhurst and Patricia Lynch helped in the plot, and organised a beautiful white wig and a dirty old coat. Mother was then very straight and it was a question of disguising her height as well as everything else. When 'D day' came, she went to her bath as usual but emerged 30 minutes later, while the two Scotland Yard men were in the pub. Patricia Lynch and Sylvia Pankhurst picked her up. She put on her wig, changed her clothes, disguised herself and went on the Irish Mail that left at 9.40 at night. She arrived safe and sound in Dublin, without having been detected. I stayed behind and saw the Scotland Yard men looking very disconsolate, walking around the place for a couple of days. Then they disappeared. Mother's arrival of course had not been unnoticed in Dublin. I think that the authorities must have decided at that time not to arrest her as it would create too much of a sensation.

In the meanwhile it had been arranged that when I received a letter or postcard or a certain signal, I was to go to Dublin. I was to stay with Dr Kathleen Lynn who was very much involved in the Sinn Féin movement in those days, and with Madeleine Ffrench-Mullen. Madeleine Ffrench-Mullen met me at the boat and I went to stay at Dr Lynn's house which was at 9 Belgrave Road, Rathmines. I stayed there for ten days or so, until it appeared that Mother was not to be arrested.

She then took rooms in North Great Georges Street. It was one of those huge redbrick Georgian houses. It was cold, bleak, and miserable. We stayed there while Mother was looking for a house.

It had originally been decided that I would go to school in St Enda's, Pearse's school. This was before the 1914 war broke out. Indeed, one of my earlier recollections is of being brought out to St Enda's by Mother and meeting Pádraig Pearse. They had a long discussion, first of all about my schooling, what courses, languages I should do and what education I should receive. Then the conversation was mainly about Irish politics. I don't remember it well beyond references to Sir Roger Casement. I had known Roger Casement fairly well as a child, because when passing through Paris, he used usually try to visit our house. I was always impressed by this tall, gaunt figure with a beard. He was always very nice to me and patted me on the head. I was also enthralled by him because the subject of discussion between Mother and Roger Casement was usually about shipping lines. Mother and Casement had conceived the idea that it was absolutely essential that some non-British liners should call to Ireland. At that period all the shipping lines calling into Ireland were British companies, either the White Star Line, now defunct, or the Cunard Line. Mother had made several attempts to get the French Compagnie General de Transatlantique to call, but this had not worked. They wanted to have non-British ships calling in, for political reasons, so that people could travel in and out without difficulty, without reports going to the British. The British companies, in addition, were there mainly to encourage emigration and the ships were used by the emigrants. The services were very bad, and they also believed this prevented Americans from coming to Ireland. So this scheme must have been conceived by Mother and Roger Casement some time back, but I remember well that he was having discussions with the Hamburg-America line in Germany in an attempt to get them to call. This was of course before World War I. I remember on one occasion — it must have been the last occasion in which he was in Paris — that he predicted there would be a war. He said that the situation was serious and that things were shaping like a war. Mother and he discussed at great length what would happen in Ireland if there was a war.

Other friends also used to call in often, and indeed, in London too,

W. B. Yeats and James Stephens, who was a great friend of Mother's and of mine. He was awfully kind to me. When I was in Paris at school, he used to take me out for a whole day. I used to collect stamps and the day consisted of bringing me to a stamp shop. I was allowed to buy any stamps I wanted. I was always troubled for fear the stamps I had chosen were too expensive but he used to tell me to forget about the prices and just take the stamps I wanted. The day would end up in Rumpelmeyer's in Rue de Rivoli where they had marvellous cakes made from chestnuts, whipped cream and meringues. James Stephens didn't eat them, but he would chuckle away while I was having them, enjoying it no end. But certainly it was a red letter day in my childhood.

However, I have been digressing from North Great Georges Street and my going to school. I don't remember at what stage it was decided to send me to school in Mount St Benedict. Finally I was sent there because it was a Benedictine school. The Abbot, the director of Mount St Benedict, was Father Sweetman, who was a strong nationalist and was involved with Sinn Féin. Old John Sweetman had been one of the first presidents of Sinn Féin in the old days and the Abbot of Mount St Benedict was a brother of his. I think he was much more extreme politically than old John Sweetman had been. He ran this very good school outside Gorey. I met the O'Rahillys, Mac and Aodhagán, who were at school there, and also James and Brian Dillon, Cecil Lavery and Cecil Salkheld. I had a good time at that school on the whole, rather unfairly. On the plea that I knew French well, I didn't attend French classes. On the plea that I knew more mathematics than the other boys, I could skip some of the mathematics classes. French schooling had been tough and thorough. I then engaged part of my time running telegrams for the post office, which was at the gate lodge of the school. It was also the tuck shop. Whenever a telegram came, a rare occasion, once a week or so, I would deliver the telegram at the rate of threepence a mile on my bicycle and used the proceeds to buy more tuck. The post office had it both ways, to a certain extent, and I also had it both ways.

We did all the usual subjects, including Irish, laboriously, English literature, and mathematics. The education was regarded as being good, liberal and broad. The teachers were interested and we had an especially good course in English literature. We were encouraged to read. I had a pair of ferrets and I used to catch rabbits with the ferrets. I used to get sixpence from Fr Sweetman for catching rabbits for the school. However this didn't last very long; either it took me too much time or was too much trouble. Incidentally, this is where I first met Máire Comerford. Máire Comerford was only a slip of a girl at that time who was assisting Miss Keogh, the house mistress, or matron. We all had rooms. I shared with Cecil Salkheld.

There were woods about, and at the beginning of the term we marked out trees. We were given one tree each to cut down and saw up for fires in our rooms. We had to plant six trees, I think, for every tree we burnt.

It was that kind of a liberal education. Also the 'Holy Man' as we used to call Fr Sweetman, used to come in for chats with us. He was a very strong, dominant personality. He used often invite six or eight of us up to his own study at night where he had a blazing fire and he puffed away at tobacco which was grown on the school grounds. The school itself extended over a couple of hundred acres and he grew quite large quantities of tobacco, called Bally Owen tobacco. He made cigarettes. While in theory we were not allowed to smoke, it was understood that if we smoked Bally Owen tobacco, nothing would be said. But, if he once got a whiff of any other cigarette – he could smell out tobacco smoke anywhere – he would be very cross. I used not smoke anything, so it didn't worry me. He had strong, republican, nationalist Irish views … a little bit of a mixture in a way, because he encouraged us to play cricket always. Cricket was regarded as a 'West British' game. They didn't play Gaelic at all, though of course this was the early days of the GAA. Fr Sweetman had spent a lot of time, before coming to Mount St Benedict, in Downside, and had probably adopted the British habit of playing cricket, and so on. But he was strong nationally, and indeed, a short time before I left, a number of us mounted an attack on a local police station. The attack consisted of matches which we had carefully put into metal pipes. We had a nail and also keys, which made explosions like shots. In the dead of night, we slipped out, five or six of us, and we banged these all around the unfortunate RIC station. Everything was closed tight and they didn't move; they thought it was a real attack. We had been 'playing soldiers' if you like. Although we had no guns, we made explosions from the heads of matches we had saved up. It made a noise in the whole locality. The police were up at the school afterwards and the Holy Man denied all knowledge of it, though he knew perfectly well that we had done it. He was chuckling away to himself about it, not exactly encouraging us but more or less saying 'about time somebody put the RIC out of this country'.

After my stay in Mount St Benedict, I was in Dublin, and took lessons in Latin, Irish and English literature from George Erwin. He was a Protestant and as I found afterwards, a captain in an IRA company in the Irish Volunteers. So his views were, quite sharp, though his influence was very good. He was a charming man who lived in Mount Pleasant Square. I used to go there and spend all day; I learned quite a lot from him. Any Irish I learned, I learned from him at that time. I had had lessons in Irish from early childhood. I also had a few lessons from Claud Chevasse in Galway. Mother had decided that I should learn Irish; she didn't know Irish herself very well. I remember the attempts; I can see them still, an Irish Grammar, an Irish book, and my mother going over various bits of Irish with me. What I remember more was that every day she would read Irish history from some big book, about two or three inches thick, I've often wondered who it was. She read all kinds of things about the Firbolgs and so on. But then I learned a lot of Irish history from George Erwin. We went from the Treaty of Limerick through to every episode which is a nationalist feature in Irish history.

There were several people who influenced my life early on in regard to the Irish nationalist revolutionary movement. On the one hand there was Mother, who taught me a lot of Irish history, culture and fairy tales, Ella Young, who was a frequent visitor and stayed with us, and of course Helena Malony. Then there was James Stephens, who was a marvellous storyteller. He used to tell me stories about the Fenians and the Invincibles, and about Cú Chulainn. He had a great impact on me. There was Fr Sweetman, who usually used to emphasise some aspect of the Irish struggle for independence during the talks in his study on the wintry evenings. In addition, George Erwin undoubtedly had a lot of influence on me. He was a strong nationalist, an Ulsterman and a Protestant. He concentrated a lot on Wolfe Tone, the 1798 Rising and that period ... republicanism, out and out republicanism. He was an officer in the IRA at the time and later on, I think, became Commandant of the 5th Battalion in Dublin.

During all this period, I wanted to get into the IRA. It was all very well to go to school and to play schoolboy pranks. The country was beginning to seethe. Arrests, ambushes and events were taking place the whole time. I used to read the newspapers avidly. I had formed a close friendship with Laurence Ginnell and his wife. They used to come to the house, and I visited theirs. I helped them with election work. I was very impressed with Laurence Ginnell; he was an MP who had left the Nationalist Party and remained in Westminster. He fought like a tiger on his own, single-handedly for a long period in Westminster. He was disapproved of by the Irish Party. He always dressed impeccably with a tall hat and long tails. A lawyer who had written some books on the Brehon Laws, he was very cultured, but irascible when it came to any questions relating to Ireland. He used to be thrown out of the British House of Commons for making speeches and refusing to sit down when called upon. I saw Laurence Ginnell a great deal.

Con Markievicz was in and out of the house quite a lot of the time. She stayed with us and was very much involved with the Fianna at the time. Through her I met a number of people in the Fianna. In another contact, at that period, I had a decisive link with the Fitzgeralds. The Fitzgeralds were a family who lived in Great Brunswick Street, now Pearse Street. They had a small shop and the father and sons did contracting work, painting work. By this time Mother had got a house in St Stephen's Green and they were doing the decorating in the house. I became very friendly with them when they were working in the house. One of them had a small garage where he used to tinker with cars. I got into the habit of going around with them. They were all in the 'B' Company of the 3rd Battalion. However, before joining the IRA, I joined the Fianna. First of all George Erwin had said that I couldn't join the IRA but I could join the Fianna; he probably suggested that I should talk to Constance Markievicz about it. He knew she was very friendly with Mother. And so I joined the Fianna and this was known to Mother. She didn't disapprove of it at all.

The Fianna was a boy scout organisation. The Commander of the Dublin Brigade of the Fianna was Barney Mellows, a brother of Liam. The object of the Fianna was 'Cú Chulainn' again: to train people for the IRA. It was a training ground and recognised as such, though denied officially. We had meetings in a place called Skippers Alley, off the quays between Fleet Street and the quays. There was a dingy hall there where we would meet and drill. There were also lectures on bits of Irish history. Madame Markievicz used to come and speak, as did Barney Mellows. The drilling included forming fours, and other military drills, barrack square drills. We also went on camping expeditions up the Dublin Mountains. We left on Saturday and would be back on Sunday night. It was quite good fun, with the added thrill that the RIC was always chasing us. We used to be very disappointed if the RIC or the military didn't arrive at some stage of our camping expedition to chase us all away again. However, this became fairly dull. I looked a lot older than I was and I decided to transfer myself. Being in the Fianna, it was fairly easy to get into the IRA; it was a good introduction.

I had some difficulty in getting clearance from the Fianna because I was under age; in 1918, I must have been fourteen. With the help of the Fitzgeralds, who were linked both with the Fianna and with the IRA — there were a good few boys — through Jim Fitzgerald, I transferred into 'B' Company 3rd Battalion. Leo Fitzgerald brought me along. He was a squad leader. I remained in 'B' Company, 3rd Battalion and was very much attached to Leo Fitzgerald, until he was killed one night beside me, in an ambush. At that time there was a lot of drilling, lessons on revolvers, rifles, even machine guns, and regular classes.

At the beginning we had endless parades. We were sent out two by two, walking about various streets, making a report on everything we saw. We were operating from Pearse Street, Great Brunswick Street as it then was. There was a Catholic Boys Club, whose name I forget now, and it was there we used to meet and from there we were sent out. We got to know the whole area inside out. The area of 'B' Company ran from Sir John Rogerson's Quay right up to the Basin and on the other side ran up to Baggot Street. It was a biggish area, and we had to familiarise ourselves with all the streets. There was no fighting then in our area; certainly there may have been a few ambushes in other areas. I think the first important one in Dublin was the attack on Lord French at Ashtown, just outside Dublin.

Concurrently with my membership of the IRA, I worked fairly actively in the 1918 General Election campaign for Constance Markievicz. She was then standing against an old Irish Party member called William Field. It was a constituency that included Thomas Street, Christ Church and the Liberties. My work was mainly typing copies of the register — the routine, humdrum work of elections. However it was all very new to me, and I remember having a terrible time with the names of the people and the names of the streets, because I wasn't familiar with those particular streets. When the election was over, the count took place in Green Street Court House. We had mounted guard over the ballot box all night. There were single constituencies in those days, just a straight vote. Madame Markievicz was elected by an overwhelming majority. William Field was badly defeated; he probably got only a few hundred votes. He was quite a character in his own right and had been very kind to me during the count. He came over and chatted to me. He always wore a big black cape and a broad-brimmed black hat. I think he had a walking stick. When the results were announced, there was wild cheering and jubilation. I felt sorry for William Field, who was an older man and looked battered and woebegone. He proceeded to get up from his seat and walk out from the Court House, passing me by quite closely. He was knocked down and immediately a number of people started kicking him on the ground. I jumped in there. I was furious, absolutely. I helped him get up. This was a man who had been their representative for a long time, who, I am sure, had done some good work in his day, who had not been particularly obnoxious, and who knew he was fighting a losing battle. I have always remembered it since, although I have very seldom talked about it. It made a deep impression on my mind, of the bad instincts which can develop in a crowd; the people who did this were cruel, utterly irresponsible and unworthy.

During this period before the truce, one thing that struck me very much was the fact that so few students from the National University were in the Volunteers. I was attending lectures in law and agriculture in UCD. I was always amazed at how few students were involved in the IRA. Of course there may have been more than I knew, but I think that I got in touch with most of them. We had meetings at the Literary and Historical Debating Society. I was a member and there were meetings at which political issues were thrashed out vigorously. James Dillon was a member and he used to make flamboyant speeches; also John Joyce, Michael Rynne and others. I got to be very friendly with Michael Rynne. He was a member of the IRA and he too was surprised at how few students were in the IRA. One would expect in a situation where the whole country was aflame that the student body would be more involved.

I remember the day that Kevin Barry, who was a student at the university, was hanged (1 November 1920). Nobody seemed to be paying very much attention. I asked a few people who I knew to be in the IRA who supported me and together we forced our way up to the roof of the college. I got Paudin Sweetman, who although he was not in the IRA, was a personal friend of mine, Michael Rynne, Kevin Haugh, afterwards Mr Justice Kevin Haugh, Kevin Maloney, later a District Justice, and Dick MacLoughlin, later a High Court judge. We reached the roof of the college, which, if I am not mistaken, was still flying a Union Jack, though of this I am not entirely certain. If it was, we certainly took it down, and hoisted a Tricolour flag at half mast over the college.

This was a spontaneous act that I was able to get done. Normally one would expect the national university of a country, when one of its students had been hanged, to have reacted. Instead of that, there was virtually no reaction from the student body. I was hauled up before the president of the college for having organised this; everybody knew I had done it. The president of UCD was Denis Coffey and he reprimanded me. However, his reprimand was in such terms that I sensed that he really agreed with me. It wasn't a serious reprimand. But I was very surprised with the attitude of the student body in UCD.

I also knew during this early period Michael Tierney, subsequently president of UCD. Michael Tierney, Michael Rynne and I used to go for long walks together. We went to Michael Tierney's flat for tea or very occasionally something to drink afterwards. We had long discussions on politics. By and large, I think Michael Tierney felt I was too extreme in my views and too involved. He was older than I was, and there was a difference in the age groups. Michael Rynne and I kept on very good terms right though.

On Bloody Sunday, 21 November 1920, I had arranged to meet Michael Rynne. I was not involved in any way in the killings on Bloody Sunday. He was not directly involved, but he knew of them. We joined forces for the time being. We expected reprisals. We were both armed and stayed together until later on in the day when we ran into Ernie O'Malley. Michael Rynne may have gone off some place. Ernie O'Malley and I joined forces and we decided that we better not stay in any place that was likely to be raided. We went and stayed in Lennox Robinson's flat. Lennox Robinson had often told me that if I wanted a bed, I could get a bed in his house. So we repaired to Lennox Robinson's house in Clare Street, a continuation of Nassau Street. I forget whether I had a key or not; I may have had one. Lennox was there and we explained to him that we were expecting trouble, and that I was availing of his kind offer. He was most gracious in receiving us. I think that shortly after our arrival, Tom MacGreevy arrived. As far as my recollection goes, Lennox Robinson prepared a meal for us. He then showed us how to play the pianola, or he put in the records for playing it. Then after a very short time, Tom MacGreevy and he decided that they had to leave urgently to visit some friends in Trinity College. I should mention that, beforehand, Ernie O'Malley and I had taken our military equipment, our revolvers, out of our pockets, and laid them on the bookcase. There was a certain look of discomfort on the faces of poor Lennox and Tom. I felt that they were leaving urgently to visit their friends in Trinity College, which was across the way off Lincoln Place, in order to get away from these two very dangerous gunmen. I can't remember if at the time Lennox was the manager of the Abbey Theatre; he was certainly a family friend who was in and out of the house on Stephen's Green. So was Tom MacGreevy.

They had hardly left the house when there were bursts of gunfire in Nassau Street and Clare Street. Ernie and I were afraid for one awful moment that Lennox and Tom were the objects of the gunfire. We rushed to the window, looking out anxiously. However we didn't see them but saw truckloads of auxiliaries patrolling the street, firing at everything they saw, including a poor man who was walking along, and who was knocked down and kicked by them. There was a lot of military and auxiliary traffic up and down Nassau Street on the way to and from Beggars Bush barracks which was their headquarters. Ernie and I played the pianola, and talked. He explained the workings of his parabellum revolver. I was familiar only with the Webleys and the Colts. I was intrigued by this big, efficient-looking weapon. And thus passed the night.

The next morning we separated. Ernie wanted to get down to his brigade in Tipperary. I went back to University College and stayed on the run.

CHAPTER II

Fianna • IRA 'B' Company, 3rd Battalion

I have already indicated that the area of 'B' Company, 3rd Battalion comprised the area running from Baggot Street down to the Quays, Sir John Rogerson's Quay, went as far as the canal on one side and as far as College Green on the other. Our chief area of activity was in Great Brunswick Street, but particularly in Mount Street and occasionally as far as Baggot Street. We never liked to go too far from Great Brunswick Street, because the lines of retreat were more difficult for us. We kept our arms in the gasworks.

My first really important military action, the first in which I was under fire, was one night in Great Brunswick Street in March 1921. For some time before that we had been going out on patrols. On this occasion we were told that our job was to protect the Catholic Working Man's Club in Great Brunswick Street. There was to be a battalion council meeting, or some important meeting, in the house. There were eight of us and our job was to go outside and protect the house from any raid by the military or by the police.

I have no specific recollection that any one person was in charge of this squad of eight people. Four took up positions on the opposite side of Great Brunswick Street and two remained at the corner of Earl Street and Great Brunswick Street. Myself and Leo Fitzgerald took up position at the corner of Denzille Street and Great Brunswick Street. We were armed. Within a matter of about ten minutes, a convoy of about five or six Black and Tan tenders and a couple of armoured cars swept up and stopped at the house. Leo Fitzgerald and I immediately got to the corner of Sandwith Street and Earl Street. From that corner we opened fire on the auxiliaries, who were then jumping out of their tenders.

The night was dark. It was very hard to see what we were firing at. We were certainly firing at the shadows of the tenders and at any moving figures we saw there. At that stage the firing from their side became quite intense. Leo Fitzgerald and I went and laid down in the middle of Sandwith Street facing towards Great Brunswick Street and fired back in the direction of the auxiliaries and their tenders. We could just see them. Suddenly I became conscious that there were a lot of sparks hopping off the pavement around us. For a second I didn't know what they were. I wondered whether I was imagining things. Then I realised that these were bullets, hitting off the paving stones. I looked up and saw an armoured car about twenty or thirty yards away, firing directly at us on the ground. By this stage I realised that our position was untenable and I said, 'Look, Leo, we'd better get back; we should get into the lane at the back of the houses and see what we can do.' I got no response from Leo. I put my hand out to shake him. My hand was full of hot blood and I realised that he was dead.

I went to the corner of a lane that ran behind the houses in Great Brunswick Street, running into some of the people who had been at the meeting. They told me that they had all left and that I should leave too. I don't know where the other six members had disappeared to, but I don't think there was any firing from their side of the street. I then realised that there was a lot of military activity around the place. There were a good few laneways in this area. I finally went into a house somewhere in the Denzille Street area and stayed there till four or five in the morning. In the very early dawn, I crawled out. I realised that my trench coat was all covered in blood on one side, blood which undoubtedly had come from Leo.

I went home to change my clothes and clean up. I concealed all this from Mother. I went down to the Fitzgerald house at nine or ten o'clock to find that Leo's body had been picked up by an ambulance and they were trying to retrieve it from some hospital. Then we had to start making arrangements for the funeral. I think the mass began from Clarendon Street at about five o'clock the following morning. We wanted to keep Leo's name and all the other details secret so that the

British police or military wouldn't know exactly who had been killed. They knew that somebody had been killed, or somebody had been hurt, but they didn't know who. I remember this occasion very clearly. It made a deep impression on my mind. This was the first time that I had been really that close to death.

I had to sit down and think for a couple of days afterwards, ask myself: *Are you prepared to face this? It's quite likely that you yourself will get killed in time. Are you really prepared to do this? If not, you'd better make up your mind, now, not to, or make up your mind to go ahead.* I had this kind of discussion with myself. I faced death quite calmly and coolly and decided, well if death is to come, there it is and I'm going to do what I believe to be right, and that is to continue.

I think until then I had been afraid. One would be. I hadn't been close to death. My father had been executed, but it was a long way from me. This was the first time that I had been right bang up against death. After this assessment, I was no longer afraid of death. I have never been afraid of death since. This was my first major military operation in the IRA. Certainly it was quite a serious one. One of our people was captured in that ambush and executed, I think afterwards, in Mountjoy.

Another major ambush in Dublin occurred rather accidentally, again in Great Brunswick Street. It was very close to the same corner, only it took place opposite Earl Street. As I have already mentioned, I had a small Active Service Unit, the Squad we called it. We used to meet there in the morning. Usually we used to go for our daily operation to Mount Street or to Baggot Street sometimes. We suddenly got a report that a number of tenders and lorries, full of British soldiers, auxiliaries and Black and Tans, had gone to the gasworks to collect a load of tar. We had a couple of men who were working in the gasworks who sent us word. The tenders would be coming back through Great Brunswick Street. About six of us immediately took up position.

We ambushed them in Great Brunswick Street. I was very worried, because there were a lot of women selling apples, oranges and vegetables who used to operate at the corner of Earl Street. When they saw us, they realised something was going to happen. I think I waved them away. I was reasonably well known in the locality and dressed rather dapperly. I used to wear a yellow waistcoat, not that I especially liked fine clothes, but I was usually dapper on these occasions. I felt that I would get away more easily with the police and in that way I was able to walk into police stations pretending to be a newspaperman.

The ambush took place and there were certainly some British casualties. The lorries were disabled and it was regarded as successful. The ambush took place in the middle of the day, which was unusual, and on a much bigger scale than the ambushes we used to have in Mount Street. They were regarded very much as hit and run.

I used to direct these ambushes. This was my squad. I was pretty well in complete control of this Active Service Unit. It grew, rather than was formed. I think some of the officers in the company were rather glad that it had been formed, for they could take a lot of the credit for the Activities of 'B' Company, 3rd Battalion. They could mark up quite a respectable number of ambushes, which could not have been marked up otherwise.

I don't remember the casualty figures. Not many in Mount Street, although we wounded quite a number and disabled some of their tenders. Our objective was to get hand grenades into lorries, to disable the soldiers, kill them and destroy the vehicle. We suffered one major casualty there, which leads me on to another story.

One of our boys who was in the Active Service Unit, Dolan was his name, was badly wounded in this ambush. He was taken away immediately by an ambulance. I had gone back to dump the arms and then went to find out where he was. Every account I got was hazy. I went down to Brunswick Street Police Station, which was the headquarters of the enemy camp, so to speak, in that area. I went straight in and said that I was a pressman and that I had heard there had been an ambush and a man badly wounded. I asked where he had been taken. This in a way is interesting in showing the rather open way in which we were able to operate. At the time it didn't occur to me that the police would know me. They told me that the badly wounded man had been taken to Mercers Hospital. He had been armed but I didn't know to what extent the police would know that. I felt that he was in imminent danger of being arrested, so I immediately started to make arrangements for removing him from Mercers Hospital.

First of all I went to make contact with Mrs Darrell Figgis. Both

Darrell Figgis and his wife were friends of the house; they used to visit us fairly often. Mother was particularly friendly with Mrs Figgis, a nice woman who was very helpful whenever anybody was wounded. She would always arrange for treatment, for a house for them and so on. So I immediately went to Mrs Figgis, told her that I had a man badly wounded in Mercers Hospital and that I was going to take him out of it. We arranged a house that I could bring him to, or where she would be, so that she could take him on to a house where he would be nursed.

By this time Dolan's leg had been amputated above the knee. I had made some enquiries at the hospital. I should mention that Mercers Hospital for some reason was always regarded as a British military stronghold, unlike the Mater, which was seen as a friendly hospital, or Vincent's. None of our people would ever be taken to Mercers Hospital at that time, because it was thought that they would be reported to the police. Speed was essential and we had to arrange for a car.

I took four hefty, big men with me, including Tom Carass, and we went into Mercers Hospital. It was night time. When we walked into the hospital, the matron picked up the phone immediately. I remember Tom Carass pushed her right back with one hand, and with the other hand ripped the telephone clean off the wall. He remained in the hallway of the hospital.

Having found Dolan in his bed, another big man lifted him up. For some reason there were spikes sticking out from the stump of the leg. It may have been for draining purposes. Anyway, we lifted him out and carried him to the car. We then brought him to where Mrs Figgis was waiting. Then he was transferred from that house to another house and was duly treated. Incidentally, he later worked in Government Buildings, and we used to have chats.

On a completely different topic, during this time I was also engaged for a good deal of my time in preparation for the defence of prisoners. Michael Noyk was the solicitor who acted for them. The junior counsel who used to do most of the cases was Charles Wyse-Power, afterwards a judge, whose family was always known to have been in the movement. He was brought in before court martial usually and only very occasionally before civil court; it was usually British general court martial.

My task was the very junior role of gathering evidence, gathering statements, preparing the statements, attending consultations, and finding witnesses. I always remember one episode which made an impression upon me at the time. We were told by the IRA headquarters that there was a possibility of rescuing two or three prisoners from Kilmainham, but not more. Therefore it was a question of making a choice. We were given the names of three or four prisoners and asked if we considered that they would be in danger when they were tried and convicted. We knew from the evidence and the inside information which we had. Especially in one particular case — I think Whelan was the man — we knew he had not been involved in the ambush and could not be involved. We advised that he was not in danger, and therefore he was one of the prisoners who could be left behind. Our judgement was wrong, though in fact he was innocent. He had not partaken in that ambush, but he was tried by British general court martial and was sentenced to death, and duly hanged on 14 March 1921. This made a deep impression on my mind because it showed how unreliable British court martial could be at that period. Indeed, it showed how unreliable judicial systems could be in regard to capital punishment. This always influenced my view a lot about capital punishment.

Another episode, of a different type, which made a deep impression occurred when I must have been away. For when I came back to 'B' Company 3rd Battalion, I was told that one of the officers in the company had ordered the arrest of a British ex-soldier in the area and accused him of being a British spy. I wasn't convinced of this, for I knew that the officer did not know very much about the area. He was seldom there. We hardly ever saw him. This man had been arrested and had been put in my charge. I was to keep him in custody until he was arrested on these charges, so he was in my custody for some days. I made it my business to try to assess him, to find out his background and other details. I came to the conclusion that he was too dim-witted to be a spy for anybody.

His court-martial was duly convened and sat. I think that

Commandant Quinn, the Adjutant of the Battalion, presided at the court martial. There were two other officers. I remember being unhappy at the way the court martial was being run. I felt that it was unfair and that the dice were loaded against the accused. By this time I was pretty sure that the man was innocent of anything and was a little bit subnormal. At the end, the court martial was adjourned until the next day to enable him to decide whether or not he would give evidence himself, to try and goad him into giving evidence. Immediately afterwards I went on my own to see Dr O'Brien, the father of Barra O'Brien, later president of the Circuit Court. Dr O'Brien had his house at the corner of Merrion Square and Holles Street, just opposite Holles Street Hospital. I didn't know him personally at the time. Indeed, I always felt very guilty about him, for we had many ambushes just at that corner, as a result of which a lot of his windows had been broken by bullets fired by the auxiliaries at us, or as the result of hand grenade explosions. However, I decided I would go and consult him. Knowing his son Barra, who was also in the Volunteers, I felt that I was free to consult him.

I explained what my problem was: I had this man in my charge who was a prisoner, but I had doubts about his mental capacity. I also had doubts as to whether or not there was any foundation for the charges against him and that I would like to bring him to be examined by Dr O'Brien, and if he wasn't satisfied as to his mental capacity, to have him certified and committed to Grangegorman. Dr O'Brien was most helpful and agreed to do this. I returned and fetched the prisoner. I took my prisoner myself, perhaps with some protests from my colleagues who were also guarding him. However, I explained that I would have to bring him to a doctor for examination before the next day. I brought him to Dr O'Brien in Merrion Square. Dr O'Brien examined him immediately, rang up Grangegorman and had him committed to the hospital.

The next morning when the court martial reconvened, I said nothing. I arrived, behaved in a most military fashion, which I had never done before. I clicked my heels, saluted them, and called them 'sir'. I didn't wear a uniform. Nobody wore a uniform. In a most solemn tone of voice I said that I had had reason in the course of the night to believe that the accused may not have been fully capable of conducting his defence, or may not have been fully responsible. I felt that it was my duty as the officer in charge of his custody to have him medically examined. I had had him medically examined by Dr O'Brien, who had certified that he was insane and unfit to withstand a trial. He had committed him to an asylum. The officers of the court martial were very cross with me. They reprimanded me for not having waited until they came to consult them. I felt inwardly some of them were just as glad that I had taken this course. I think that they had made up their minds to convict him and sentence him to death.

This confirmed the impression I had that military courts, juntas, and indeed, ordinary civilian courts in judicial processes are very unreliable. Certainly death sentences should never be carried out. I have no doubt that this man would have been sentenced to death, and would have been shot, except for my stratagem. I was chary of all this: perhaps I was more sensitive because I was a law student and had a lot of sympathy with the people who were charged and tried. I had had this other instance of the man who had been convicted by a British general court martial and hanged, though I knew he was innocent. I was also chary of the people who were prosecuting. I felt that they didn't know enough about the case and it was a question of their getting a scapegoat. That their shooting of a British spy would be good *pour encourager les autres*. I don't think there were any British spies around the area, actually. I think that probably many people were executed as a result of this kind of drumhead court martial who probably should not have been executed and shot by the IRA.

I think the Republican Courts operated fairly and justly, but they were not entrusted with capital cases. They were trying usually ordinary civil actions and ordinary local crimes. Capital cases were still entrusted to court martial; that is capital cases relating to the IRA, relating to the war at the time. It also made me feel strongly that capital punishment was most fallible and that the judicial system was also fallible. This was indeed largely confirmed afterwards by further experiences I had at the Bar. All these earlier experiences influenced my work at the Bar later on. Wherever there was a question of the death penalty, I certainly put in far more work and far more care than I would have put in to any other case. I had a sense that justice was important. I started off with a strange idea of being a farmer and a lawyer, of having a small farm in the country, living from the farm, and doing an occasional law case, for interest or to be able to vindicate justice from time to time. This was probably very idealistic and probably a youthful concept. This was the concept I started off with when I began studying both agriculture and law at the same time in UCD.

Sometime before the truce, I had been brought in by Michael Collins, Eamonn Price, who was Director of Organisation, and Eoin O'Duffy and asked to undertake a mission to Counties Wicklow, Wexford and Carlow. I was to try and 'step up' the activities of the IRA in those places. They explained that one of their immediate objectives was to have all the RIC barracks closed in those counties. These were the only areas in the country where there were still RIC barracks functioning. In all other areas the IRA had forced the RIC to retreat from isolated stations to main stations, usually with the British military. I think my first step towards the accomplishment of this mission was to visit the battalion councils in Wicklow, Carlow and Wexford, just to ascertain what the position was, and to try and obtain statistics as to the strength of the volunteers there. I also tried to form an assessment as to their capacity to start a fresh burst of activities. However, I am not quite certain whether or not this is what I did first. I do know that I did attend a battalion or brigade council meeting in County Wicklow. The battalion commander's name was Gerard. He had, as an assistant, a much younger man named O'Carroll, who struck me as the most active person in the area. The Intelligence Officer for the unit was Gus Cullen, a solicitor who was an old friend of mine, and the Quartermaster was Christy Byrne.

The relationship between the IRA and the Dáil was ill-defined. It depended largely on the different areas in the country. For instance, in some areas, the local brigade commander could be a TD. In other areas the TD might have nothing at all to do with the IRA. I don't think the Dáil influenced the IRA, I think it was more the reverse. For instance, in the west, most of the IRA commanders were TDs and had quite a lot of influence in the Dáil.

The non-military members of the Dáil never tried to give orders to the IRA. There was in the IRA itself a certain resistance to orders from the Dáil government. The Republican government was functioning fully at that time. At the time I am talking about, Cathal Brugha was Minister for Defence and therefore the supreme commander of the army. The Chief of Staff of the army was Dick Mulcahy. Cathal Brugha was a strict disciplinarian. He was very concerned to ensure that the IRA did not carry out acts that were hard to justify or defend in the Dáil or in public. Every day he would send sheaves of enquiries to the Chief of Staff or to the Adjutant General of the IRA. The Adjutant General at that period was Gearóid O'Sullivan, and I worked in his office at that time.

Most of my work in his office was taken up with investigating complaints received from the Minister for Defence; for example; that five volunteers were reported to have got drunk in a public house in Kanturk, Co. Cork. There was quite a lot of truth in some of these complaints, but the tendency of the Adjutant General was to try to minimise these things. Brugha was most persistent in obtaining information. There were many files which contained repeated requests from Cathal Brugha for information. We tried to give explanations, though it was not always possible because travelling was not easy and one couldn't furnish an explanation for something that happened in Cork, Donegal or Galway without sending somebody down to investigate it. Brugha was sympathetic, extreme in his viewpoint and rather straight-laced. He never drank and I think he disapproved of people who did. Collins and a lot of his staff used to drink a good deal. Brugha had a different temperament, honest and straight. Generally, in our feelings towards Brugha, a dichotomy (a split would be too strong a word to use) occurred between the IRA volunteers, those engaged in the fighting, and those who were regarded as the politicians. For a volunteer to refer to somebody as a politician was an expression of opprobrium. It implied that 'he wasn't really much good', that he was 'only a politician, don't mind him'. Brugha was not referred to so much in those terms, though a little bit, I think everybody respected him because he was so absolutely dedicated. He was never in favour of compromise. I have no idea of the relations between Brugha and de Valera, but I would say in retrospect that they didn't get on. Brugha was probably much more extreme, more straight-laced on republican principles than de Valera.

Brugha and Collins: I don't know what their personal relationship was at that time before the truce. I imagine it would have been rather strained, because they were such different types. Brugha would have been all the time criticising or demanding explanations from Collins and from Mulcahy. Mulcahy's reaction to Cathal Brugha's queries would have been one of discipline and of giving full account. Collins' reaction would have been, 'Oh tell the old so and so to get to hell out of this and not to be bothering us. We have too many things to do to be doing this kind of work.' Certainly this was the attitude of Gearóid O'Sullivan, the Adjutant General for whom I was working. O'Sullivan and Collins were very close and had much the same attitude. They both drank a good deal and both would have resented all these queries coming down from the Minister.

Brugha and Austin Stack would have been friendly, on the basis of both being extreme in their political viewpoints. Here I should explain that de Valera was always regarded as being somewhat suspect. This was on account of proposals he had made while in America, referring to some form of relationship (between Ireland and Britain) as existed between either Puerto Rica or Cuba and the United States. Many references to this can be found in the Treaty Debates where he was accused of already having compromised the national position. So he was regarded as a moderate and a person who was prepared to compromise on the question of the establishment of a free independent republic. Austin Stack and Cathal Brugha would have been quite inflexible on this.

Let me make it clear that, as far as the mass of the movement was concerned, probably the public did not harbour any of these suspicions and did not voice them, though I think there was always among Sinn Féin and the public generally, a feeling that de Valera would compromise at some stage. He became popular because first of all he was a very good orator and would carry a big crowd with him. His speeches were emotive, well conceived and well delivered. Also I think that people who had sensed that he might compromise a little felt that he was a safe person to support. It is very hard to recapture exactly the atmosphere of that period. Arthur Griffith was definitely regarded as somebody who would compromise, who would accept something much less than complete freedom or independence. Stack, Collins and Cathal Brugha would have been regarded as extremists in the government. Arthur Griffith, Seán Milroy and others would have been regarded as people who compromised; de Valera as the 'in-between', holding the scales between the two wings in the government.

Griffith we didn't have any dealings with. He had made several statements to indicate that he thought we should settle for something less. Griffith was never a force in the army at all. All the older people had tremendous respect for Griffith. He had taken an active part in the building of Sinn Féin. It is very hard to reconstruct that period without having looked at the growth of Sinn Féin, of the Irish Volunteers, of 1916 and of the arrests of the people who were imprisoned in Frongach after 1916. Eoin MacNeill was regarded as having let down the ideals of Irish republicanism by not going out in 1916.

Going back over the period just before the truce and my own experiences then. After having visited the three counties, I decided to set up a flying column in Wicklow consisting of the whole of the Brigade staff. I did this really to try and ascertain whether or not they were capable of taking part in a fight — to a certain extent to test them. Unless they could be effective in a flying column, they would not be in a position to set up flying columns in a county and to undertake military activities. Therefore, I decided to try this first. I brought down with me, from my own company, 'B' Company 3rd Battalion, Dublin Brigade, one of my most active men, Jack Hunter. We met the battalion/brigade staff and I told them I was going to mobilise them into a flying column. Our task, I said, would be to try and attack a number of isolated barracks in Co. Wicklow in order to force the RIC to withdraw from them. I was in a hurry, because my instructions were to get things cracking as quickly as possible. Tremendous progress had been made and I think that already there had been preliminary negotiations for a truce: the IRA leadership wanted to see this other part of the country which had been dormant suddenly flaring up. This would encourage the British to realise that they had to come to terms.

I knew that negotiations were taking place and that the British were thinking of some compromise. Indeed, I think that this had been published in the papers and also one could gather it from an exchange of letters which had taken place between Lloyd George and de Valera. So that the question of a truce, compromise, cessation of activities was in the air, and my instructions were really to accelerate this process. This would increase the pressure on the British and make them realise that there was no area in the country which hadn't an active IRA unit. Accordingly, I mobilised the battalion staff within the next forty-eight hours. We started off as a flying column with kit and all, sleeping out in the open. Quite a lot of time was spent trying to ambush military convoys between Wicklow town and Rathdrum at a sawmill near Glenealy. We mined the road very carefully and waited, but no convoy came, to our disappointment. Then we tried to attack the local RIC barracks in Avoca, but found that there was nobody in the barracks. Turning our attention to Rathdrum, we planned a major operation there. This would be difficult, firstly because of the large number of RIC in Rathdrum. Apart from that, there was a big British military encampment in Avondale just a half mile away, so that it had to be very much a hit, then run attack on the barracks. On our way to the barracks, we ran into a number of RIC men, and opened fire on them. Although we had planned to take the barracks, we did not dare do this now. I had arranged for a getaway from Rathdrum. I had detailed four or five men to dig a trench across the road and had arranged for a motorcar from a volunteer in the Wicklow Brigade to be on the other side of the trench. This was so that we could retreat on the road leading to Glenmalure valley. We couldn't be followed by the British military because the one road had been blocked. We would then have gone across the mountains, towards Laragh, or in that direction.

When our plans miscarried, we went for the trench, which was to have been dug in the road, and the motorcar. But there was no trench, and no motorcar. So we took to the fields. My brigade was not very used to marching or strenuous exercise. We had to run up to the mountains overlooking Glenmalure. I should mention that at the time Mother had a small house at the head of the Glenmalure valley. We had left our heavy equipment in the house. My intention was to retrieve our heavy equipment and then to carry on to attack a police station somewhere else. Instead of that, we couldn't reach the house at Glenmalure because the British military had overrun the valley with many lorries. They also had an aeroplane looking for us. This was quite a new development at that period. So we had to move with a fair amount of caution on top of the Glenmalure mountains. I think that wherever the military were at hand, the British took the attacks seriously. The RIC would take the attacks seriously too, but they really had lost heart by that stage; they didn't want to fight and get killed. All that night, we were crawling on top of the mountains. We were a little bit handicapped because we had only small side arms. We had left our equipment in the house in Glenmalure, which afterwards was duly raided by the British military. They took all our arms. These were pretty antiquated rifles. Apart from my automatic colt, the rifle I was using there was an old Martini rifle. Though quite a good rifle, this would load only one bullet at a time. I don't know where the Wicklow Brigade got these arms. Practically every unit in the country had arms, though some of the weapons I had were antiquated and terrible.

I first tried to reach the house to retrieve the weapons, but I couldn't because the military were below in the valley in lorries. I changed tack and went for Laragh, Annamoe and Glendalough. In the course of the night I put out my ankle by falling down a boghole. We made for the Glendalough Hotel. We knew the proprietor of the hotel and the family, the Richardsons, who were not themselves in the IRA, but were sympathisers. There I learned that a truce had been declared.

My immediate reaction was one of considerable annoyance. I had a feeling that this was quite wrong, that we were on the way to really 'make things hotter'. I had been rather horrified to find so little being done in these parts of the country and a lack of support for the IRA and Sinn Féin. I felt that this was due to bad organisation and that with very slight organisation and pushing we could have built up quite a strong unit in all that eastern coastal area. This would have been easy to do.

After spending a couple of days allowing my ankle to recover, I decided to go to Dublin. I went partly by sidecar, partly by bicycle and partly by train from Bray. I tried to see my commandants. I saw Eamonn (Bob) Price first and told him how I thought the truce was a tremendous mistake, how we could have done a lot more, how we could have got much better terms by continuing for another couple of months. I described my experiences in Wicklow and that area, saying it was only a matter of time before activities could be built up and indeed, activities right through the country could also be stepped up. But he said, 'Ah well there it is; they have decided on these negotiations. Don't take this too much to heart. This will give us a pause, a breathing space during which we can reorganise and restructure some of the units which were not active.' He meant by 'they' the government, the politicians, de Valera. He tried to reassure me quite a lot that I needn't worry, that Collins would never agree to this and that nobody else would agree to this truce. Mulcahy wouldn't have agreed to this unless it was to provide the breathing space so as to win right on to the end, with no question of compromise. That is what Price said.

I don't know if the military were consulted about the truce. I imagine that the cabinet was consulted, which would have included Michael Collins, Cathal Brugha and all the members of the government. I wasn't at that level, so I don't know exactly what consultations took place before the truce. I am sure that the truce wouldn't have taken place unless Collins had agreed to it. The cabinet papers should show whether or not there was a vote taken, and if it was a unanimous decision.

Bob Price then said we must hurry up and rebuild our forces. We needed training. He started to talk to me about setting up an officers' training camp, which we duly did in Glen na Smol. We had taken this big house at the head of Glen na Smol valley. The commander in charge of the camp was Dinny O'Brien. It was an extremely well run camp, and Dinny O'Brien certainly had put a tremendous amount of work into it, organised before I arrived as Adjutant. Afterwards he was in the Free State police force and was killed in some ambush. The camp had been started up very shortly after the truce. We had a squad, and we trained staff to do the canteen work. There would have been about fifty officers at the time, drawn from different parts of the country. I first underwent some training there in map-reading in which I was very interested. After that I took over the map-reading classes in the camp. But it was really tough work. We used to begin at 5.30 in the morning and the day wouldn't finish until eight or nine.

We gave the unfortunate trainee officers who came there a really hard time. They were made to drill, run up and down the mountainside, all kinds of things. The grand finale was two nights before the last day — the course lasted about ten days — we would spread rumours throughout the camp that the truce had broken down and that hostilities might resume very quickly. We might not be able to finish the course and they might all have to go back to their units. We would then provide them with detailed instructions as to what they might do if they were attacked. Rumours of that kind would be spread quite easily in a camp. Then on the second last night, the alarm was sounded at three in the morning. Myself and a few others would run down the Glen na Smol valley and start firing a few shots in the air. This was taken to be an attack. The results were interesting. Quite a large number ceased to obey orders, running off in all directions. We always got them all back afterwards, and they all had marvellous excuses. They would say that their one idea was to get back home to their unit and that if they followed the instructions they had been given, they might have been captured. But it always created a great scare … the last major exercise at the end of every training period.

The success in each area depended upon the local leadership, usually on one man. He would be very active, form a flying column, a small active service section from seven to twenty men, who would carry out attacks on British posts wherever they saw them, courageously and fearlessly. They would plan these carefully. They would then have the support of the other volunteers – maybe there might be 500 or a 1,000 in the area – but it would only be that small nucleus doing the fighting. These would have the initiative to do things.

There were other training camps, organised by different divisions and different brigades throughout the country. This was organised by GHQ. I don't think it was a breach of the truce. At least it certainly never crossed my mind at the time.

CHAPTER III

'In a war you must try everything'
Despatch runner to the delegation • Gun running

After a period of about six weeks or so while I was in Glen na Smol, Collins sent for me. He said he wanted me to accompany him with the negotiating team to London. He said he was taking Tom Cullen, Liam Tobin, Joe Dolan and me. So I naturally felt flattered at being picked out. Although I felt honoured, I said that I had already been given an assignment by the Director of Training. I pointed out to Collins that I would have to get permission to give up the other work I was doing. He said you better see the Chief of Staff about that. It took me a day or so to find Mulcahy. He had an office during the truce period in Abbey Street, not far from the Independent buildings. I saw him there and told him that Collins had asked me to go to London with him. He disapproved of this, and said that it was 'far more important for you to carry on with your training. There's no need for you to go to London with Collins.'

So I went back to Collins, feeling crestfallen. I reported that Mulcahy said I couldn't go and that I should stay at my job. Collins used a few lurid expressions and said to 'tell him to go to hell. I want you to come, and you're coming. Go back and tell him that you're coming, whether he likes it or not.' So I went back to Mulcahy and in much more polite terms explained that Collins seemed to be very disappointed and had asked me to go back to see him. He seemed to really want me to accompany him … to arrange for a quick getaway for the delegation, if it were needed. Whereupon Mulcahy said 'All right, I'll talk to Collins about it. You had better go.'

By this time the IRA had become very popular. It was a question of everybody getting on the bandwagon throughout the country. Whenever a parade was called by a battalion or company, hundreds would turn out. They would have marches, they would drill. They would fall in and parade outside churches on Sundays and give a display and sometimes become quite obnoxious. The IRA was getting bigger, not necessarily better in quality, but numerically stronger. The sudden popularity was due to success. The IRA had won. In 1916 the Irish Volunteers didn't have more than at the very most 5,000 people in the country who would support them. There had been this sudden conversion of the country over the past few years to an extreme, nationalistic, republican policy. The IRA had forced the British to agree to a truce, and the IRA practically ran the country.

Local courts had been established right through the country. Usually it was the IRA who enforced the decrees and who ran the courts. Witnesses were procured by the IRA and so on. So there was quite a civil administration being set up, mainly by the IRA. There was rather a good relationship during all that with Sinn Féin. The courts were usually manned by Sinn Féin judges, but the IRA were present in the court, playing the role of the local police with regard to the court.

Those of us who had fought before the truce had a mixed reaction to this popularity. On the one hand, it showed tremendous success: we had more power than ever, these people could all be recruited and trained, if necessary. It showed that we had more support right through the country than before. On the other hand, I felt the whole time that the truce had been a mistake. We should have waited for another three to six months until we were strong enough to increase our activities. I had been concerned with the shipment of arms, when I had been in GHQ, my other life. I knew that we had arms, that we could ship more. Indeed, I was engaged in that also during the truce period while I was still in the training camp and also in London. I had been involved with Michael Cremin, who was then Director of Purchases for the IRA. I had also been involved with Liam Mellows, who was Director of Munitions at the time. Part of my activities had been connected with the purchase of arms and the importation of arms to Ireland.

43

When I arrived in London, the mission was already established in two houses, one in Cadogan Gardens and the other in Hans Place. There was quite a divergence between the two houses. Cadogan Gardens was where I stayed with Michael Collins, Liam Tobin, Tom Cullen, Joe Dolan, and Dan McCarthy. As far as I was concerned, I was not part of the political mission. My task was theoretically to make arrangements for a quick getaway in case the truce broke down. I was also to carry despatches between Dublin and London. Liam Tobin, Tom Cullen and Joe Dolan were not part of the actual political mission either: they were there really in order to supervise safety and intelligence arrangements for Collins. Liam Tobin was our direct superior. Dolan always accompanied Michael Collins, whenever Collins went out or even to Downing Street. I think Tom Cullen used to go too: they went as a kind of bodyguard. They were armed throughout and so was I. Collins would have been armed too. I am not sure if Collins was armed when he was going to Downing Street, but certainly Dolan, Tobin and Cullen were armed. I often remember them coming back from Downing Street; they would take their guns from their holsters and put them on a shelf or into a press.

Most of my time was taken up running despatches from London to Dublin. Many of these I delivered directly to de Valera or to Kathleen O'Connell, who was his private secretary. She would give me, in turn, despatches to bring back. Travelling was by the Irish night mail. It left London at 9.40 every night. I travelled on the night mail at least twice a week, backwards and forwards. I seldom spent more than a day in Dublin. Very often I arrived in the morning and left that night. Of course, since I didn't read the letters I did not know what the contents were. In retrospect, I presume they were letters from the delegation. I knew that a lot of the despatches were written by Erskine Childers, who was secretary of the delegation, and I suppose some by Robert Barton and George Gavan Duffy. Collins wrote private letters to people such as Seán Ó Muirthile who was the IRB man. My function was to bring all these letters backwards and forwards. I would have assumed then, that the letters from Barton, Childers and so on were to de Valera and to the Secretary to the government connected with the negotiations and to more official formal matters. I would assume that the letters between Collins and Gearóid O'Sullivan and Ó Muirthile were to keep the IRB and some of Collins' friends in Dublin informed as to the course of the negotiations.

There was a tremendous dichotomy between the two houses. We were in Cadogan Gardens. We were regarded as the 'military' house because Collins was there, the rest of us were there and Dan McCarthy was there. I don't know why Dan McCarthy should be regarded particularly as of the military house: he was very largely IRB and he was probably there in that capacity. The other house included Arthur Griffith, George Gavan Duffy, Robert Barton, Erskine Childers and secretaries. I spent time in both houses and I think I used to have my leg pulled by my pals, Tom Cullen and those who would say, 'what are you doing going over to the politicians' house?' I knew the other house and I knew Barton very well. He had been of help to me during the truce and later on when I ran a camp in his grounds, in Wicklow. I knew Childers slightly, though not as well as I knew Barton. I got to know George Gavan Duffy and respected him very much. I regarded him as an important lawyer.

Arthur Griffith I didn't know very well. But I had learned from Mother and from the history of the earlier part of the century that he was an important nationalist. Even though he might not be extreme, he certainly should be treated with a great respect. I used to go over and have afternoon tea with them from time to time in Hans Place. I used to play bridge with Barton, Gavan Duffy and a man called Charters whose position was always nebulous. I could never find out what his role was or what he was doing. He certainly was suspected of being a British spy for a time. We played bridge which was rather an amusing way of passing the time. I was also rather glad of it as a reaction to my other colleagues in Cadogan Gardens who did far too much drinking, everybody, Collins included. There were bottles of whiskey around the place and everybody went to help themselves whenever they wanted to. They may have been drinking when they went out, but I didn't go out with them. In Hans Place, there was much less drinking, though I was rather horrified when I learned that Griffith was also drinking.

There was little contact between the two houses. This may be a slight exaggeration, but as far as I can remember, I was the only person who visited from one house to the other, and was on friendly terms with people in both houses. I don't remember Collins and Griffith being together, but I am sure they must have met and had long discussions. I was in London one day, then off to Dublin the next, so that a lot of things would happen which I wouldn't be aware of. Nor do I remember being conscious of Collins going out to visit friends in London. I have heard the accounts of the various houses visited by Collins and other members of the delegation in London, but I was not aware of any of this. What I do remember mainly in Cadogan Gardens were the long sessions of drinking at night by my colleagues and sometimes by Collins and Dan McCarthy. They had brought over with them a waiter from the Gresham, a housekeeper and some maids. I remember there was a great 'hoo-hoo' on one occasion: Arthur Griffith had gone off with a couple of the girl secretaries, Miss Lyons and somebody else, to a theatre. They had lost their way in the tube, eventually got to the theatre but had to come back. This was a great source of merriment at the time. The drinking was excessive and I became conscious of this rapidly. I was rather revolted by it, though I did drink a good deal with them. But I felt it was having a bad influence on the delegation, on Collins, on Dan McCarthy and on Eamon Duggan. I felt that they were letting down the country, that matters were not being taken sufficiently seriously, that alcohol was neither the best help with, nor preparation for, negotiations. I am quite sure the British knew. I am certain the British had agents placed in the houses and knew everything that happened.

We know from reports since that time about certain things which happened. For instance we know how Michael Collins went out a good deal, had some relationship with a woman. I had no knowledge of this: it is something which I have learned since from discussions with Rex Taylor. My main occupation was in making the night mail and returning.

One day I remember an incident. I was sitting playing bridge in Hans Place with George Gavan Duffy, Barton and Charters. Griffith wasn't with us; he kept aloof. We had been having tea and Collins suddenly erupted into the room. He was returning from Downing

Street. He said, 'What's this about these guns? What about this shipment of arms that has been caught in Germany?' Then, to Gavan Duffy: 'Why didn't you tell me about this shipment of arms? I know nothing about it.' And Lloyd George threw this across the table... a shipment of arms in Hamburg had been found. Collins was inclined to blame Gavan Duffy for it. Gavan Duffy said he knew nothing about it. I said, 'Yes, that's quite right, but I know a good deal about it. There is a shipment of arms in Hamburg that is being brought over on the *Santa Maria*.' I would have had something to do with this I imagine under Michael Cremins' orders, and I think that Collins also knew about it. But I think he had thought it was another load of arms which Gavan Duffy knew about. Gavan Duffy had been Irish Ambassador to Berlin. However, poor Gavan Duffy didn't know about it, and Collins had been very annoyed with him. Then I explained that it was pretty urgent that I should go there. Collins said, 'Alright, see if you can try to salvage these arms. Above all make sure that you give no further evidence about shipments of arms, because Lloyd George raised all this, and I denied all knowledge of it.'

I took off, there and then, for Hamburg. In those days there were no planes. I went by night ferry from Harwich to Antwerp. It was a quiet way of going across and little police attention was paid. From there I went by train and contacted Jim McGuinness in Hamburg. McGuinness was an absolutely marvellous man and a very able sailor. He came from Derry and been on the Byrd expedition to the South Pole. He ran all our arms shipments. At that period we were operating at two different levels: a steamer with engines called the *Santa Maria* of which McGuinness was skipper and a small steamer between 1,500 and 2,000 tons called the *City of Dortmund* which we had bought, or had some shares in. 'We' would have been the IRA, the Department of Purchases or the Department of Munitions. I never knew what the distinction between Purchases and Munitions was. All I know is that Michael Cremin was very competent on all these things. The *City of Dortmund* used to run into the Port of Dublin with a legal cargo. Underneath this, well below in the holds, there would be some arms ammunition, usually brought over from Hamburg. Otherwise the *City of Dortmund* appeared to be a regular ship, carrying on a lawful business. The *Santa Maria,* on the other hand, was a gun running ship. McGuinness had one defect in that he used to drink once he got to port; never on a voyage but as soon as he berthed, he used to go off on a batter. More often than not he would end up in a police station. When I got to Hamburg, I think I did actually find him in a police station.

The buying and the loading of arms was done in different ways. Cremin used to organise that a good deal and Bob Briscoe was also involved in the purchase of arms. On this occasion, I went straight to the Harbourmaster of Hamburg who turned out to be Karl Spindler. He had been the captain of the *Aud*, the ship which had tried to run guns in 1916, and was captured by the British. I can't exactly remember how I got to him. I think it may have been through friends that I had had in Berlin. I may have visited them there first, or got them to come to Hamburg, Herr and Frau Grauber. She was an Irish American married to a German member of parliament, and she was always a source of considerable strength and help to me. I think it was she who put me on to Spindler. I went directly to him and laid my cards on the table. I said we were running arms from Hamburg, that we had this steamer, the *Santa Maria*. The arms were somewhere in the docks but the British secret service knew about them. It was a question of getting the arms off quickly and secretly.

He cooperated to the fullest extent possible and helped me to get hold of McGuinness. By arrangement, the arms were taken out and dummy cases were inserted instead. For safety's sake, in case the operation had been noticed, the arms were loaded onto another ship. During the next night, the *Santa Maria* pulled up alongside the other ship. The arms were transferred to the *Santa Maria* and off she went with a load of arms to Dungarvan. The arms would come to Helvic Head and there different arrangements were made. Lorries were available and the arms were immediately distributed to the various units. Cremin arranged all that.

So the mission was accomplished, the arms were got out of Hamburg, the *Santa Maria* was out, and once on board McGuinness was completely in command of the ship. Sometimes plans regarding securing of arms took three to six months to mature. Other times they could go through very quickly.

The truce had been sold to us on the basis that we needed time to strengthen the IRA in every respect and to get more arms in. I suppose I was chosen for this largely because I was so keen. I had opposed the truce so much, they felt in that way I would realise that everything possible was being done to train recruits and to acquire more arms. So the purchase of arms went on right through the truce. There was no question of countermanding any orders or of not importing arms. We were told to be very careful when doing it and not to be caught.

If the truce was not to break down, presumably all these arms would have been used to arm the IRA which would have been regarded as the lawful army of the government of the Republic. Concurrently with the arms deals in which I was involved, we were also getting arms from America. We got large quantities of Thomson sub-machine guns. I had been down to Cobh to collect a load of Thomson machine guns which had been landed.

Indeed I remember on one occasion before the truce or at the beginning when Collins instructed me to investigate the possibilities of an arms deal. He had received a letter from somebody in the Clan na Gael in America saying that they had made contact with a man who was probably a crook, who claimed that he would be in a position to obtain and deliver large quantities of arms from France. Details of the operation were very sketchy. Collins sent for me and instructed me to go and meet this man. We knew nothing about him. The appointment had been made from America by Clan na Gael for a given date, which must have been for a week ahead of the time when Collins told me about it. My only instructions were to meet this man, whose pseudonym was Jones, not a very imaginative alias. He would be in a café on the docks in Boulogne. I found it. I was to wear a pink carnation in the lapel of my coat. This was in fact very unsuitable as I realised later. The café was in a windswept corner of the docks and was a low level café for which I was dressed rather dapperly with my carnation and a pair of gloves, not at all in keeping with the surroundings. It made me conspicuous.

Immediately when Mr Jones arrived, he shook hands, said something which I had been told he would say and I greeted him as Mr Jones. We left the café to discuss this arms deal. We may have gone to the house of a friend of his. Mr Jones had been wanted by both the French and the Belgian police for robbing some jeweller shops, and as I gathered, for murdering in one case the jeweller. This only emerged as we went along. His proposition was: he admitted to being a crook. He was wanted by the police. He said that he had a gang with him and that one of his principal allies and fellow gangsters was a man who was foreman in a huge arms dump. This dump had been established by the British army on the French coast between Boulogne and Calais. It wasn't exactly under military control but it was under the control of a British civilian contracting firm called Piquet. He also had some other subordinate who had been involved in various types of criminal activity with him and knew the captain of a ship who was used to gun-running and contraband handling. The first step we took was to visit this camp which was a couple of miles long. In sheds, pretty well unguarded, were vast quantities of British army equipment from the war. Apparently all the arms which had been left by Britain, or captured from the Germans, had been gathered at this spot. I spent a day with Mr Jones going through all the various hutments. These were going to be stolen, loaded first onto a lorry and then to a ship. We could have taken a couple of thousand rifles and no one would have noticed. There was no one to check anyway.

On the second day I met some of his co-conspirators. Then a fire broke out, somewhere in this vast area. Of course a fire was highly dangerous on account of these explosives. Fire alarms were rung all over the place. There was a small little railway running inside this huge encampment and he and I got onto the railway with every other human being in the place. We got to the outside of the camp where we were all questioned one by one. I was asked why I was there. I had separated myself very carefully from Mr Jones. I said that I had been working along the shore and I turned in there. Suddenly there was a fire alarm and I saw everybody getting onto these trains and I too got onto them. This was accepted and there was no further ado. Then I waited for Mr Jones and we went to have a discussion with the captain of the ship. This was a very eerie experience.

It was a small steamer, I suppose five to eight hundred tons, dingy and dirty. The crew were mainly Chinese. The captain could have been any Asiatic nationality but spoke French. He could have been from Vietnam or Cambodia. I discussed the whole venture with him. I tried to discuss prices and a long controversy ensued between Mr Jones and him about the price. At the end the relationship between Mr Jones and the captain of the ship didn't appear to be so good.

The next day Mr Jones insisted that I should go with him to see the foreman who had been a criminal with a fairly long prison record. We went to his house which wasn't very far from where all the arms were kept. He had a particularly good wooden house. We went in, but the man of the house was out. We were greeted by his wife. We waited for him to return and as soon as he saw us he said no, I'm through with everything illegal. I have a good job and am making good now. I'll have nothing more to do with anything like this. Mr Jones pleaded with him, saying that there would be no danger. They could make a lot of money on this deal, the arms wouldn't even be missed. But he would have nothing to do with it and we left. Mr Jones was very cross. We had walked about a quarter of a mile when he said, I want to go back; I'm not going to let him get away with this. He went back and returned with a handful of notes. He had blackmailed the foreman.

By this stage I had realised that the whole venture was quite impossible. Even if we had managed to get the guns loaded on the ships unnoticed, I could not see this ship making the Irish coast. The arms would have been missed and the whole British fleet would have been after it. It was a mad hat venture. I went back to Collins and told him that we shouldn't pursue it further. I believed the people in Clan na Gael in America who had advised us were not very responsible. However, Collins said: 'You must try everything. In a war you must try everything.' So that was that gun-running expedition.

The last I saw of Mr Jones was on a return journey perhaps to Amiens. He was nervous that day of police following him. In the train he suddenly said, 'I've seen a police face I know passing down the corridor.' The train slowed down and he opened the door and jumped out.

It's very hard to know the feeling at that time of Germany towards England. All that I know is that they were quite prepared to help Ireland. Anybody who had been in the German army was friendly towards Ireland and was anxious and willing to help. Certainly there was never a moment's hesitation in Karl Spindler's mind and he laughed heartily saying, 'Well, I'll at least have got one load of arms into Ireland now.'

These were arms that Germany had during the war. They had probably been stowed away secretly from the Allied intelligence. There was probably a lot of that going on at the time. There was, I believe, a strong move among the German army officers to build up a secret stock of arms. They wouldn't mind giving them or selling them to Ireland because they believed they might be put to a useful purpose. There was still a strong element of 'anti-Alliedness'. The Allies had beaten them in the war, and therefore they were not specifically sympathetic to the Allies and to Britain, more so, I think than the French.

CHAPTER IV

'An economy of British lives'
Truce • Treaty • Execution

I had complete confidence in Collins. I had great admiration for him. I regarded him as a much more effective and capable leader of the IRA than I did Mulcahy or Brugha, although I had nothing against either of them: on the contrary, I had great respect for them.

The first worry about Collins really occurred one evening in Cadogan Gardens. Collins had come back from the treaty negotiations in Downing Street. There were a few of us there — myself, Dan McCarthy, Liam Tobin, and Tom Cullen anyway. Collins described to us an event in the course of that day's negotiations. He pointed out how astute Lloyd George was, trying every trick in the bag to try and convince him to remain in the British Empire. Collins described how Lloyd George, who was very small, had put his arm around Collins' waist, and had brought him over to a big map of the world. In this the Empire was marked out in red. Lloyd George said: 'Look, Mick, that's the British Empire and we need you to help us to run it.' Collins mentioned all this merely to indicate how wily Lloyd George was and also, presumably, to let us know that he would not be influenced by any devices of that kind. But I got the strange feeling, there and then, that Collins had been influenced by all this.

I remember we had a long discussion afterwards. This was really sparked off by Dan McCarthy when he said that, of course, there was no question of Ireland being completely free as a result of negotiations. They would have to fix on some compromise. I became very indignant at this. We had a long argument and I think Tom Cullen and Liam Tobin supported me. But from that evening on, I felt that Collins had been impressed by Lloyd George's arguments. He had been impressed by the possibility and even the desirability of remaining in the Commonwealth, provided Ireland was given an equal share in the responsibility of the Commonwealth.

Before the negotiations his views would have been completely against any participation in the Commonwealth. He had an extreme viewpoint. That is why we had confidence in him. I would have said that before the treaty negotiations, Cathal Brugha, Austin Stack and Michael Collins would have been regarded as the people who would never compromise. We felt that Arthur Griffith and many other members of the government were people who would compromise, indeed some had indicated so. De Valera held the middle course between them. Collins was certainly regarded as one of the most solid republicans there and this is indeed what gave confidence in the negotiations.

It was quite clear from the discussion that night that Dan McCarthy, who represented to a certain extent the IRB viewpoint, was prepared to accept membership of the Commonwealth. I had been brought into the IRB but I wasn't particularly anxious to join. I went to one meeting, somewhere in Parnell Square. It was a long, solemn meeting, rather dull and boring. I didn't participate in the discussion. I gathered that they didn't meet often. They discussed partly the relations between Sinn Féin and the government of the Republic, and the Volunteers. I don't remember clearly who was present apart from Seán Ó Muirthile and Jack Moloney. We all sat around a big oblong oak or mahogany table. There would have been about twenty-five to thirty people around it. The IRB didn't do much that I know of, beyond maintaining a kind of secret society within the IRA and the Sinn Féin movement, not many IRA people were in it. Collins and the others who were in the IRB with him used the IRB influence in support of the treaty. In other words, they had better control of the IRB than they had of the IRA. I don't think the IRB itself had very much influence on the treaty: as far as I was concerned, I regarded them as being of an older generation living in the past a bit. They were not facing the realities of that day's struggle.

I think it is likely enough that Collins remaining with the IRB was an influence in the minds of Cathal Brugha and of Austin Stack, who had left. There was a supreme council of the IRB and Collins was a member, but I don't think he attached an awful lot of importance to it. However, that's merely an impression. On the other hand, I can quite well see that Cathal Brugha and Austin Stack could or would resent anybody who stayed on. The IRB was essentially a secret society that was operating within the republican movement. Therefore, both Stack and Brugha would have had suspicions as to what Collins was doing, what his purpose was. The only meeting at which I was present had none of the fighting men that I knew of there, except possibly Tom Cullen.

I was in Dublin when the treaty was signed. I had been running messages backwards and forwards and happened to be in London towards the close of the negotiations. I was completely opposed to the treaty, firstly on the grounds that I had been opposed to the truce. I felt we could have got much more if we had waited. Secondly, I felt that the imposition of allegiance to the crown would never be acceptable and should never be accepted. Thirdly, the treaty would probably involve the partition of the country which again should never have been accepted. Collins arrived back. At that period we had offices in the Gresham Hotel. I was at our office, early in the morning, waiting for him. There were others there including Eoin O'Duffy. We all welcomed him, I was probably cooler in my welcome. He came over to me after a couple of minutes and said, 'I suppose you're very disappointed and disheartened by all this but there was nothing else I could do.' I said yes, I was completely fed up with it and probably expressed the reasons for my disappointment. And he said, 'Well, I thought that's the way you would feel.'

For me it was quite a blow, because my friends, people like Tom Cullen, Liam Tobin and Collins, people I'd worked with, were all on the treaty side. I was more or less bereft of personal friends in the movement.

I think that the first thing which I did, politically, was to go and see de Valera, and to convey to him my support for his opposition to the treaty. I knew where de Valera stood because he had rejected the treaty publicly. Also I offered my services to help him in any way I could. He was then about to open an office in Suffolk Street in order to try to keep the movement together. He asked me would I help him in that. I agreed, and so I worked with him and Kathleen O'Connell in the office. In a way I gave up military activity and took up a political role. At that time, nobody knew where anybody else stood. This was before the treaty had been debated in the Dáil.

I also had disagreements at home. Mother was at that time very much in favour of the treaty. I could quite well understand her point of view. Most of her lifetime, the struggle had largely been for Home Rule, for some measure of independence and control of our own affairs. To Mother, this looked like a tremendous step forward. It would only be a question of time before we had complete independence. While I understood her point of view, I didn't necessarily agree with it. Having been close to the IRA, having worked in it and known the position of the IRA in the country, I felt that we should have gone on further. There would have been no question of having to accept an oath of allegiance or to accept the partition of the country, or indeed accept any other conditions which were in the treaty.

So Mother and I fell out on this. When I say fell out, we weren't bitter, but we agreed to disagree. We ceased to exchange views very much – political views.

I next went to see Rory O'Connor, who was the obvious leader emerging on the republican side. There was the Chief of Staff, Mulcahy, who accepted the treaty, Collins, and a lot of senior officers who accepted the treaty. The only well-known person on the IRA side who opposed the treaty was Rory O'Connor, he was then Director of Engineering. He combined that post with Officer Commanding, Britain, in charge of IRA units in Britain.

At that time there was a lot of indecision. Much depended right through the country on the lead given by the local IRA leaders. I am thinking of areas in the west which I knew quite well from my earlier days … people like Michael Kilroy, OC 4th Western, took a very strong line against the treaty. So did Tom Maguire, who was the leader of the 3rd Western Division, and also Liam Pilkington, Director of the Sligo Division. They immediately took a very strong line against the treaty and that influenced the people under them, most of the rank and file with them.

Many thought that this was a device, that soon Collins would again take leadership, put an end to the truce and resume fighting for the republic. That idea was spread through the country by many of the pro-treaty people and indeed many of the republicans who couldn't concede that this was acceptable. And it took quite a long time for people to really take sides, in that sense.

The actual giving over of Dublin Castle to an Irish government and the gradual evacuation of British troops from all over the country influenced the rank and file. It had a tremendous effect on Mother, for instance, and lots of people of her generation. It also probably had a great effect on many people in the IRA. However, they recovered from that and realised that it didn't mean very much unless there was going to be freedom, that we were not going to see the treaty leading to a position where Ireland would be kept within the British Empire with an economy of British lives ... as I think Churchill put it at that time, in order to justify the treaty from their side.

We now had a situation in which Ireland *was* to be kept within the empire with an economy of British lives.

During this period there was a great deal of discussion and soul searching among different people. I remember discussing the treaty with Ernie O'Malley and several people whom I knew in the country in the IRA. It was all a very genuine discussion, a search for what was the right thing to do. Then it was felt that the British were putting pressure on Collins and that Collins would break.

We had contacts with Collins on a great many things connected with the north. Collins promised to give us all the assistance he possibly could so that the struggle would continue in the north. Arms were handed over in substantial quantities, in lorry-loads, to the IRA in Dublin, to us, to Rory O'Connor. This was when we were in the Four Courts and beforehand. We had been planning beforehand. Several consignments had gone up already to the north. As far as I was concerned, all the gun-running arrangements that were made before the treaty had continued. Our dealings were with Collins. There were some with Mulcahy, but there was a much greater bond of friendship between Collins and the IRA than in dealings with Mulcahy. Dick Mulcahy wasn't such an endearing type of person as Collins was. Liam

Lynch and the Cork people were very much against the treaty, but Collins, being from Cork himself, there was a certain bond of friendship there all the time. So, most of these things were probably organised unbeknownst to the government. Now Collins never told us this and I don't know what he told other members of the government. Judging by their attitude, by people in the government who have written, by people like Blythe, it is very unlikely that he did tell them. For instance, right up to the day of the attack on the Four Courts arrangements were being made: indeed, on the very day of the attack, a large contingent of arms was transferred to the IRA from Beggars Bush barracks and left the Four Courts for Donegal.

As to why the Four Courts was attacked, it's difficult to separate what is hindsight with what one felt at the time. At the time we felt that the British were exerting strong pressures and were insisting on it. There were very strong rumours, I don't know how true these were, that the British had trained some gunners to man the guns outside the Four Courts. There were also rumours that some British officers were there, supervising the operation of the guns that were shelling the Four Courts. There was nobody in the Free State army capable, or with any knowledge of artillery. Our impression was that this was being done mainly under British pressure.

Divide and conquer … to get the Irish to fight together with an economy of British lives. The sooner civil war could be unleashed, the better, the more likely would the treaty be finally enforced upon Ireland.

Collins himself had probably very divided views. I think that he hoped he would be able to carry through the treaty and use it as a stepping stone for the republic and this was running through the back of his mind, justifying to himself most of his actions. On the other hand, he had loyalty to most of his colleagues in the Provisional government then, Dick Mulcahy in particular, though not an overwhelming loyalty: in some respects he would have preferred the people on the other side. For instance, he had great respect for people like Tom Barry, Liam Lynch and all the Cork IRA commanders, whom he would have known. To that extent his loyalties were divided.

Perhaps this is to a certain extent what was tried later on at the time of the negotiations leading up to the Statute of Westminster. This was a tremendous departure from the British Empire then. I think that Kevin O'Higgins would have seen this as carrying out Collins' intention of using the treaty as a stepping stone towards the achievement of a republic. The real architect in the negotiations with regard to the Statute of Westminster was Paddy McGilligan, with the help of Jack Costello and Hugh Kennedy. FitzGerald, although involved with External Affairs, was ill at that period and does not seem to have played a prominent role.

I attended nearly all the Dáil debates on the treaty, nominally as an officer maintaining guard there. In fact I was really there because I was interested and made it my business to be assigned the task of assisting the guard. I would have arranged this through Liam Tobin or Tom Cullen, with whom I remained on good terms throughout the whole of that period and indeed during the civil war.

My recollection of the treaty debates is somewhat vague … a series of long speeches, predictable on both sides. I was very impressed by Mary MacSwiney's speech. It was long and widely criticised at the time. I must say it made a deep impression of logic and integrity on me. I was much more impressed by the anti-treaty speeches than the pro-treaty speeches. This would have been because I had already formed a subjective view. Most deputies took the predictable line and the split became very obvious. Of course of lot of speculation had gone on beforehand as to which side people would take. Naturally it was the sole topic of conversation from the time the treaty was signed in London until the Dáil debates. That would be a matter of some weeks and we had our own assessments, lists of how people might vote. There had been a lot of canvassing, exercise of pressure by different IRA units who were watching carefully to see how the representatives of their area would vote in the Dáil, but I was obviously wrong in that judgement.

I probably also hoped that Collins would detach himself from Griffith's view. The differences between the two of them had become much more obvious by now. There would have been a possibility that Collins might adopt the attitude: yes. I signed this; now I realise that it is about to split the country in two. Therefore it may lead to a civil war, so I will not vote for the ratification of the treaty, even though I did sign it. Robert Barton and George Gavan Duffy, who had both signed the treaty had voted against it.

One of the matters which surprised me about the debate was the little amount of reference given to the partition of the country. It was a long and detailed debate, but partition was hardly referred to except for a few speakers like Pat McCartan. Otherwise most of the speakers concentrated on the issues of national sovereignty, the oath of allegiance and matters of that kind. This absence of reference to the north may have been due to the fact that they thought the Boundary Commission would define far more natural boundaries, and secondly, the Council of Ireland would have been formed. This had been envisaged under the 1920 Act. There would be some form of unifying administration. It is quite strange, looking back now, how few references there were to the partition of the country by the treaty.

It is difficult to remember what I did after the ratification of the treaty by Dáil Éireann. I was active in an anti-treaty branch of the IRA and Sinn Féin and I worked with de Valera in Suffolk Street. I helped in finalising plans for the Irish Race Congress which was to be held in Paris in January 1922 and which was under organisation for at least a year or two beforehand. The Irish Race Congress was a very grand project that I think had been fathered by de Valera. Its aim was to bring people of Irish descent from all over the world, not only from the United States, but also from the Argentine and countries in Europe where the Irish had played a prominent part, who would be able to support Ireland's struggle. It was intended to be mainly cultural, but also with political influence, as an adjunct to the fight for Irish independence. De Valera wouldn't be stopped from going to it. I know that he went with the approval of the Dáil and the government and that some monies had been made available for it. Indeed, the monies were inadequate, as I learned during the course of the Race Congress. My first task was to help in organising the journey of de Valera, who naturally had no passport. De Valera was disguised as a priest and an American passport had been organised for him. Fr Shanley, an Irish American priest, was travelling with him. We finally set off for Paris. Seán Nunan also came. We drove to Rosslare and took the Rosslare-Fishguard boat. We went to London where I remember one small episode. De Valera wanted to buy a new fountain pen. There was a particular pen or nib he wanted, so we went to a special shop on the Strand. He then proceeded to try out the fountain pens. I was watching him. To my horror he proceeded to sign his name, Eamon de Valera, on a sheet of paper, in order to try out the pen. I gave him a strong kick and took the piece of paper away quickly. He realised that he had, by mistake, written his name.

We stayed in London only for one or two days. We went on to Paris where Seán T. O'Kelly was ambassador. De Valera was very pleasant to travel with, but didn't find it easy to keep time. One always had to keep an eye on his not missing trains.

When we arrived in Paris, Seán Nunan, Fr Shanley, de Valera and I, we stayed at the Grand Hotel in great luxury. The Congress was very large, several hundred delegates. It was presided over by the Duc de Tetuan, an important personage from Spain of Irish descent. He barely spoke English and this made the Congress difficult, particularly as there were no such things then as amplification or simultaneous translation. There were representatives from all over the world. I did not follow the work of the Congress too closely for I was too busy with the practical arrangements, such as arranging dinners, lunches, who de Valera should meet, and so on.

De Valera was the principal person from Ireland at the Congress with the title of Chairman or President. Seán T. O'Kelly was active also. The Congress must have lasted for the best part of a week. My anxieties were concerned with financial matters, worrying how I was going to pay all the bills. In the end I had to borrow some money.

De Valera's extravagance was, I think, a little out of character. I think that Seán T. was running the embassy in Paris and was living in the Grand Hotel. It was the biggest and most expensive hotel in Paris at the time. Seán T. was inclined to be rather lavish. He had certainly done very good information work in Paris. The Paris press was sympathetic to Ireland. I remember during the Black and Tan war, huge posters showing Cork in flames. So he had done quite a tremendous job with public relations in Paris.

I would like to relate an incident that happened years afterwards, but it is connected with this visit to Paris. Several years after the civil war, around 1925/26, after Kid and I were married, we were living in Paris. We had a favourite restaurant, which was not as expensive as it is now, the Ramponneau in the Avenue Marceau. It was extremely good, it still exists, and is one of the best restaurants in Paris. When we had some money, Kid and I would go and have a meal in the Ramponneau. I noticed that the patron of the Ramponneau, who was also *maître d'hôtel*, used to be friendly and looked at me curiously time after time. One day he came over and said. 'Now I have you. You're Irish.' I said, yes. 'Now I know who you are. I was *maître d'hôtel* in the Grand Hotel at the time of this Irish Race Congress. I used to supervise the services for M. de Valera and yourself. You had adjoining rooms and I came in with the waiter who brought your breakfast in the morning.' And so I recognised the man then, fairly easily. He went on to say that he wanted to tell me a story, adding that 'it doesn't matter now, but it certainly gave me a lot of worry. While you were there, representatives who announced themselves as being from the British Embassy but who were obviously British secret service agents, arrived and offered me very large sums of money for your waste paper basket and any papers I could find from your room or M. de Valera's room. It was a tempting offer, a sum of money which would have enabled me to set up business. I was very tempted to accept it. The next morning I came into your room, as usual, with your breakfast. You were asleep. But I saw protruding from under your pillow the handle of a revolver. This shocked me and I returned to discuss the matter with my wife. We both decided that I should have nothing to do with the British secret service offer. I rejected it that day.'

After the Irish Race Congress, we returned to Ireland. I continued to work with de Valera for some time. However, I got more and more involved in the reconstruction of the IRA. I was appointed Assistant Director of Organisation to Ernie O'Malley. Most of my work consisted of drawing up various forms and of compiling from them statistics of strength of the different units in the army; of organising and forming units where there were none, while Ernie was carrying out a systematic inspection of all the divisions, organising as he was going along. One arms deal, in regard to which I certainly got my instructions from Michael Collins, was when he showed me a letter which he had again received from the Clan na Gael in America. I still have a visual memory of the meeting I had with Collins in the Gresham Hotel, at our offices. Eamonn Price was present at that meeting. The letter concerned the possibility of obtaining large quantities of arms from an organisation of German officers, through an American who had been sent over. They were prepared to sell them to us. The Clan na Gael people who wrote the letter warned, however, that they had no real knowledge of this man named Hoover. Michael Collins instructed me to meet him and investigate this proposition. Although I have no idea of the time or date of this meeting, I can fix the date at the end of this expedition. This episode started at the time when my relations with Collins were such, that though he knew I was strongly against the treaty he would entrust a mission of this kind to me. He knew I was working with Rory O'Connor at the time, I am sure, because I never made any secret of that. The instructions I received from Collins were in the Gresham and so must have been after the truce had begun. I think it was after the treaty had been signed, and that, I think, was the last I saw of Collins.

What makes me think it was after the treaty was signed was because I remember thinking that Collins had probably assigned this mission to me as an indication if not an assurance that he was regarding the treaty as a stepping stone to the republic, not as a final settlement, that this was merely the breathing space. Despite everything he was prepared to continue arming the IRA, and had entrusted me with this mission to obtain very substantial quantities of arms. It may have been before the prohibited army convention of the IRA went ahead on 25 March. Strangely enough, during all that period, my relations with the Collins side of the IRA were quite friendly, that is Tom Cullen, Liam Tobin, Michael Collins, Eamonn Price – I never quarrelled with them during that period.

I probably spent some weeks with Hoover. I arrived back in Dublin some time around 11 June 1922 after a long and tiring journey. I had left Germany on Friday morning for London via Brussels and Ostend, arriving there the next evening just in time to catch the Irish Mail at Euston by which I arrived in Dublin before 8 a.m.

I went straight to the Four Courts where, after having a wash and some breakfast, I saw Liam, who told me he was glad I had come back as a convention had been summoned and that nobody could find the papers in connection with delegates, so immediately I hurried off to make all arrangements required. Our department arranged all the secretarial work of the convention.

There was a good deal of vacillation and doubt as to particular units of the IRA at this time. Frank Aiken, who was OC 4th Northern, had not declared his attitude clearly, whether he would go with us, go with the Free State, or remain outside. Also there was a good deal of doubt as to the attitude of the 1st Southern Division. It was felt that Liam Lynch and Liam Deasy were so eager to find a compromise that they were trying to patch things up. It was felt that in the course of trying to patch things up with Collins, they might reach a compromise which was unacceptable to the rest.

I had, at one stage, become very suspicious of Hoover having double dealings behind our backs. Hoover had gone to the Shelbourne, but I had arranged to meet him in the Four Courts. I would have liked to be there when he walked unsuspectingly in and was arrested, but I had to be in the Mansion House, so I left instructions with the OC of the Four Courts for his arrest. I then went to the Mansion House, where I spent about an hour inspecting the credentials of the various delegates.

This convention was summoned to consider the army unification proposals and Tom Barry's resolution on declaring war. Some of the proceedings remain a blur in my memory, but nearly everybody spoke and some made long speeches at that. Liam Mellows made a depressing speech which showed clearly that there was a split in the Executive. Rory and Liam saw the huge mistake it had been for Barry to bring forward such a proposal to a convention. They knew it might lead to the withdrawal of part of Cork from the republican army. At the same time they understood that this was the only policy which could be consistently followed by us.

It was by far better to break off from those who were prepared to compromise on such a vital question, that of the control of the army and the working of the treaty. It probably would have been better if the split had come before, however weakening it might have been. It was far more weakening to have the army controlled by people who, although quite sincere, did not put their heart into it and who still believed that our opponents could be trusted in negotiations. It must be remembered that there was hardly a promise made by those who negotiated with us on behalf of the provisional government which wasn't broken by them. So it was in this frame of mind that Rory put up a short but firm defence of the war proposals. Everybody was depressed and solemn.

The question was put sometime around 8 p.m. Peadar Breslin and I were the tellers. The motion was passed by a couple of votes, but was challenged on the grounds that a brigade was there which wasn't represented at the last convention. That objection was upheld, a new vote was taken, and the motion was lost. There was more discussion, during which Rory said to tell Liam Pilkington and some other members of the Executive that if the compromise proposals were brought to the convention, he was leaving it. These proposals came and about half the delegates got up and left. Rory, Liam and Joe McKelvey held a hurried consultation outside the room and decided to have a meeting of the convention the next day in the Four Courts. This was announced to the delegates who had come out with them, and Liam told me to go and announce it to the rest of the convention and to get his hat which he had left behind.

I went in and got Liam's hat. Cathal Brugha was speaking. Cathal had been strongly against Barry's resolution, but was also strongly against the compromise resolution because he thought an agreement could be found and that this wasn't the best time to declare war on England. I waited for a pause in his speech and then announced that a convention would be held in the Four Courts the next morning. There was an absolute silence, and I could hear my steps like shots from the top of the room to the door. A few more delegates came out.

Things came to a head after the general election, and following the assassination of Sir Henry Wilson. One of our officers, Leo Henderson, was arrested, and so the following day Ernie O'Malley and I went out and arrested Ginger O'Connell and brought him back to the Four Courts. Then on 28 June the Four Courts garrison was attacked using British equipment. The shelling lasted for several days. We surrendered on 30 June. That was the commencement of civil war in the country. We were brought to Mountjoy jail, and I spent most of the civil war period in jail.

We were delighted of course, when de Valera threw in his lot with what then came to be called the Irregulars after the attack on the Four Courts. We had still certain misgivings that he might compromise on certain issues. However, we were delighted that he had shown that measure of unity. I think there was a belief among the people in prison that there would be a closing of ranks in the republican movement which would succeed, finally, in overthrowing the Provisional government. We were delighted when Frank Aiken and the 4th Northern Division came in, in August 1922.

When we heard of Griffith's death on 12 August 1922, there was no rejoicing: on the contrary, it marked the passing of a father figure in the Sinn Féin movement, possibly not regretted so much on the IRA side because we looked upon him as a compromiser. He was still held in respect for what he had done in the past during a very lean period of the building up of Sinn Féin and literary revival movement, *United Irishman* and so on.

We did hear of Collins' death, and we were all very sad. We had had respect for Collins, and as far as Rory and I were concerned, though not necessarily as far as the rest of the prison was concerned, it was the last hope that Collins would detach himself from the Provisional government and join with us again.

We heard that Pádraig Ó Máille and Seán Hales had been shot by the IRA in Dublin, I think on the quays. Here I should mention that for some time before that, preparations were being made to transfer a number of us to the Seychelles Islands or to St Helena. I don't know how we heard this; we seemed to receive plenty of intelligence as to what was going on outside. On the night of 7 December we heard rumours that some of us were going to be sent to either one of these islands immediately. I didn't pay very much attention: I forget what time it was in the evening or night when Paudeen O'Keefe arrived with a squad of soldiers and officers. They were swinging guns, Paudeen O'Keefe was tight, cursing about the place and ordered Rory and I to get up and to dress. He gave us something like twenty minutes to pack our things to get ready to leave. During this time Rory and I speculated as to what was to happen. I said, trying to cheer up Rory, although I wasn't quite certain, 'Oh well, we're off to the Seychelles Islands now. This may be no harm at all.' O'Keefe came back and opened the cell door, shouting, 'You, get back to bed, you don't need to dress. Rory O'Connor has to come along, but you don't.' So I helped Rory to pack his things. Rory had some money with him, including the silver and gold coins that had been used by him at the wedding of Kevin O'Higgins a short time before. He wanted to leave all the money he had with me. I insisted that he should take it with him. I said, 'Well, on the Seychelles Islands, gold sovereigns may be invaluable. You might even be able to buy a ship with them, and leave!' So I sewed them into the belt of his trousers and a short time afterwards he went off, and I said goodbye. At the cell door I saw Liam Mellows going off and Joe McKelvey and Dick Barrett. Dick Barrett I remember well going down the long metal staircase, singing 'The Hills of Donegal'. Whenever I've heard this Donegal song since, it has always reminded me of that picture of Dick Barrett going with all his things in a bundle; he had put all his things into a blanket, which he carried as a bundle on his back, singing 'The Hills of Donegal'.

I went back to the cell and tidied up. I folded up Rory's blankets and tidied the rest of the things which he not taken with him. He had left me the game of chess, which was stolen afterwards from me by one of the soldiers I think. I didn't sleep.

At about six or seven in the morning I heard volleys of shots. It was a holy day and we had Mass. I knew before Mass that they had been shot. You could read it on the face of the soldiers… Canon MacMahon said Mass and he announced it. Our relations with the church and the chaplain were very strained at the time. Canon MacMahon and the regular chaplain refused to give us absolution unless we first of all were prepared to say we were sorry for having opposed the elected government of the people, or the Provisional government, and to sign a piece of paper to that effect. Of course no one did; we resented this bitterly. It was the complete abuse of power by chaplains and priests who should have at least stayed out of it even if they were pro-Free State. They had no business to use their religious functions in order to try and force the acceptance of political status which had been refused.

Hence our relations with Canon MacMahon and the chaplain were not good. But I forget on that morning whether it was he who sent for me, or whether I went myself. I went into the sacristy with him and there he immediately produced a piece of paper. 'I implore you to sign this,' he said. 'If you don't sign, you will be the next to be executed. And I don't know who else of your comrades will be executed, so you must all sign this now.' I really got furious and launched into a tirade against him and the abuse of his function. As a representative of the church and of God on earth, he was trying to use his religious function in a moment of crisis such as this, when he knew, or should have known, that we were under such pressure to get us to sign the document. I was really outraged. My outrage must have been conveyed to Canon MacMahon who suddenly sat down and burst into tears. He held his head in his hands and cried. Then he said, 'The most terrible thing about all this is they were executed on a holy day, and this is against Canon Law. You cannot execute anybody on a holy day.'

This even made me more vindictive because he realised that this was wrong, but for the wrong reasons; that it was merely because they had been executed on 8 December on the feast of the Immaculate Conception. I explained to him that the fact that it was a feast day or not did not matter, that it was the fact of executing men who were prisoners without any trial, without any charge, without any opportunity to defend themselves and for a political purpose. So we continued to argue, and he put back the piece of paper. He had wanted to leave the paper with me, but I refused to take it. It was a typed sheet, undertaking that I would lay down arms and recognise the Provisional government and the constitution or whatever it was at the time.

We kept talking: he was leaving by the stairs which led down from the sacristy and on to the front gate. The sacristy was over that portion of the prison. I went down with him. The soldiers who were on duty opened the gates, the small doors in the main gate of the prison. He and I walked down the front avenue of the prison and suddenly I realised that I had left the prison. Without any thought of escape, I turned around, walked back, and knocked at the door to get in. Of course this was a piece of complete madness in retrospect, but I was so shook that it never occurred to me to go on walking. I don't think that

Canon MacMahon had noticed it either because he was so upset, still arguing about 'terrible' things, and should we not sign, and so on. I found my way back into the prison, but I had to get guards to open the gates. I think that they were so upset that they didn't notice I had gone out and come back in again.

I would find it very hard to find any justifiable explanation for the conduct of the church at that time. I think that the only reasonable explanation would be something like this. The Irish bishops had very close contacts with the British government. They had been financially and administratively dependent on the British for educational facilities in Ireland. They had developed a close connection with the British administration in regard to matters like financing Maynooth, financing education generally, the power of the clergy and interests of the clergy. The British government had used the clergy as part of their establishment in the same way as the Church of England acted in England. There had been that long tradition. There was a feeling against anybody who rejected the British government and rejected the Irish Party, which had been very close to the church. The Parnell split beforehand had given strength to the conservative wing of the bishops. They resented, some very strongly, for example Bishop Cohalan in Cork and Cardinal Logue, though he said little. I think they were completely opposed to Sinn Féin and more so to the IRA which they saw as red riot and revolution. The Russian revolution had taken place sometime before and to them this was evil, and in some respects this was a reflection of the Russian revolution. Communism was not used as a catch-cry then, as in later years. However, I think the bishops may have used the concept as a stick with which to frighten the people. They were really pro-establishment and that is the only explanation which I can think of for their conduct.

I should qualify all that by saying that many members of the clergy, and some bishops, disagreed with the attitude of these particular bishops.

I do not know whether or not this is in context, but I do know that on account of the attitude of the church in Ireland and in particular on account of the chaplains in the prison (the absurd requirement of getting the prisoners to give political undertakings before giving absolution) that representations were made in Rome to the Vatican. This happened either through Count Plunkett or some emissary of the Vatican who was a papal count, and also through Mary MacSwiney in a letter which was smuggled out of prison by her. These resulted in a papal nuncio being sent by the Pope to Dublin. Monsignor Luzio arrived in Dublin in March 1923. He stayed in the Shelbourne Hotel and had to go and visit bishops individually and informally: normally a papal nuncio would be received and probably be put up by the archbishop or cardinal.

Either as a result of Monsignor Luzio's visit or otherwise, it may have been after the executions of Rory, Liam, Joe and Dick, seven additional chaplains were sent in. We could go to confession to any one of eleven different priests. Among those, there would always be two or three who would give absolution without requiring any undertaking. This, I thought, made a complete farce of religion. It meant that we went to confession, went around until we got the one priest who would give us absolution. It was argued in defence of this that it was left to the conscience of each confessor. I think it was probably as a result of directives from the Vatican that they had no right to refuse absolution. I have heard brief accounts of the report Monsignor Luzio made after his return to the Vatican, one of which was from the then President of the Irish College, Monsignor Hagan, and also from the General of the Carmelites, Father Magennis.

Strangely enough, we didn't discuss the executions or why those men were chosen at that time. We were all shocked, hurt and pained. It was an awful blow. We had become very friendly with each other and we had come to like one another. As far as Rory O'Connor was concerned, my relationship with him was as an uncle and nephew. I was so fond of Rory: he was such a nice man. I developed quite an admiration and a respect for him. In the same way I was very fond of Joe McKelvey who was full of life and bounce. I knew Liam Mellows less well. Dick Barrett I knew well because he was a lively Cork man. Indeed, I also used to wonder how it was odd for him to be singing 'The Hills of Donegal' going down the stairs that morning

After Rory's execution I remember my feelings in the cell. I spent a few days alone. I carefully folded Rory's blankets neatly in a corner:

three blankets, a sheet, and a pillow slip. I used to do this every day. I kept them there that way for some days. I also put away the set of chess which Rory had made during the time when we were in jail. He had carved them out of pieces of wood with a penknife. And I put those away feeling that I must keep these as a kind of memento. We had developed a certain order in the cell. We had each folded up our blankets and put them into the corners, using them to lean against as a kind of an armchair during the day.

Several days passed by and then I decided I might as well use some of Rory's blankets. It was cold at night. I remember having a funny kind of feeling that in a way I shouldn't use them, they are his blankets, but then arguing with myself, well, he's gone after all, and I'm sure he would like me to use them. We used to sleep on the floor and I could use them on the floor. After a few days Seán Buckley was brought in. He was a TD from Bandon, West Cork. He came and shared the cell with me. He was a nice charming man, elderly in my eyes then, probably about sixty. I think that he was put in my cell so that I would look after him a little bit and so that he would cheer me up. He wasn't well part of the time, he had a bad cough. I got fond of Seán Buckley: he was a pleasant cell companion. We used to talk a good deal, long discussions at night about the civil war, every aspect, and naturally about Rory.

I cannot remember ever really having come to any conclusion as to why the executions had taken place. The execution of Dick Barrett and Joe McKelvey was completely incomprehensible. Dick Barrett was not a very senior IRA officer. True, he was from Cork and from the 1st Southern Division. Joe McKelvey was the OC of the 3rd Northern Division. This was obviously lining up with the British completely as far as we were concerned. The 3rd Northern Division included the Belfast area, and Joe McKelvey was the commander of that whole area. There was the kind of feeling: was this done at the request of the British or not? Did they want Joe McKelvey out of the way? Rory O'Connor was an obvious choice as one of the big leaders. Liam Mellows was also a well-known leader. As reprisals, I could see that the enmity, and I won't mince words here, I can see that there would be the personal enmity of certain members of the government towards Rory

O'Connor and towards Liam Mellows. They had opposed their philosophy. I would say that Blythe and some of these members would have felt a type of bitter enmity towards them. The whole thing of course is incomprehensible and the one thing which surprised me most about the executions was Kevin O'Higgins. O'Higgins had a legal training, and I think he was honestly and sincerely devoted to trying to establish some rule of law in the country. I am surprised that Kevin O'Higgins would have consented or been a party to the executions.

Apart from that, I don't remember very much because I was in prison. Then we started off that long tussle for escape. There was an escape attempt, the first steps planned by Peadar Breslin who was the OC of the wing at the time. I can't remember whether this was before or after the execution of Rory O'Connor and the other three. It meant overpowering the guard. However, something went wrong and a sentry was killed. One of our prisoners was also killed.

A lot of my impressions on developments from June to December 1922 would have been as the result of judgements formed after discussion with Rory O'Connor in jail. The belief was that sooner or later Collins and some members of the government (among those Rory O'Connor included Kevin O'Higgins, who was a close personal friend of his) would realise that an end should be put to the civil war and that we should come to terms on the basis of some republican step towards repudiation of the treaty and insist on demanding further concessions by Britain. There was considerable disappointment when we realised that they were becoming the instruments of British policy in Ireland and were more and more carrying into effect the Churchillian policy of keeping control of Ireland with an economy of British lives. This ran through my head most of the time. I wondered how men who had been so courageous and such strong nationalists had got to the stage of fighting a war, more or less on behalf of British interests in Ireland.

I should like to make this comment, before going on further. I don't blame de Valera in any way for the civil war. I do blame de Valera for not having participated in the treaty negotiations, or for not having taken adequate steps to ensure that the delegation would act continually under the control of the cabinet as a whole. It has always struck me as fantastic that the delegation, the plenipotentiaries in

London, should not have returned to Dublin every Friday evening and returned to London every Monday morning. There was a complete loss of contact and loss of touch between the members of the cabinet at home, de Valera, Stack, Brugha and so on, and the delegation itself. This I blame de Valera for. The various despatches that I carried backwards and forwards seem to be the only link for the exchange of views. Telephones were not used in those days; telephoning from Dublin to London was very difficult. He should either have gone as the leader of the delegation himself, or alternatively have taken steps for keeping in much closer touch with the delegation as a whole and with individual members. From my experience later on as Minister for External Affairs, I certainly would not have allowed any delegation of officials to go to negotiate even a minor trade or other agreement, with the British or any other country, without being in daily contact with them, finding out exactly what was happening from day to day and giving them very clear instructions as to what they could or could not do, what they should or should not do, what they could or could not agree to. I should and would ask them to come back if necessary. I think that during the treaty negotiations de Valera should have insisted on the delegates coming back each weekend. There was no reason why they couldn't. In those three months it should have been a rule that they come home every Friday evening and return each Monday. De Valera had not created the opportunity to enable him to maintain the personal contact that he should have had with each member of the delegation. It wasn't enough to receive reports from Childers. I was particularly conscious of this, because I was conscious that I was the main link between the delegation and the cabinet. It seemed to me odd that they didn't go back, probably because of the fact that I went backwards and forwards so frequently, so freely, and I had no real difficulty in doing it.

CHAPTER V

After a time, two or three hundred of us were transferred to a new camp which had been built at Newbridge. I remember the journey well; it was a big operation. We were taken in lorries from Mountjoy to either Kingsbridge or Sallins and put onto a train. We were all handcuffed. I remember finding a packet of hacksaw blades in the bottom of the lorry. I could never make out whether or not it was a friendly soldier who had left these, but naturally we got going with the hacksaw blades and proceeded to saw our handcuffs. This was done very quietly. I sawed the handcuff off the man who was handcuffed to me, who as far as I can remember was Paddy MacHanley. He was a big hefty man, and it became very painful for him because his wrist was bigger than mine, and of course when I was coming to the end, I was cutting through his flesh as well. But he was very courageous and he said, go on, go on, and we finally got the handcuff off. It was bad management and bad planning on my part, because my wrist was much smaller and I could have cut a handcuff on my wrist much more easily.

We were on the train when we finally got our handcuffs off. Some of the others had cut through their handcuffs. We were all sitting in compartments: strangely enough we had no soldiers with us. They were in special carriages interspersed throughout the train. At one stage the train slowed down and one of our companions, Cunningham, who knew the countryside, opened the door, jumped out of the train and disappeared down the embankment. The machine guns fired on him, but apparently he got away. The train stopped a mile or two beyond, but by that time it was like looking for a needle in a haystack.

Finally we got to Newbridge, where we were put into this camp. There were about two thousand prisoners from all over the country. There were also big camps in the Curragh, Tintown Number One and Tintown Number Two.

Newbridge was a mixture of huts and old unused military buildings, most of whose windows had been broken out. There were stables as well which were also used. I was in a wooden hut about sixty feet long, with beds pushed very close to each other. I suppose there would have been thirty to forty in a hut. The people who had come from Mountjoy with me were all together. Next to me I had Jack Plunkett. He was a son of Count Plunkett and he was always a little delicate. He had an elder brother, George, who was much stronger and who looked after Jack. George was on the other side of Jack. After a while, Jack and I used to play chess. Jack would get very annoyed when I beat him and really took it as a personal insult. Of course, as I improved, I did beat him fairly often. But then for a couple of days we wouldn't play chess, and he wouldn't talk to me.

We had another character in the hut called Chummy Hogan from Terenure. Chummy was quite a rough and tumble character. Then there was also Donnie O'Reilly who was as young as I was, or younger. Chummy, Donnie O'Reilly and I used to pal around together a good deal and planned a whole lot of tricks here and there.

It was very difficult to maintain discipline in the camp. It was hard to get people to obey orders. The camp was organised militarily with a headquarters and a Camp Commandant, Tom MacMahon. I had some position on the camp staff; I was an intelligence officer. We made Chummy Hogan the OC of the hut because he was the most untidy and disorderly of the people there, and we felt that it would make him tow the line, get up in the morning and so on. Fatigue parties were appointed every day. Their duties were to clean out the huts, do all the chores. Another fatigue party would go to fetch the food, and so on. As intelligence officer, I watched out for opportunities of escaping. I also had to find out what tunnels were afoot because every small group was running some tunnel or escape project of its own. These were badly planned, unsuccessful and brought on attention. And so, part of my job was to try and find out what escape projects were on so that we could try and pick out the best ones. We had one major escape project, a tunnel, of course, and it was built fairly well, but was finally caught. Another one was started then.

I was watching daily a big ten-ton military lorry that brought bread into the camp. It used to come into the compound. The prisoners would carry the bread out of the lorry and on wet days it had a tarpaulin on top; otherwise it was open. When the bread was taken out, the tarpaulin was taken off and thrown on the ground. When the bread was off, the tarpaulin was thrown back into a heap on the bottom of the lorry.

Having watched these proceedings for a long time and having volunteered to take part in the unloading of the bread on these occasions, I decided that this would be one way of escaping. So one nice, misty, wet morning, I unloaded the bread and I made a dive in afterwards, under the tarpaulin that was in a heap on the bottom of the lorry. I had planned this fairly carefully, worked out the number of seconds, minutes and so on, that it would take for the lorry to go through the first gate, around the compound itself, and then I had estimated the amount of time it would take to get onto the Curragh road, because it went from Newbridge to Kildare. I wanted to stay in the lorry, just until it was out of Newbridge town, before it got onto the Curragh plain itself. There were a few bunches of trees there. I knew the road fairly well and I decided that this should be the place where I would jump off the lorry, so that I would have some cover from the trees, whereas if I were on the Curragh plain I would have no cover and could be seen for miles.

So I got into the lorry, under the tarpaulin. The gate out of the compound was a double gate; the lorry pulled up at the first gate, the soldiers came, searched the lorry and signed the form saying they had checked the lorry out. I wasn't detected; being a wet day favoured things – they wanted to get back inside their huts. The second gates were opened and the lorry trundled off. After a very short space of time the lorry stopped and, as far as I was concerned, this was an unscheduled stop. I didn't know what happened the lorry from the time it went out of my sight to the time it went back to the Curragh. Then suddenly there was a tug, and another tug, and heavy things had been thrown in, hitting me on the head and piling up around me. I didn't know what they were. They turned out to be bread boards. The officers and the non-commissioned officers used to get special cakes which were brought on bread boards, and empty boards were being thrown into the lorry. Normally the tarpaulin should have gone down under their weight. I heard one of the soldiers say: 'Hey, there's something under the tarpaulin, go in and have a look.' And soldiers came in, and there I was under the bread boards. I was brought into the guard room. And I thought I was in for a hammering, but I didn't get a hammering. They were very cross and rather amused. So I stayed in the guard room until some time that night, and then I was transferred back to Mountjoy, into 'B' wing this time.

By and large I was rather glad, because you had a certain degree of privacy in Mountjoy which you didn't have in a camp, living with thirty or forty fellows in a hut and having to maintain discipline — people got on each other's nerves. It made life more difficult. Personally I never minded solitary confinement. I was in solitary on several occasions and it never worried me at all. I would read if I had something to read. I would pace up and down the cell and think of different things. I had no regular system. I used to sleep a lot, but it never really got me down, particularly if I had something to read.

I was in solitary confinement for three days the first time I was in jail, and all I had was the Bible. So I amused myself reading bits of the Bible, and pondering on it.

However, this time when I got back to Mountjoy there were a lot of the younger men from the West in. Tommy Kettrick, Tommy Heavy, Tom Derrig and others. We decided to start off a plan of escaping. I was sharing an end cell with Tommy Heavy. We took a cell right near the inner end of the wing: that is the end nearest the circle. Mountjoy is built in four big wings that are joined in a circle at the centre, the axis. Somehow or another I had been able to get half a razor blade, and we started cutting the bars off the windows of the cell. We did it slowly, and carefully so as not to make noise. We used to select our time very carefully. We cut in a slant so as we could take the bars out and fit them in again, and they would stay put. We would cover up the place we had cut with soap and dirt. Having done this (we had no very concrete idea in mind), I thought that the first essential was to try and get out of the cell itself, and do a certain amount of reconnaissance in the grounds so as to find out if there was any possible way we could get out over the outside wall.

The first thing of course was to find out exactly where each sentry was, and what their beats were, how long they took to walk from one post to another, when they were inspected, to get to know their whole routine. So for many a night, either Tommy or myself used to go out, with sheets and blankets tied together, slip down to the ground and crawl on our hands and knees around the grounds of the prison inside, sometimes lying quite flat, to watch the movements of the sentries and the military guards in the prisons. It wasn't easy to think of any scheme whereby one could climb over the wall. The sentries had a beat at the foot of the wall inside. Also the sentries were on top of the wall, in special nests which had been built for them. That would make it difficult to climb the wall which was very high; we would have needed some way of making a ladder to hop us up the wall and down the other side. So it didn't prove to be very encouraging. Tunnels were still being caught on the ground floor by the windows.

One day, a group of us were discussing the matter with Dr Tom Powell from Galway, the mastermind of the project for our tunnel. This undoubtedly was one of the best organised attempted jail breaks that every occurred in Ireland. Tom Powell had a brainwave, that instead of trying to start a tunnel from the ground floor, or the basement, we should start from the ceiling, or the roof. There were four floors in the wings. We should do this by breaking into the space between the ceiling of the cells and the roof. It was a v-shaped roof and there was a space of about ten feet between the top of the cells and the top of the roof, and a slant of course. But there was plenty of room. At one cell at the end of the wing there was a big round steel trap door with a padlock which was used by warders or workmen when they had to attend to the water heating system which was hardly ever used.

So the first step was to get a key for the padlock. This was rather easy. We had a key in no time. Then the tunnel itself was organised and carefully planned. Tom Powell had a small group of four or five who helped and gradually we recruited about thirty prisoners into the escape plan. We had to be careful, because we knew that informers had been put into the wing of the prison with us in order to find out if there were any tunnels. We had to make sure nobody would talk loosely. We organised them and swore them all to secrecy in the most formal fashion. The plan was to go up into the space between the ceiling and the roof, right up to one of the main chimney stacks. There are two big chimney stacks in Mountjoy, you can see them from the outside. We would break into the stack which was nearest to us. This was no mean task because it was very heavily built with granite rocks. Then we would make a ladder, go right down to the basement, and start digging a tunnel there.

We had succeeded in having four prisoners more in the cell than the authorities knew about. This was essential, so that at any time we could be four prisoners short. If there was a sudden count, four prisoners could still be working away in a tunnel. There were no lists of prisoners, just numbers. The authorities must have made attempts to draw up a list, but they knew exactly how many prisoners were in each wing because they used to count us at different intervals. The operation on the tunnel went very well. We broke into the main chimney stack. We had to make special clothes to work in. One of the big dangers was that the guards would notice clay or soot on our hands or clothes; the chimney had a big, thick coating of soot inside. So we had to take special working clothes in, strip and get into a kind of pyjamas. Naturally pyjamas were ideal for this kind of thing, so our operations extended to the task of stealing some pyjamas here and there from our colleagues. When they were missed, there would be some trouble!

In the space in between, the clothes used to be washed, we had a team doing nothing else but washing and ironing clothes and getting them ready, so that when we came out, there would be no trace of anything on them. We also had the lighting department. We made the lights from tins, melted fat from meat, and a wick made from blankets. As fat was in great demand, it was therefore necessary to have three or four men working on the issuing of rations, to extract some fat from the meat. Sometimes part of the ration was severely reduced, when we ran short of fat for the lights!

There was one great occasion, in regard to pyjamas. Captain David Robinson was in our wing, he had lost an eye in World War I. A titled lady friend of his sent him four pairs of beautiful silk pyjamas, with his initials embroidered on them. And one by one they disappeared, much to his annoyance. We used to be very tickled, working with whomever was wearing these beautiful silk pyjamas.

The tunnel proceeded. I was the first or second person to go down the ladder. I have forgotten the measurements, but it was a ladder long enough to reach from the top of the roof of the wing, right down into the basement. It was made of bits of blankets, bits of sheeting, bits of wire, anything we could get; it used to swing around in the middle of this chimney which was a rather terrifying experience. Side by side with this ladder, we had a hand rope, made out of blankets too. You could hold on to this going down, so even if anything went wrong with the ladder we had a back-up. I used to do my regular shift: allow 20 minutes for going down the ladder, work for 30 to 40 minutes in the tunnel, and 20 minutes for going up the ladder, when I would be relieved by somebody else. There were always two down below at the bottom of the tunnel, and two on top, keeping an eye on the ladder. Then it was a question of having a tremendous wash and scrub. There were tanks there, for the water supply when the hot pipes were on. However, the hot pipes were not on, so we used these tanks for washing. Luckily, after working away for about a month, at the tunnel proper itself and the job of cutting out the chimney through granite and stonework, we finally got to the clay. The clay had to be brought back. Accordingly as the clay was dug, it was put into a pillow slip, or a sack which had been made, and then brought right back and hauled up to the top, then the clay was carefully emptied out at the edge of the roof, and the sacks were returned and refilled. It was a very highly sophisticated and complicated operation. But at the end of about a month or so, one day, I was digging away doing my shift. Suddenly I went through to a metal shaft and a gush of air came out, blowing out my life. This tunnel was barely two feet by eighteen inches high, and you were lying on your tummy the whole time. At first I got a fright as it was so unexpected but it turned out to be a blessing. We had broken, by accident, into an airshaft that went under the jail, which we knew nothing about. By this airshaft, we were able to get right up to the end of each wing, and to start digging from there to get out. It was very close to the wall.

However, at this time, October 1923, a big hunger strike started in some camps; I think in one of the Tintown camps in the Curragh. Prisoners were striking against bad conditions and for release. This was discussed by all the prisoners and they decided to go on hunger strike. The same thing happened in Mountjoy. Each wing separately discussed the hunger strike and decided to refuse to eat.

Our tunnel group, naturally, didn't want the strike. On the other hand, we didn't want to oppose the strike, or we would have been accused of being cowardly, opposing steps that might bring about the release of all the prisoners. We argued this out very carefully ourselves: we said that if our tunnel succeeded, most of the people in the wing would be able to escape, but only a handful might not be caught again. Certainly it wouldn't help the thousands in other prisons. Therefore, we couldn't seriously oppose this hunger strike.

The hunger strike then started. This was October/November, so the prison authorities decided to turn on the heating. They switched on the hot water pipes, but there was no water in the pipes, and no water flowing; the heating system had been completely disrupted by our tunnel. We had used all the water in the tanks and had used the piping for tools. And so they went up to investigate what had happened and found the tunnel. It was a disaster because I think it was the most perfect tunnel or escape operation that had ever been envisaged.

I was blamed for the tunnel, of course, with two or three of the leaders in the prison. It was decided to shift us from Mountjoy to Kilmainham, where there would be more security. At this time we had been on hunger strike for four or five days and I had pains in my stomach, cramps. I was feeling depressed at the tunnel going to waste, and not at all cheerful at the prospect of a prolonged hunger strike, or of dying on hunger strike.

That night, they arrived to shift us to Kilmainham Jail. I was in bed and refused to get up because I wasn't feeling well. I was then dragged out of my cell in my pyjamas and yanked down the stairs. I remember well being pulled by two soldiers down the stairs, bumping at each step, which did not improve my physical condition at the time. I was thrown into the bottom of a lorry, feeling cold and miserable. There were four or five of us in the lorry, including Michael Price and Daithi O'Donoghue, an old Sinn Féiner and IRA man, and military guard. I would say about fifty prisoners were being shifted.

For some extraordinary reason, apparently our lorry lost its way or lost the rest of the convoy. I think there was a crowd gathered outside the gates of Mountjoy at this time. Our lorry went virtually towards the Berkeley Church near the North Circular Road and stopped just at the church. The officer and the soldiers jumped out to discuss the next step with the driver and an officer in front. I suddenly decided to sit up, and look out, and low and behold there was nothing to prevent me from leaving. So I slid away promptly in my pyjamas and dashed across the road. I looked back and saw Michael Price. It was about three or four in the morning and so it wasn't easy to identify people. And then I saw somebody else coming out, and somebody else, and then I heard shouting. The guards had finally noticed that the prisoners were all escaping and were firing wildly around the place. By this time I hopped up into a little laneway opposite the side of Berkeley Road or Berkeley Chapel that went northwards. I travelled on this and heard soldiers coming at one stage, so I jumped over a wall into a garden and lay there until they had passed and then got back again. After that I was moving up a lane when I heard steps coming up another lane, so I crept very carefully. It was only one person. I reached the corner, and hit my nose against a pair of shoes and a hand. It was Michael Price, who had also escaped, and had got into another laneway. But Michael Price had taken off his shoes and for some extraordinary reason was holding them in front of him. The shoes were the first thing that went around the corner and hit me on the nose. We then joined forces and went together.

We travelled quite a long way. My general plan was to cross the canal. The only place I could think of on that side to get to fairly conveniently was Maureen Buckley's house. Her father was subsequently made Governor General by de Valera. It wasn't far: our whole problem was to get across the canal. So we lay in different places, waiting for a good opportunity. Shots were being fired around the city; it was still more or less semi-civil war period. We could hear lorries and armoured cars searching for us all over the place. We got near Cross Guns Bridge on the road to Glasnevin and lay there until there was complete quietness. Then we walked briskly across the bridge. Some corporation official came along, putting on or off lights, or listening to water pipes, or some such function. I remember well – how ridiculous one can be – saying to Michael Price, let the two of us walk very straight and upright, and he'll just think we're coming back from a party. So we both walked very straight, Michael Price still carrying his shoes in his hands in front of him, I in my pyjamas, and walked past this man as if nothing had happened!

At some later stage, after we had crossed the bridge, two soldiers came tearing out. I certainly didn't feel like racing very much. But when we got near them one of the soldiers said: 'Knock me down, for goodness sake; knock me down quickly.' I couldn't have knocked anybody down at the time and he threw himself onto the ground, groaning, with the other soldier apparently looking after him. We never came within striking distance of each other. Afterwards he was court martialled for cowardice in not catching me. And they gave a long detailed account of how they had fought, tried to catch us, we had hit them back. I don't know why he asked me to knock him down. They were probably friendly and he obviously didn't want to take us.

We finally got to the Buckley household in Iona Drive, Glasnevin. By this time I suppose it was about four or five in the morning. We knocked at the door, rang the bell, and finally, after a long delay, Mr Donal Buckley's head appeared through the window over the door. I had never seen before, and have never seen since, a man wearing a regular proper night cap with a tassel at the end of it. He looked out with his night cap and his beard, and asked who I was. I explained, trying to keep my voice down. Then he had a confab with Mrs Buckley inside and said: Well, if you are Seán MacBride, you will be able to talk to me in French! So I talked to him in French and explained that I had just escaped and would be grateful if he could let us in. So Mrs Buckley came down and let us in. All the lights were put out; luckily they had chicken, and we were given cold chicken. I must say I was careful and didn't eat very much. Michael Price ate more than I did. Then we went and lay down, staying for two or three days, and a car came and fetched us. Maureen Buckley wasn't there, she was away on holidays, and that was the end of that episode.

Afterwards, though my memory isn't very clear, I stayed in various houses. Andy Cooney was also on the run, and we stayed with Kit Cassidy. Then I remember going down to the west of Ireland, to Galway and Mayo, making contact with the 4th Western division, with those who had remained there and were not in prison. Afterwards I went with Michael Carolan, who was Director of Intelligence in the IRA. He was building up files on those who had been spies in the various prisons and internment camps. There was no fighting during that period really.

My recollection is that the 'ceasefire' and 'dump arms' order was issued as a general order first of all, and then probably de Valera promulgated it or published it. After the fighting stopped, there was a period of 'stock-taking'. There was a good deal of heart-searching as to what should be the next move. The IRA had clearly been defeated in the civil war, and it was really a period during which the IRA leaders in different parts of the country were trying to make an assessment of the situation and what lay in the future. There were many different views of course. Some were opposed to the 'ceasefire, dump arms' order. I remember going around the country meeting various IRA commanders and discussing the situation with them, obtaining their views and reporting back. All options were considered, but there was no plan behind it. Plans were being made to hold an IRA convention at some stage or another, to consider the situation, but there was no strong dissident element. There were of course several dissident groups. I think they were mainly regional. There were, on the other hand, many IRA men who wanted to return home to a quiet normal life. But I wouldn't say that there was any strong movement in the IRA pointing in any particular direction at the time. It was more a period of reassessment and a recovery from a serious defeat.

The IRA had been very badly defeated. The executions left a tremendous amount of bitterness in the country. The figure seventy-seven came from a count of the number of executions which were taking place. I don't think there were more, but what I am not sure of is whether or not the four, Rory O'Connor, Liam Mellows, Dick Barrett, and Joe McKelvey were included in this figure. I have an idea that there were seventy-seven in addition to these four. There had been a number of assassinations, of course, of prisoners killed while trying to escape, or killed under interrogation. Some of the methods used by the Free State army had been pretty awful. One remembers in this context Ballyseedy, and incidents of this kind.

I doubt if these acts would have been organised directly by the government. I think, indeed, that Kevin O'Higgins was very worried about the situation within the army and within the police, and was making a serious effort to try and prevent execution and brutality. He was the one person in the government who was adamant about trying to stop it. Possibly some of the other members of the government didn't mind about it, I would say people like Ernest Blythe and those weren't really worried as to what happened. Mulcahy was against any form of indiscipline. He was a strong disciplinarian himself, and I think he would have stopped it. Kevin O'Higgins was very much a law and order person who believed in the rule of law and who didn't believe in any individual action by army officers throughout the country. There were some elements in the Free State army who were brutal and who were behaving in an indefensible fashion from time to time.

However, getting back to the IRA: in a broad general way we were planning a convention. Then the question of future control of the IRA came up fairly sharply. There were those who resented the fact that de Valera and the government of the Republic, as it was called, should have control of the IRA. In this period they had assumed more power than had been intended at any stage before, because of the defeat of the IRA itself. So that de Valera's government was regarded as having usurped too many of the functions and responsibilities of the IRA at the time owing to chance, and probably a little bit deliberately too: because from the point of view of the government, it was a very unsatisfactory situation to be government of a country in theory, but to have an army which was acting independently.

I don't know what funds the government had then, but they had enough apparently to finance the payment of staff officers in the IRA. It was the Minister for Finance who paid and in that way exerted a good deal of control. It never occurred to me where the funds came from. Some were probably a remainder of the funds which the IRA acquired during the civil war. Also there had been a republican loan floated. I think some of these funds had been kept in America and were then used by the government of the Republic. I think that this was one of the arguments used by de Valera at the time as to the necessity of having a government: a government could raise a loan and could utilise the existing monies obtained by way of loans. Some were also Clan na Gael funds. As far as headquarters staff was concerned, there was no real dissension at that time. I remained an active officer on the headquarters staff of the IRA as Staff Commandant. At some stage then there were various groups trying to form political parties. And there were various incidents arising out of these attempts, or when the police or army raided some place when the IRA was trying to hold a meeting.

I was working with Pa Murray who was Adjutant General. We had our offices at Roebuck House at the time. Pa Murray was a competent Cork man, a pleasant person to work with, silent and efficient. Mother had started a jam factory at Roebuck House in order to provide employment to people who were coming out of jail. There was a tremendous amount of victimisation on the part of those who had been pro-Free State. Generally speaking it was the business people and the pro-Free State people who had been supporting the government. The CID at the time made a habit of raiding places where republicans were being employed. And Mother started this jam factory, which in point of fact did not provide much employment. It did provide a few jobs, here and there.

I have forgotten when exactly, but it was in or about that period, 1924-25, that de Valera sent for me. He asked me if I would be prepared to go on a mission with him to Rome. Archbishop Mannix from Australia, who had been a very strong supporter of the republican cause, was coming over to Rome. De Valera was anxious to meet Mannix but didn't know whether the archbishop would meet him or not. So he asked me if I could go with him and arrange an interview.

I arranged a false passport for de Valera — just a question of changing the photograph on the passport of some priest, and getting a new photograph of de Valera dressed in clerical clothes. This was duly done and we drove down to Rosslare, and went from there to Fishguard. We spent possibly two days in London, during which we secretly met Art O'Brien who was the Irish republican representative in England who had been in prison and was eventually released following some law cases. We also met McGrath, Irish consul there.

Then we went on to Paris where we met Leopold Kearney and had long discussions with him. I remember an incident which annoyed me a lot. I left de Valera with Leopold Kearney at his flat. I went to gather up the luggage, get the tickets and put the luggage on the train. They were to meet me at Gare de Lyons. Kearney swore he would bring him on time, but they arrived an hour after the train had left, and I had to take the luggage out again.

We decided that we would go to Florence. De Valera would stay in Florence while I went to Rome to find out whether Archbishop Mannix would meet him and to make all the necessary arrangements. I duly did this. I went to Monsignor Hagan, President of the Irish College. Monsignor Hagan contacted Mannix for me. I met Mannix, who said he would be delighted to meet de Valera.

We had many long discussions with Monsignor Hagan and with Archbishop Mannix. De Valera had private discussions with the archbishop, lasting two and three hours. Apart from these, there were also long general discussions in the Irish College. Monsignor Hagan gave a lunch to which notable Irish prelates who were in Rome were invited. But all this was supposed to be kept very secret. I had investigated the possibility of an audience with the Pope, but I discovered that this was not on, nor had the idea been at all well received by the Vatican. Indeed Monsignor Hagan himself was somewhat against it because he himself was in some difficulty. While he was friendly himself to de Valera, he did represent the Irish bishops who, after all, had excommunicated de Valera amongst the republicans.

However, in addition to these discussions, we had long discussions with Fr Magennis, General of the Carmelites. I am a little confused as to whether or not there are two branches of the Carmelite order. There are the discalced and the others. The discalced Carmelites are the

Clarendon Street ones. Fr Magennis was from Whitefriar Street. They were always traditionally nationalist, republican and progressive. The Carmelites are a very important order in the Catholic Church. Fr Magennis was a close friend of Liam Mellows, who had been executed in December 1922. He gave us a very full account of all that was happening in Rome during the executions. He had made a desperate effort to try and get the Vatican to intervene, but had not been successful. The Irish College, I think, took the side of the bishops and was therefore anti-republican, pro-treaty and Provisional government. This was not necessarily a reflection of Monsignor Hagan, who was extremely friendly to de Valera on a personal basis, but it was the attitude which he, as representative of the Irish hierarchy, had to maintain in Rome.

Fr Magennis was, on the other hand, quite independent. I remember well his telling of the efforts which he had made. He had repeatedly discussed the matter with the Cardinal Secretary of State, he had repeatedly asked for an audience with the Pope, but the Pope always declined to see him when he found out it was about events in Ireland. He finally saw the Pope on one occasion, but he cut him off very abruptly. Although the Carmelites did have houses in Ireland, the policy of the hierarchy did not concern Fr Magennis, so as a last resort he decided on a plan of action which he described in great detail.

On some fixed date annually, the generals of the different orders went separately to visit the Holy Father, and to bring with them the contribution from the whole order. Fr Magennis had to do this on behalf of the Carmelites. I have forgotten now the sums involved, but they were very large sums, millions. The practice was that you would have the audience, and when leaving, would place an envelope with a cheque on a side table which the cardinals who were with the Holy Father would take.

In any case, Fr Magennis had been more or less brushed aside by the Pope and pretty well told that it wasn't any of his business. He was given to understand that the church was not anxious to take any action or take any steps which were regarded as inimical to Great Britain at the time. So when the day came for him to go up to the Vatican to be received formally as the general of the Carmelite order, and to bring his contribution, he went up to the Vatican and sent away his carriage.

He was received by the Pope. Discussion ensued about the order, and the progress the order was making throughout the world and he again raised the question of Ireland. He said that this was causing the order considerable concern, particularly in Ireland because the Whitefriar Street Carmelites had always been closely linked with the national movement. (Indeed, I remember in the 1920 period funerals at four and five in the morning to avoid police activity, and I think it was even Fr Magennis who was Director of Whitefriar Street at the time.) So he raised all this and said that this was causing grave concern to the Carmelite order throughout the world, Latin America, the United States, New Zealand and so on. But he got the cold shoulder from the Pope, who coldly remarked that he had already expressed his views on this. And so, after twenty minutes or half an hour of an interview, Fr Magennis took his leave without leaving the envelope containing the cheque which was the contribution of the Carmelite order.

He meandered through the Vatican, he said some prayers in St Peters. He then walked down the town, visited some nuns who were ill in hospital, or in a home for old people and went to visit some Irish priests. He took his time, and returned to the motherhouse of the order only at about nine o'clock that night, having spent his day wandering around on foot in Rome, visiting the sick, looking in shop windows and behaving like an ordinary citizen. He found three cardinals waiting for him. They pounced on him immediately and said: 'Where have you been? We have been waiting here all day.' He said, 'Oh, I went to see Sister _____ in hospital and Father _____' and he went through all this. Then he asked what the matter was. The cardinals told him that he had never left the cheque when he left the audience. Magennis said 'I know. I thought the Holy Father was not interested in the views of the Carmelite order, and so I kept the cheque in my pocket when he told me this, and I went and visited the sick instead.'

They were very annoyed with this, and said: 'Will you give us the cheque now?' And he replied, 'Oh no. If the Holy Father wants to see me again, I'll certainly go up to see him. And then, I'll consider the position of the cheque.'

And so an appointment was made immediately with the Holy Father. Here my memory gets a little vague, but I think it was the next morning that Fr Magennis saw the Holy Father and discussed the position with him. Finally, the Pope agreed to send a papal legate to Ireland. In those days there were no nuncios in the country. Ireland was still regarded as being under the jurisdiction of the papal legate in England. The Irish bishops weren't particularly keen on having representatives of the Pope sitting in Dublin. Be that as it may, I think it was as a result of this interview, although I'm not certain, that the Pope sent Monsignor Luzio to Ireland. Again when Fr Magennis brought up the Irish situation, the Holy Father said: 'I have already indicated that I am not prepared to discuss the Irish situation, deplorable as it is, with you.' Fr Magennis persuaded the Vatican that not only were people in Ireland concerned, but it was probably much more important from the point of view of the Catholic Church that the Irish American population was concerned with the excommunication of republicans. It will be remembered that the nuncio had to stay in the Shelbourne. This had caused considerable shock in the Vatican. It was said that Monsignor Luzio in his report (which I did not see, but heard several accounts of it) had stated that there were 26 popes! Hagan told us some of this, but Fr Magennis told us a lot more. I am quite certain that Monsignor Hagan reported what was said by Archbishop Mannix and de Valera to the Irish hierarchy.

De Valera used to give me accounts of these discussions the night after they took place. We were sharing the same bedroom in a hotel in Rome. I think he was formulating in his own mind, while talking to me, further possible courses for future political developments in Ireland. Archbishop Mannix had been urging him that it would be essential for him to accept the status quo, that is, the establishment of the Free State government. In other words, Mannix urged upon him the policy which afterwards became Fianna Fáil policy in 1925/26. Mannix had been pressing very hard, saying that this was the only way in which de Valera could really place the Irish hierarchy in an indefensible position, if he came out openly, accepted the status quo, and sought election to the Free State government, so that he could participate in the political development of the country. I felt at the time that de Valera accepted this viewpoint and had been convinced by these arguments. We had very long discussions running into the night as to whether this was advisable or not.

I put forward all the arguments against acceptance of that position. I argued that if it was once accepted that Ireland was part of the British Commonwealth and that the Irish Free State was the lawful and legal government of Ireland, it was reneging completely on the republican position, and the position which de Valera occupied himself as the nominal President of the Republic. It was also reneging on the theoretical constitutional position which had been established in regard to the Second Dáil, and particularly on the judgement of Mr Justice Crowley who had delivered a long judgement on behalf of what was in theory supposed to be the Irish Republican Supreme Court. For a time it was the bible of both Mr de Valera and Miss MacSwiney as to the constitutional status of the Second Dáil and of the Republican government. I have no doubt that it was really in the course of this interview that the idea of founding Fianna Fáil was formed by de Valera. Indeed it was quite possible that the Vatican had had a say in getting these ideas formulated by Archbishop Mannix to de Valera. The Vatican could have seen this as one solution to the rather impossible situation which existed in Ireland, in which the Vatican was put in the position of having to stand over the attitude of the hierarchy, which included standing by the Free State and the executions which were taking place. It wouldn't surprise me at all if Mannix had not then indicated to de Valera that he had discussed the matter with the Vatican authorities and that they were urging this course. If this course were adopted, they would certainly make it their business to make the Irish hierarchy change its attitude and they would appoint bishops in future who would have a more neutral outlook. Certainly that policy seems to have been put into operation from that moment on.

Appointments to the Irish hierarchy by the Vatican seem to indicate that they realised that republicans should be recognised by the church in Ireland. I think de Valera considered the friendship of the bishops important. He also considered the opposition of the bishops important. De Valera himself was a strong Catholic and religiously minded. He resented of course the opposition of the church. He was excommunicated, although I don't think he took the excommunication seriously. But he did feel that it was very damaging to the whole position of the church. He knew that he undoubtedly had the support of approximately half the population of Ireland, perhaps more. He felt that the church by its opposition to republicanism was alienating from itself a large segment of the Irish population. Indeed it did do this. Many of those who were refused absolution in prison refused to practice Catholicism as a result of this.

So we returned from Rome after four or five days. And I think it was shortly afterwards that arrangements were being made by de Valera to start a party. I certainly felt that Archbishop Mannix had made strong lodgement in de Valera's line of thinking at the time, and that he was going to start a political party which would recognise the Free State parliament and put up candidates for election. But no direct approaches were made to me at that time.

However, shortly afterwards I had a visit from Frank Aiken, still Chief of Staff of the IRA. I had seen very little of Frank Aiken. I didn't really know him well at all until after the civil war. Somehow or another, our paths hadn't seemed to cross. I had been working in the Adjutant General's office and also with Michael Carolan in intelligence. I felt that Aiken's hesitancy before the outbreak of the civil war had been one of the factors which had probably caused the civil war. I think that the then Provisional government had reckoned that the 4th Northern Division, of which Frank Aiken was commander, would not have taken the republican side. From their point of view they considered that, at best, the 4th Northern would have joined them, or at worst would have remained neutral. I think that if they had felt that Aiken would take the republican side, they would have hesitated more before issuing an ultimatum to the Four Courts. To that extent, I regarded him as being to a certain extent to blame for the outbreak of civil war. It was his type of attitude, the same type of attitude that Liam Lynch had, which precipitated the civil war. It gave a false impression of the strength and depth of republican feeling on the anti-treaty side. Aiken was possibly more 'to the right', more on the pro-treaty side than Liam Lynch. I wasn't surprised when Aiken succeeded to Lynch as chief of staff. But it didn't worry me really. I reckoned we had lost the civil war completely at the time, and that probably the chief of staff of the IRA should be somebody who had taken that viewpoint. That he would probably be more effective in trying to regroup and reorganise the republican movement than somebody who had been more extreme and who would have criticised openly and constantly the more moderate elements of the Republican government and the IRA. I didn't know Liam Lynch very well. I regarded him as a strong silent man. I decided he couldn't have risen to the position of OC of the 1st Southern Command unless he was really able. The 1st Southern Division officers all respected him highly and thought he was a very able military leader. This I did not know. I did regard him as being somewhat of a compromiser at the time.

I felt that the 1st Southern Division shilly-shallied too long before coming into action. Possibly we had all built undue faith and pinned undue hopes on the effectiveness of the 1st Southern Division as a military unit. We also probably did the same thing in regard to the 4th Northern Division, Frank Aiken's. For some reason while we felt the other military areas in the country, the western divisions, would stand their ground, we never expected that militarily they could recapture the country.

Con Moloney was from the 2nd Southern Division from Tipperary. He later married Kit Barry. He was Adjutant General during the time of the civil war. I didn't come across him very much during that period. I knew him subsequently fairly well. I was in prison during at that time. I was not able to form any estimate as to his military ability, but he struck me as a good, capable man.

Ernie O'Malley I knew very well for a long time. I knew him from the Black and Tan era before the truce. I had worked with Ernie quite a lot on a number of different occasions. I was very fond of him. I think he was a good military leader. It is very hard to judge who is, or who is not, a good military leader. He certainly had read up a lot of military tactics, and had read all the classical books, Clausewitz and all the classical military statutory books. But he certainly was extremely courageous and inspired confidence, and was regarded as one of the best leaders. O'Malley and Barry were probably regarded as the two best leaders in the field. I thought very highly of Tom, courageous, very able, rather impulsive in his judgement. He had certainly been one of the foremost leaders in Cork, quite a different man to Lynch, in the way that he would have been a much more active military commander in the field than Liam Lynch would have been.

I came across Liam Deasy not much then, nor indeed afterwards. He was regarded as being Liam Lynch's right-hand man or administrator, not regarded as being a great military leader. Dan Breen was closer to being like Tom Barry than the other military leaders of the period. He was courageous and generously impulsive.

During all this period I was very close to Máire, Seán and Annie MacSwiney. They were very worried about Muriel, Terence MacSwiney's widow, and their child, young Máire. I went to Germany to meet Muriel and to see the child. But I was in close touch with the whole family.

Anyway, Frank Aiken had sent word that he wanted to see me. He told me about starting Fianna Fáil, and mentioned the army — saying this would be the best way of taking over the army. They would get elected and take over the government. They had been discussing the possibility of the role I would play, and that I would become, I think, adjutant general, if not chief of staff of the army. They would give me a very high position in the army and I could build up the IRA. It was a definite offer of position, in the event of Fianna Fáil, or de Valera gaining office. I rather resented this. First of all I don't think I ever had any ambition of having a high post in any army. I couldn't see myself as a professional soldier, officer or general. I had done this with a considerable amount of dislike, partly because I considered it my duty to try and help the country at that time. I don't believe in wars as a method of solving anything. I believe that only as a last resort do you have to resort to violence and to force. I felt that the 1916-21 period had created such a situation. I was much less sanguine as to the justification of opposing the treaty by force of arms, though yes, I think it probably was justified in the light of the situation which existed then. I had absolutely no ambition of being a military man. I had been a military man by accident during a certain period of time. I also resented very much the idea that Aiken thought he could bribe me by the offer of a position in the army, or indeed in anything else, in order to get me to agree to a policy which I didn't think was particularly sound. It was a considerable error of judgement on Aiken's part, and indeed on de

Valera's if he was involved. Even if I had been offered a legal or constitutional post I would have said no. I think that the question of pensions also arose in this discussion with Aiken, and this horrified me. Indeed, I was entitled to a military service pension. I was awarded a medal, which I accepted. But I refused to take a pension because I had not done anything believing that there might be financial benefits accruing from it. I had volunteered for all this and therefore did not wish for, or desire, a pension.

Sometime in 1924/25 Frank Aiken and Michael Carolan gave me a mission to try and trace substantial sums of money that had been lodged in German banks, particularly in one bank in Hamburg before the outbreak of the civil war for the purchase of arms and for the payment of shipments. My task was to try and ascertain where the money was, and to try to recover it. The information at my disposal was somewhat slender. The principal account had been kept in a bank in Berlin. I think that Dr and Frau Grauber were able to assist me in finding the actual bank, and in making contact with the manager. These monies would have been there probably from the truce period, or possibly before that. They would have been collected by the IRA or by the government of the Republic.

As far as I remember, Robert Briscoe had been involved in opening and operating these accounts. He had given an account (here I am vague) that certain sums of money were still there. Robert Briscoe acted as an agent for the republican forces in the purchases of arms in Germany. He had no official position as such. The director of purchases had been Liam Mellows. Other people involved were Mick Cremin, but I never came across Briscoe in the headquarters staff. I knew he was there. I knew he had contacts in Germany which enabled him to arrange arms deals. I met him on one occasion at Helvic Head where we were expecting the *Santa Maria* to come in with a load of arms. However, I investigated matters as far as I could. I found that there had been fairly substantial sums of money in this bank account and that they had been withdrawn fairly recently. When I returned to Dublin I wrote a report on what I had found addressed either to the acting president, chief of staff, or Minister of Finance. I indicated that I thought it would be worth ascertaining certain information from Mr

Briscoe and also that a look should be taken at Mr Briscoe's own bank account and financial standing, as he appeared to have emerged as a fairly wealthy man at the end of the civil war. I should say that there had been reports in the press or in the Dáil that certain agents had been purchasing arms both for the IRA and for the Free State army, collecting commissions on both. I think that the suggestion was that Mr Briscoe, or some friends of his, had been involved in these transactions. However, my memory on this is very hazy, but it is all embodied in a very full and detailed report which I prepared at the time.

It is also possible that I sent a copy of it to the director of intelligence who at that time would have been Michael Carolan. But that was not the end of the report. Some time later a copy of the report was captured by the CID in one of our offices, possibly in my own office.

One day, quite accidentally, I met Peter Ennis in Dublin. He came over and said he had been very interested in reading my report on Mr Briscoe's operations. He thought he should tell me that he had brought Briscoe to the castle on one occasion, sat him down and got him to read the report there and then. Briscoe appeared to be very shocked. Peter Ennis, who was then head of the CID in Dublin, was extremely interested. He told this story with great glee. He asked me whether Briscoe had ever spoken to me about this report. The strangest part of the story was that he had brought Briscoe in and shown him the report which indicated clearly that possibly some of these funds had found their way to Mr Briscoe's own personal funds. But Briscoe had not given an explanation saying why this couldn't be so.

A further development on that particular episode was that some time later, when Fianna Fáil was formed and Mr Briscoe was being put forward as a possible candidate, somebody raised this issue within the party. Seán Lemass then wrote to me asking me if I would make a copy of this report available and if I would be prepared to give evidence and information to a committee which was being set up to investigate the matter. My reply was that in as much as the content of the report which I had prepared was at the request of the government of the Republic and the chief of staff, I did not feel it was open to me to make use of it, or to give copies of it to anyone. As far as I remember, I said I would be quite willing to give evidence of what I knew. I also pointed out that

Mr de Valera and other members of the Fianna Fáil Executive had also seen it, so that therefore this was known. I took the stand that what I had done in my official capacity had to remain privileged until such time as I was permitted to release it.

I cannot remember when exactly it was that I was sent for by Frank Aiken and given copies of a despatch which had come from Larne internment camp, run by the British military. I have forgotten the number of prisoners, but there were several hundred prisoners there. This despatch indicated that they were working on a tunnel which they hoped would be successful, and that the end of the tunnel would open on the seashore. Therefore it was essential that there should be boats available to take the prisoners from the sea shore, as soon as the tunnel opened out. They were to make signals from the shore that would be seen, and could we send a small boat to the prisoners to collect them and bring them to safety.

As far as I remember they estimated a period of about two months before the tunnel would be completed. So Frank Aiken asked for my suggestions as to what should be done, what kind of boat would be required and so on. I had always been interested in boats, sailing and indeed ships of all kinds. It was also well known that I had been involved with the shipment of arms from Germany before 1921, during the war and afterwards, to Ireland, and that I knew all about ships.

My first idea of course was to try and locate Jim McGuinness, skipper of the *Santa Maria*, who had run the guns from Germany on a few occasions. However, I wasn't able to locate him. I heard afterwards that he had become harbourmaster of Leningrad for a time. He had had various adventures, but certainly was not readily available in Ireland. So I then proceeded to look around for a suitable boat. We didn't have many funds available. The idea was that we would purchase a vessel, carry out the rescue operation and then decide whether we would keep the vessel or dispose of it. I discovered that there were two submarine chasers from World War I in Belfast, in reasonably good condition, which were for sale. So I impersonated a retired British navy officer — I assumed the name of Lieutenant John Swift who had done part-time duty during the war. I was buying one of these vessels for an uncle of mine who was a retired admiral living in Southampton. I negotiated the purchase of the boat, which required some repairs, though not many. There were some plates under the propellers which had corroded and had to be replaced. During the course of this I became very friendly with the manager of the Workman Clark shipyards in Belfast, who undertook to carry out the repairs for me. I supervised the repairs and through the manager I got to meet the harbourmaster and other officials in the port of Belfast.

In the meantime I had to start recruiting a crew. The boats were timber, about 80 or 90 feet long, with two very powerful petrol engines, not diesel. So I decided that I needed a good engineer and I got Tony Woods. Besides, Tony was a friend of mine and active in the IRA. I also got Tommy Heavy who had some experience of boats and was active and full of energy and enthusiasm for a proposal of this kind. Thirdly, I got Frank Barry, a sailor from Cobh, who had been in the IRA in Cork. I brought my crew to Belfast and kept them discreetly out of the way. I thought it might look odd that the whole crew came from the south. So they were not much in evidence in Belfast; they worked on the engine and that kind of thing. Finally the boat was ready and we decided to have a christening party. The boat was christened the *St George*. Until then she had a number. The harbourmaster, the officials and other dignitaries from the port and shipyard came to this official christening.

In the meanwhile I had to try and keep contact with the prisoners in Larne camp the whole time. This was no easy matter. My main contacts were through the Bradys, Kay, Frank and Beatrice, from a fine nationalist republican Belfast family. The parents and some of them lived in Belfast, but they had a house in Dublin as well. So there was a regular coming and going between Dublin and Belfast. They were kind and helpful to us, and also maintained contact with the people who had links with Larne internment camp. Beatrice finally joined the Carmelite order in Dublin.

However, to cut a long story short, we decided to leave Belfast, as all the reasons for remaining there no longer existed once the boat was finally finished. We had to hang around for some time outside. And then we got word suddenly that the tunnel had been caught. We were not prepared for this. We had to make a whole set of new plans. What would we do? We decided that we would sail down to Southampton, actually, and leave the boat there. There we would decide whether we had use for the boat, or should sell it. It was a saleable commodity at the time because it was in very good condition and had been done up and looked very smart. However, just as we were leaving Belfast Lough, a storm broke out. We had a very bad time because some water got into the petrol tanks, mixed with the petrol and finally the engines conked out completely. We were unable to carry out repairs. It was a bad storm. We were blown out – a north wind blew us down the channel, then an east wind blew us into Dundrum Bay off the coast of County Down. We finally ended up on a sandbank off Newcastle in County Down. The ship was holed, but not badly. In any case, we were resting on a sandbank. When finally the lifeboat came out, it took us ashore. There was an enquiry later at which I criticised the coastguards for not seeing our distress signals earlier. We had been flashing 'SOS' but they hadn't seen them. So there was quite an enquiry held at which I appeared and gave evidence. I appeared as Captain Swift. We weren't questioned much because the coastguards were more or less on the defensive.

Then we proceeded to try and recuperate the ship. First of all we tried to refloat it, but were unable to do so. I should also mention that in the interim period somebody had tried to 'hi-jack' the ship. If there is a shipwreck with nobody on it, anybody who can board it can claim two-thirds of the value of the wreck. Some locals tried to do this and we actually had a lawsuit in the northern courts which we won hands down. The judge commented that it reflected rather badly on the local population that they should try to avail of this shipwreck to make some money out of it. Finally we dismantled the ship, and sold it in bits and pieces.

I had spent a good deal of my time in Ballykinlar camp, where the British military officers invited me to their mess. It was around Christmas and I had two or three parties there with them. I then returned to Dublin, safe and sound, having broken even financially as a result of the sale of the ship's parts. It was quite surprising that we were not found out because photographs were taken when we landed and published in the Dublin papers of the crew of the St George. Nobody recognised us. I suppose some people did in Dublin, but it didn't percolate back to the British intelligence.

CHAPTER VI

Marriage and life in Paris
Reflections • Jail

Kid and I then married. We got married in University Church, St Stephen's Green at six o'clock in the morning of 26 January 1926. I was on the run and had been so since I escaped from prison. I was living in Sandymount and had arranged with Tom Daly to be my best man. Tom Daly was a brother of Charlie Daly from Kerry who had been executed. I had arranged for Tony Woods, a close friend of mine who had a garage with his father in Donnybrook, to pick me up to bring me to the church. Tony Woods said yes, yes, but he thought I was pulling his leg and he never turned up in the morning. However, we were duly married. The marriage was supposed to be a great hush, hush secret. But there were, nevertheless, about two or three hundred people at the church, at six o'clock in the morning.

Then we went to live in Paris. We had to do something, so we decided that we would go to Paris, take a holiday and look around. We had no definite plans as to what we would do besides taking a break. I was anxious to take a break and so was Kid. She was involved too. She had been in prison, on the run, at the Four Courts and so on. The civil war had been a pretty tough episode. We took a small flat in the Rue d'Annonciation in Passy, close to the flat that Mother had before the war in Paris. We took a half-flat there; it was sublet and I did some newspaper work from Paris.

Ernie O'Malley joined us for part of the time in Paris. Ernie had been very badly shattered during the civil war. He was a little bit odd at that time. He was wandering around different parts of Paris; he couldn't stay put. He used to arrive, stay with us, and then move on.

A couple of amusing episodes happened. On one occasion, an acquaintance of ours, a colonel in the French Army, Colonel Lacassi, invited me to have lunch with him. We talked away during lunch. During the course of lunch he was trying to find out what I was involved in. It turned out that Colonel Lacassi was in fact a hired officer in the Deuxième Bureau. This was the military intelligence department of the French army and a very efficient military intelligence it was. He knew Seán T. O'Kelly well and was the colonel in charge of Irish affairs. So he said: 'Well the reason I have been asking you all these questions is that the British apparently think that you are up to something. If you are doing something, be careful. All your letters are being opened and read.' He had come to tell me this of his own initiative and I was rather surprised because I didn't know him well. I had been told beforehand by Leopold Kearney that an application had been made for my extradition. These applications, Kearney had told me, were made by the Irish representative (who wasn't fully accredited) to Paris and by a man who was attached to the British Embassy but who represented the Irish government who claimed I was wanted. It was quite correct. I was wanted in Ireland because I had escaped from prison. On the same basis a great many other people were also wanted. So Colonel Lacassi mentioned all this, warning me that the British had asked for my extradition and that I should be careful. He said it was not French policy to extradite and claimed that they had told the British government that they had no intention of extraditing me unless there were positive charges. If this were the case, they insisted that the British government would bring forward the evidence. And Colonel Lacassi went on to say that even though the British had asked several times, France had a tradition of receiving political refugees and that they regarded me as an Irish political refugee. He added, 'We also regard Mr O'Malley as an Irish political refugee.'

On another occasion he said my mail was being opened and read by the British secret service. He offered to put an end to this if I were prepared to cooperate with the police in catching the people who were responsible. He would only do so if I would give an undertaking that I would not make any publicity out of it. Apparently, every Wednesday night when my wife and I went out to have dinner with a friend, Dr Catherine Lynch (a standing engagement), they had bribed the concierge, obtained a key to our flat, and read all the documents, taking copies of some of them, and going away again before we came home. This had been an established practice once a week.

It was arranged on one occasion we would catch them in the act. So we went out on Wednesday night in our normal way but, instead of going to our friends, went to a café. Colonel Lacassi was there with some of his men and they raided the flat, caught two men in the act and brought them to the local police station. It turned out that they were employees of the British Embassy. They were given a lecture by the local Commissionaire of the police. They were told it was an offence against French law to break into anybody's house, or to read papers, or to take copies of papers. If they were caught again, he warned, it would be very serious and they would be sent to jail. And they were let out on that understanding.

This brings to mind a previous incident. It was when Mother was living in Paris in the Rue de Passy. She had a cook who was devoted to her. The cook's son was an invalid, and was learning photography. Mother arranged for the cook's son to come and live in the house, and to do his photography work from there. This he had been doing for some time, until one day she was told by somebody in the police service that all her letters were being photographed in the house. It turned out that this faithful French cook and her son were photographing all her correspondence. A stop was put to this of course.

I should mention another amusing incident which occurred in Paris during this period in which Colonel Lacassi was also involved. This was subsequent to the episode when the French arrested the British secret service agents who were raiding our flat every week. Colonel Lacassi got in touch with me, saying he wanted to see me. So we had lunch together. And he said: 'You know your friend, Mr O'Malley, a nice man, but what is he doing?' I said I didn't know but that he was badly shocked and wounded during the war. So he said, 'We are a little bit worried, because he is now acting as chief military adviser to Colonel Macia, the leader of the Catalan separatist government here in Paris. And they are nice people, very decent; we allow them stay here, they have a good deal of liberty. Unfortunately, however, they are planning an invasion of Spain next Saturday afternoon. This is a little difficult and awkward from our point of view. It is neither sufficiently well organised, nor sufficiently strong, and the Spanish police are bound to have agents in their ranks and probably know all about it already. They are planning to take the train from the Gare d'Orleans, Gare d'Austerlitz next Saturday afternoon. They intend to go to the frontier, disembark and invade Spain. There are probably about thirty or forty of them going on this train. So it creates a very awkward situation for us, because we don't really want to do anything hostile against them. I was wondering whether you could do anything; perhaps you could talk to your friend Mr O'Malley, and possibly even see Colonel Macia. Perhaps you might dissuade them from this expedition.'

I knew Colonel Macia and so I sallied forth to see him. He lived outside in Vincennes. I remember taking a taxi to the place where the headquarters of the liberation movement was. I was received very formally at the entrance gate. I paid off my taxi, much to the disgust of the guard. I wasn't very wealthy, and had no funds from any place to finance these little operations. There was a guard inside the gate in some kind of uniform with a rifle. They had thrown the gates wide open and were very disappointed that the taxi did not drive right in. It was a big house, a kind of château, in which he lived with his headquarters staff. I walked in and was received in a big room with great formality and ceremony as the representative of the Irish Republic. There, at the end of the room, sat Colonel Macia in an armchair at the middle of a table, surrounded by his advisers. There were long speeches of eternal friendship stressing the connection between the liberation movements of Ireland and of the Catalan people. This went on for a while and I wondered when and how I was going to have an opportunity to tackle my mission. There was no sign of Ernie O'Malley.

I should mention that Ernie O'Malley had never mentioned to me his connections with the Catalans, only in a very vague way. He had kept this as a dark secret to himself, naturally enough. When I saw no opportunity of talking, I said, 'I would like to have a word with Colonel Macia,' but he said, 'Oh, say anything you have to say here. You needn't worry; these are all my advisers, you can talk quite freely here.' I said that I was a little worried because I had heard that they were planning an expedition the following Saturday. And he said, 'Oh, you know about it, yes? Our good friend General Mr O'Malley must have told you about it.' I assured them that General O'Malley hadn't told me, that he had been quite discreet, but that I had heard about it elsewhere. I added that because this was so, then many others had probably heard about it. And this would cause quite a good deal of danger. It was quite likely that the French police knew all about it and that the Spanish secret services knew all about it also. Therefore, when they arrived at the frontier, at Hendaye, they might be killed or arrested or trapped or something like this. So he said, 'Yes, yes, perhaps you are right, but it's very awkward because we have made a lot of arrangements. We even have the tickets bought.' Apparently they were going to take the train quite openly in Paris. However, he said that they could postpone it. He added, 'I'm sure your advice is sound, coming from a representative of the Republic of Ireland, so we'll call it off.'

And it was called off. But some two or three weeks later I had an urgent call from Colonel Lacassi saying thank you very much for having it called off the last time, but they're at it again. They want to go off next Saturday. Could you see them? And could you talk to General O'Malley and attempt to discourage him from arranging these expeditions. So I had to repeat the performance. Again I had to make appointments and go out to Vincennes to their headquarters, and meet Colonel Macia. On this occasion he was more reluctant to call it off. He said, 'Well, we can't keep putting off the liberation of our people. If you really insist, we'll call it off this time, but we can't call it off again.'

Again two or three weeks later, I got another call from Colonel Lacassi, saying, 'They're at it again. It's next Saturday.' I think Saturday must have been the day when you could get excursion rates. But they got the same tickets always, just restamped and redated. Of course it provided a marvellous opportunity to the French to know when they hoped to go and also to the Spanish secret services.

So for the third time, I went off to Colonel Macia who firmly said, 'No, no. We've put it off twice on your good advice, but we can't put if off any more.' I reported to Colonel Lacassi that this time they wouldn't put if off. He said yes, it was a pity, but he thought that that was how they would react. He continued to say that 'they had planned this for a long time and our problem is whether or not we should arrest them on the French side, and prevent them from falling into the hands of the Spanish and being possibly shot. But if we arrest them on this side, they will blame us.' However, it was decided to arrest them as the best means of protecting them.

And the following Saturday they duly left for Spain, but were arrested by the French police just before they reached the frontier. They were taken off the train and brought back to Paris. They were told not to try any more invasions. But the French were very tolerant. Colonel Macia remained in Paris and ran his government in exile, and ultimately during the Spanish civil war set up a government, and was President of the Basque Republic, which survived a year or two. I think he was then assassinated. He was a charming man and the Basque people are charming people.

We had many odd incidents of that kind, because Ernie used to succeed in running into different complications here and there. He was arrested on one occasion in Italy and held by the Italian secret police. They got in touch with me through the French secret police and we arranged to have him released.

We were in Paris for the best part of a year. I did some newspaper work, articles for the *Herald Tribune* and we returned home in December 1926. When I returned from Paris I was no longer on the run. At that stage they had released all the prisoners. And I think that they had given an assurance to Kid's uncle Frank Bulfin, and also to my own uncle Joe MacBride, both Cumann na nGaedheal T.Ds who approached the government and asked them what their intentions were, saying it was perfect nonsense that I should continue to be on the run. This would probably have been a factor contributing to our decision to return.

When we returned, I recommenced my law studies. I think I got credit for some of the lectures I had done before. We also had the jam factory at home. We were running *An Phoblacht*, the republican newspaper that had been restarted after the civil war. I was writing for it.

The first news I had of the assassination of Kevin O'Higgins in July 1927, was while I was having my lunch in a restaurant in Brussels, reading the evening paper, *Le Soir*. The first item which caught my eye was 'seventy-seven' which I knew could only refer to Ireland. At that time, all mention of events in Ireland usually referred to the fact that the government had executed seventy-seven IRA leaders. The headlines ran 'The man responsible for the 77 executions in Ireland, assassinated'. There was a photograph of Kevin O'Higgins. It came as a complete surprise to me, because I was not aware of any particular antagonism to Kevin O'Higgins on the republican side at that period. On the contrary, it was generally felt that he was trying to restore law, and that he disapproved of any individual assassinations or acts of violence undertaken by the CID or the military. The CID had become a little of a law unto its own at the time. It arrested people illegally, detained them illegally and so on. Kevin O'Higgins was working strongly against them. My own first suspicion at the time was that he had intervened and insisted that one of the mutineers, or a man associated with the mutineers, Captain Murray, should be tried for having very brutally murdered a military policeman who was suspected of having passed information to the IRA. This unfortunate man (I think Bergin was his name) was tied to a lorry and killed that way. Captain Murray was put on trial, convicted and duly sentenced to death. I think that Kevin O'Higgins had been one of the persons who had insisted on his being put on trial and who was probably opposed to his reprieve. Again, I am not sure, nor am I sure of the sequence of events in regard to that. The report of Captain Murray is in the Irish Reports under the *Attorney General* versus *Murray*.

I felt at that time it was quite possible that some of the mutineers, or some friends of Captain Murray, may have carried out the assassination of Kevin O'Higgins. I don't believe that still, though it remains a possibility. I have never found out who assassinated Kevin O'Higgins. I have heard the reports of different republican groups and individual republicans alleging that they carried it out. But these reports are so numerous and conflicting that in the end I began to disregard them all. There is a strange tendency — I don't know whether it is only confined to Ireland — that when something of that kind happens, somebody has to claim credit when they think they render themselves popular for doing it.

At that time we were running the jam factory at Roebuck. I was getting some fruit pulp from Belgium or Holland, and some equipment for the jam factory. I had met, either on the Irish mail boat or on the mail boat from Dover to Ostend, Major Bryan Cooper, the Cumann na nGaedheal MP for Sligo, a strong right-wing Cumann na nGaedhealer at that. We chatted, we might even have had a drink on the boat together. This was the day before the assassination of Kevin O'Higgins so accordingly he knew I could have had nothing to do with it. In those days there were no planes and travelling from Brussels to Dublin was a long journey.

Some days after I got home, suddenly, in the middle of the night, the police erupted into the house, came into my bedroom and arrested me. They handcuffed me and took me off to the Bridewell. I was treated quite roughly and I was charged there with the assassination of Kevin O'Higgins. I told them that this was nonsense; I wasn't even in the country at the time. But they paid no attention to this. The chief superintendent, a young man who I think was in the IRA, was there. Here I will relate an interesting sidelight. I was put on an identification parade at which a number of other prisoners, about fifteen, paraded with me. I think it was the gardener of the O'Higgins house, together with another witness, who identified me as having been the person who had assassinated Kevin O'Higgins. I mention this because it shows how unreliable identification can be. Probably the identification parade was rigged, and my position was indicated to the witnesses by the CID, which was at that time active and bitter. But the result remains that I was then identified by at least one or two witnesses as having participated in the assassination in Dublin, when in fact I was in Brussels.

Major Cooper was rather indignant at all of this. He knew that it couldn't have been true because we had met on the way to Brussels and he told the government this. But the government didn't heed him. The evidence they had was very slender. A special emergency powers act was passed, enabling them to hold me for an indefinite period on a charge of alleged murder. As a result of this, I was duly locked up in Mountjoy prison and brought up in the police courts under this act. I was the only suspect held. The act meant that I had to be brought before a magistrate in the Dublin district court. This was Mr E. J. Little. Mr Little refused to apply the act, denounced the act, and denounced my arrest. He said that it was highly improper and that it was in contravention of the rule of law. Whereupon the government then took an action against him in the High Court, to compel him to make an order holding me. This came for trial before Mr Justice Hanna. He decided that the government was entitled to pass this law and that I should be held in custody. A report of this case will be found in the Irish Reports of that period. And I was duly held in Mountjoy for two or three months, I should think. I was the only political prisoner in Mountjoy at that time.

I remember that time very well. There was a man in Mountjoy who had been sentenced to death for an ordinary murder. He had been a worker on the Shannon scheme and had murdered a German ganger. They had gangers and supervisors for the Irish labour force which was working on the Shannon scheme during that period. The name of this condemned man was Cox.

I remember these details fairly clearly. I was alone in the prison at the time, so I made an offer to the governor, an old-time British prison governor, himself a little odd, to exercise in the same yard as this man called Cox. He finally decided that he would let me if I had no objection. He said it would be a good deed on my part to help this man for the rest of his days. So I exercised with this man, Cox, in the yard where the hang-house is. I talked and walked with him. It was as if you were undergoing an execution yourself. Let me add hastily that this was not the intention of the governor or the prison authorities. They felt that since I was in solitary confinement, it would be a relief to have somebody to talk to. I remember well, because first of all Mr Cox told me all the details of his life, about his wife and family. We used to exercise together for about two hours a day, so naturally I got to know a lot about him. What really horrified me was that first of all we exercised in this yard next to the hang-house where he was to be executed, and secondly, there was a workshop in this yard. Through the rather dirty windows of the workshop I could see his coffin being made by a warder and some convicts for at least a week before his execution.

This was a subject he never touched upon, but I am sure that he must have seen it just as I saw it. I was there finally and left him late the night of his execution, when his wife came to say goodbye to him. It was really horrifying to see. She was shrieking, weeping and in a state of collapse. That was the last I saw of him. My cell was close to his cell. His cell was next to the hang-house. Next morning I heard the trapdoor, saw Pierrepoint and saw the warders, the chaplain and the governor passing by, before, and after the execution.

That experience enabled me to live through what executions were like. I must say it was a rather horrifying experience which helped to convince me firmly that capital punishment should be done away with for anybody. Oh, there were no merits in this particular case. I think Cox had murdered this German supervisor. He had done so quite brutally, I think to rob him.

Another episode happened later, which was rather amusing in contrast with that grim experience. There was a character at that time in Dublin. He was one of those characters who dressed oddly, wore a frock-tailed coat and top hat, bedraggled. He used to beg and address passers-by. I think his name was Edelstein. He was quite a character, knew Shakespeare and knew lots of poems. In prison for not paying debts and in my wing, Edelstein was my next companion in the prison yard after Mr Cox had been executed. He had all these stories and was very amusing and entertaining. He was a little bit mad. Finally he was released after spending three or four days there.

A couple of days after his release there was tremendous activity. The governor was pacing up and down outside my cell all day long. More warders were put on and extra police were brought in, flicking the light on me all night so as to see I hadn't escaped. Finally the governor came to me after a day or so of this unusual activity and said, 'It would simplify things a lot if you told me what arrangements you made with Edelstein to rescue you.' Edelstein had, apparently, on his release, written me a letter saying he was attending to all the arrangements I had made and it would be not long before I saw the last of Mountjoy. From this letter, the authorities understood that I had made some escape arrangements and used him as a messenger. This was the last thing I had in mind. I certainly wouldn't have used Edelstein as a messenger. But this had thrown the authorities into uproar. I told the governor that I thought he was being had by the perverted sense of humour of Edelstein, who was probably getting his own back on the prison authorities. I think this point of view was finally accepted and all these extra security measures were stopped.

It was probably a few weeks later when suddenly in the middle of the night I was released without any further ado. And that was the end of that episode.

CHAPTER VII

League against imperialism
Saor Éire • Career • IRA

During the late 1920s I didn't belong to any party. I was loosely connected with the IRA. Naturally we were always discussing the future of Ireland and different political issues in the world. Peadar O'Donnell, a close friend, was most active in these discussions. I had known Peadar for some time. He was a great talker, storyteller and writer. My wife and I knew himself and Lil very well and we saw a good deal of each other. He was always bubbling over with energy and different schemes. The real trouble was that he used to forget his schemes and plans from one week to another. I used too say, 'Well, Peadar, did you do anything about this idea you had last week?' And he would say, 'What idea?' So from a practical point of view it wasn't very helpful.

During this period, an old childhood friend whom I had known in Paris, Chato Padaya, contacted me. An Indian, he was a friend of Madame Cama, with whom I had stayed in Paris often. It was not in the pacifist, but in the active, revolutionary movement that he was engaged. There was always, even in the Gandhi period, a revolutionary 'wing' to the Indian liberation movement, that was not very active, but which had extreme views. Chato Padaya had been involved with these. Somehow or another he ended up in Berlin, I think it was from there that he contacted me. He came to see me. He was engaged in organising an anti-imperialist conference of all the anti-imperialist forces throughout the world, India, Egypt and so on. This congress was finally held. It was regarded as a landmark in the fight against colonialism throughout the world. First of all, a preliminary meeting was held in Brussels in 1927 and then afterwards the Congress of the League against Imperialism was held in Frankfurt in 1929. It was an important congress and was regarded as a turning point in the history of the liberation movements throughout the world. Hitherto they had been working in isolated quarters. This appealed to me very much because I felt that if all the various movements in the colonies got together, one could put an end to British imperialism, and indeed to any other form of colonialism in the world.

Now I don't remember the details of this congress very well. I remember that Nehru was there. It was the first time I had seen Nehru. Ho Chi Minh was there, as a young man. I don't remember much of those two. I remember much more of an Indian leader whose name was Singh. But Singh is such a common name that it doesn't mean anything. He was imposing, with a beard and a big turban. Peadar and I were very much taken by him. Peadar O'Donnell had come to the congress with me. Singh came to visit us in Ireland afterwards. Later I think I heard that he had been assassinated in India by the British.

So this led us to a good deal of ideological thinking and discussion. Peadar felt that nationalism as such was past and we should concentrate on international socialism. I agreed with him to a certain extent, but not all the way. I felt that we needed both nationalism and internationalism. I felt both should work hand in hand in order to put an end to colonial and racial rule throughout the world.

Fairly active during this period also was Frank Ryan. He was part of the younger generation of the IRA. Frank Ryan was from Tipperary. He was the editor, for a long time, of *An Phoblacht* and was much inclined to follow Peadar O'Donnell's policies and an extreme left-wing line. I didn't think it was workable. I didn't disagree with the fundamental policies which they had, but I felt that they were not practical. I felt that nationalism was very important and that we should keep nationalism to the forefront while at the same time working towards world socialism, without necessarily accepting socialism as it was being practised in the Soviet Union or elsewhere in the world. Frank Ryan was in the IRA in Dublin and was arrested on a number of occasions. Many people were arrested fairly frequently for one thing or another by the CID during that period. One never knew quite why, or the reasons for it. I was arrested two or three times, Peadar O'Donnell was arrested, George Gilmore used to be arrested. This was quite a frequent occurrence. I thought Peadar and Frank were somewhat impractical in putting socialism to the fore in the late 1920s, rather than nationalism. This was discussed at IRA conventions. I took the view that the IRA should remain as it was, pledged to the achievement of the complete independence of Ireland and the establishment of a republic, and that it was for the political party and for the government to then decide what kind of a republic it should be. I felt that if anything was to be done in that line, it should be done through a political party. Finally a compromise was reached, and it was decided to form a political party. There were endless arguments as to the constitution, the aims and objectives of the party. Finally a party called Saor Éire was set up. Saor Éire was launched with a great flourish of trumpets. Discussions had taken place between myself, Peadar, George Gilmore, though George didn't feature so much at the time, Maurice Twomey, Michael Fitzpatrick, Donal O'Donoghue and Con Lehane. A constitution was evolved for Saor Éire. It was on the basis of this constitution that I agreed to take an active part in the setting up of Saor Éire. This didn't please Peadar very much. Peadar would have felt that he would like to run Saor Éire by himself.

I wasn't enthusiastically in favour of Saor Éire because I felt that it would provide a weapon to the government against republicans at that period. There was nothing very startling in the Saor Éire programme. It was modelled to a certain extent on the programme of the First Dáil. What did amuse me was that while Saor Éire was to a large extent Peadar O'Donnell's child, I was the one who went off to organise it and finally ended up in jail on account of Saor Éire. I was the only victim of Saor Éire at that time.

There was to be no formal relationship between Saor Éire and the IRA. There would of course have been some people on the Executive of Saor Éire and some people who would have been on the Army Council or Executive of the IRA. Somehow or another, after the denunciation by the hierarchy and by the government of Saor Éire, it seemed to fade away to a certain extent. I don't think that those who were in favour of it pursued it very much further.

It was during that period that George Gilmore came very much into prominence. He was arrested several times and obtained a good deal of sympathy from republicans who had been persecuted. George Gilmore was in the South Dublin Battalion. He may have been the Commanding Officer of the Battalion or just an officer in it. I remember he was arrested and ill-treated on some occasions. There was another organisation started, mainly by George Gilmore, called the Republican Congress. I don't know how it came about: I was not involved in it nor was I clear what its policy was. It was intended to be more to the left of the IRA and I think more to the left of Saor Éire. I don't think it had a very specific programme of action. So it didn't really get very far. I was given the task of trying to organise Saor Éire throughout the country. My idea was to work my way back from the south from Kerry and Cork to Dublin, organising branches of Saor Éire. Tom Daly was quite active at that period, he was Charlie Daly's brother from Kerry. I remember I was staying in Tom Daly's house. Concurrently with all this, the then Cumann na nGaedheal government became very active on Saor Éire and decided to outlaw it.

At one stage when I was in Kerry after attending some meetings in Tralee, I was returning to Tom Daly's house, 'Firies', and was held up on the road by a large number of men in plain clothes and cars, obviously CID. But they had sheets over the bonnets of the cars so that the numbers wouldn't be visible. They were armed with rifles. They arrested me and threatened me, saying that unless I left the country — left at once — I would be shot. I then proceeded on to 'Firies' and stayed there. They took up guard. They came into the house actually, and sat there as permanent guard, around the place. The man in charge was Superintendent O'Mahony, whom I had reason to come across later in my legal career. This shows the lawlessness which still existed at the time. I used to drive around Kerry with this escort of maybe twenty CID men, armed with rifles, from place to place.

They finally arrested me. I was charged in Listowel. They also arrested a number of Kerrymen who were at a meeting with me. I appeared in Listowel district court. There were military guards in the courthouse and so on. I asked the then district justice if this was a civil court or a military one. He said it was a civil court. I asked, 'Then why is the army in possession of your courthouse?' He said yes, it was improper and he ordered them to leave. After about a week of being brought up in courts here and there, finally I was discharged. We were all discharged. I think the government probably had done both, arrest and release.

Concurrently with all this, General O'Duffy, who was then chief of the guards, visited the bishops, possibly with Mr Cosgrave and other members of the government, and certainly conveyed to the bishops that Saor Éire was a dangerous communist organisation that was out to destroy the church and establish communist government in Ireland. To a large extent this was the kind of thing which I foresaw in the developments urged by Peadar O'Donnell and George Gilmore at the time. While this was not their intention, their language and methods would leave it open to the government to charge them with being Marxists, trying to overcome and overthrow the government and replace it with an atheist and a communist government in Ireland.

The red scare was very much in evidence then. The bishops again issued a pastoral letter, not unlike the one they had issued during the civil war, more or less outlawing Saor Éire. This created quite a furore. Subsequently I was able to obtain from some of the bishops copies of some reports which were given to them by Eoin O'Duffy and some members of the government, which were complete fabrications. These reports completely misrepresented the position of Saor Éire. As well as the government and Eoin O'Duffy who were our adversaries, there was also Fianna Fáil. Fianna Fáil regarded Saor Éire as a rival organisation to them. They remained silent, but as we were being arrested, they had to protest against our arrest. Later, on another occasion when there was a strike of busmen or tramway men in Dublin, Saor Éire and the Army Council of the IRA issued a statement in effect giving their full support to the strikers. This also led to a wave of arrests. These arrests were made under emergency power legislation. It is really fantastic, if one looks through the statute book of that period, or indeed since the setting up of the state, the number of special powers acts, public safety acts, offences against the state acts and emergency legislation of every kind which was enacted. We probably have more emergency legislation and repressive legislation on our statute books than any other country in the world. I think that the methods they used only served the purpose of putting them out of office in the end. First of all the reports they acted upon were completely unreliable and were grossly exaggerated. The government at that period was bent on remaining in office; this is demonstrated by the fact that the chief commissioner formed a movement with the intention of remaining in office.

There was an improvement when an action was brought, in which I was involved in instructing solicitor and counsel at the time against a number of police officers for having tortured and beaten up prisoners. I wasn't at the Bar at the time. The case came for hearing before Mr Justice Davitt, who, very courageously gave a decision against the police and found them guilty of having committed assaults and other illegal acts on prisoners. This was a turning point to a certain extent. Those who believed in the rule of law, like O'Higgins had, were bent on establishing the rule of law and making it work. They were prepared to stretch it here and there in favour of the government and against republicans. But gradually the time came when they must have thought: well, if the rule of law is to prevail, we must apply it impartially. I felt that Cahir Davitt was due a lot of credit for being the first judge really to assert the rule of law against the state. There had been an attitude up to then that a police officer or a CID man or a military officer could do no wrong.

This was important from my point of view. During all that period, I felt that there were a number of people on the Cumann na nGaedheal side who did want to get back to normality, and did want to assert the rule of law and the legal system, and have them function objectively. On the other hand, many of my colleagues in the republican movement didn't agree with me. They felt that the more we got the legal system to operate fairly and impartially, the more credence it would have. I always felt a certain amount of difficulty whenever I wanted to bring test cases to the courts on account of that. This was the first case. We had a number of test cases afterwards, all on the same issues. But certainly this was a point of divergence between me and my colleagues in the republican movement at that period. The Free State government was not willing to do anything without necessary legal powers. They passed all these various acts. But the purpose of the acts was to suspend the ordinary rule of law. These acts were usually passed at the instance of the Attorney General. I think Jack Costello, who was Attorney General for a time, was responsible for getting a lot of these acts passed in order to avoid the rule of law from being disregarded completely. Therefore it was necessary to pass all these acts to suspend the operation of the ordinary law, and to enable the police to act illegally, in such a way so as they could not be brought before the courts.

I've always had a high regard for Cahir Davitt as a judge. I always thought he was a very good judge. By and large, I had a fairly high regard for some of the judges, not all of them. Tommy O'Shaughnessy, a hand down from the old regime, was completely partial, not fitted to be a judge by his temperament. Other judges like John O'Byrne were very good. He became a judge in the High Court and Supreme Court afterwards; as did Cahir Davitt. Tom Finlay was also a very good lawyer. He was one of their main prosecutors, and Cecil Lavery was another of their main prosecutors. Indeed on one occasion I was prosecuted by Cecil Lavery and Tom Finlay in Green Street, and tried by John O'Byrne before a jury. I was acquitted. This was all before I became a barrister.

I became involved in the *Irish Press* newspaper; Frank Gallagher asked me if I would like to work on the paper as a sub-editor. This would have been my only source of income, apart from Mother, who had an income of her own and was very generous. But her income was also dwindling as a result of various things happening.

So I worked on the *Evening Telegraph*, the editor of which was Bob Egan. The chief sub-editor was Joe Anderson, who was extremely good. The *Irish Press*, first issued on 5 September 1931, was republican at the time. Mr de Valera wisely, as a first step, had begun to raise money for a paper of his own which would be independent.

There was one famous occasion on which Mr de Valera was making a major policy speech in Dáil Éireann prior to the constitution. I was working on the *Evening Telegraph*. I remember this well because the *Telegraph* was the same as the *Evening Press*, its equivalent. Mr Chamberlain had made an equally important statement in the House of Commons in London. Working on evening papers is always hectic. We had three editions in the afternoon, and they had to be changed quickly, because we wanted to try and give a new appearance to the paper for each edition. At the end, when all your editions are out, you sit back at 5 or 6 o'clock and look at the results of your handiwork. We were all sitting around in the subs room looking at the edition which was produced. Suddenly a groan of horror arose from all of us. We had put a good five inches of Mr de Valera's speech into Mr Chamberlain's speech and a good five inches of Mr Chamberlain's speech into Mr de Valera's speech. Such a look of horror on our faces: Bob Egan, the editor, paled absolutely. I thought he would faint. These things happen on a paper; it had happened on the stone when the paper was made up. Somebody had by mistake, when shortening the speech, decided to lengthen it again and had transferred the two pieces of type from one to another. So then we had a discussion as to what we should do about it. There were two views. One was that we should immediately phone up Mr de Valera and apologise, the other, which was mine, was that we should stay put, and as likely as not nobody would notice it. This latter course was adopted and in fact nobody noticed. It shows how carelessly these papers are read, the evening papers. They read the headlines, they knew the speech by de Valera, they knew the speech by Chamberlain. But nobody had bothered reading through the text. Or if they had, they hadn't noticed. Or if they noticed, they were good enough to stay quiet. This must have been before the strike, for I never went back to the *Irish Press* after the strike.

The newspapers then, the *Irish Times* and the *Irish Independent,* were very different to the newspapers of later years. The *Irish Times* was openly pro-British and conservative, under the editorship of Bob Smyllie. Even in its news services, it was not objective. The *Independent* was Free State and very anti-republican. The old *Freeman's Journal* had disappeared during the civil war. So the only two papers left in Dublin were the *Irish Times*, out and out pro-British and the *Irish Independent*, out and out Free State, and pro-bishop as the bishops were very closely identified at that period with the Free State and the treaty. So far as republicans were concerned, they had no organ through which their voices could be heard. Censorship had been lifted and de Valera quite properly and intelligently conceived the idea of starting a paper that would be independent and that would put forward the republican, anti-treaty viewpoint. He had collected a lot of money in America and all over the world for this. Indeed I inherited some shares in the *Irish Press*, which Mother bought at the time.

I also worked for a while as a sub-editor on the *Morning Post*. I never regarded the policy of the paper I worked for as having anything to do with my own policy, any more than a printer would. My relations with the *Irish Press* were terminated by an indirect incident. Most of the evening papers in Dublin at that time were sold by newsboys in the streets, hundreds of them, barefooted little urchins, freezing with the cold. It was a fashion and a habit in those days to sell stop press editions of the papers if anything new happened after the paper had gone to press. These unfortunate youngsters were usually exploited by some sub-dealers. They were in a shocking condition, ill-clad, ill-clothed and underpaid, probably a pittance. I don't remember what they were getting as commission for selling the papers, but Jim Larkin had decided to organise them into his union, the Workers Union of Ireland. Jim Larkin had been a big figure during the earlier part of the century and a tremendous figure during the 1913 strike. After that he had been in jail in America, but later returned to Dublin and started to organise the Workers Union of Ireland. Jim Larkin was inclined to look upon all republicans as being drawing room republicans who preached certain principles, but never put them into practice. He often criticised them. Strangely enough he also criticised all those whom he considered to have strong left-wing views, such as Peadar O'Donnell.

But he organised the newsboys in his union and they had a strike. I was then a member of the National Union of Journalists, the NUJ. So when he organised the newsboys and called a strike, my sympathies were all with the newsboys. I felt that they were probably the most underprivileged group of human beings in the city of Dublin, if not in the world. Some of the transport workers had decided to down tools in the *Irish Press*. I raised the matter with the journalists. I explained that I didn't think we should cross the picket lines and I thought we should give our support to the newsboys in their efforts to get decent conditions of work. The attitude of most of the journalists was: well, are we all agreed on this? Unless we are all agreed on this, we should do nothing. And they looked in particular to Dick Fox, who was then also sub-editor on the *Irish Press*. Dick Fox has written a number of books. He was by way of being very much theoretical, a left-wing thinker and philosopher. And they looked to Geoffrey Coulter, who was also in the *Irish Press* and had been in jail. However, for some reason which I have never quite understood, they opposed the idea of downing tools and joining the newsboys on strike.

I took it on myself to join the picket line and I joined the newsboys picketing the *Irish Press*, much to the horror of the journalists and management of the paper. I then joined the union for the duration of the strike. It was rather amusing. I didn't know Jim Larkin well, but they had a hall in Marlborough Street, a Workers Union Hall there. I went over and when I arrived Jim Larkin was addressing a meeting of the strikers. It was to a packed hall on a miserable wet day, to a crowd of cold, shivering urchins. Jim was in full spate of oratory, addressing them about the misdeeds of the *Irish Press* and of the management, of the capitalist system and indeed the journalists who should know better, people like Seán MacBride, Dick Fox and Geoffrey Coulter who instead of being out on the side of the workers were on the side of the bosses. By this time I was at the back of the hall listening to all this, somebody had noticed me and had passed Jim a note saying that I was there. Then Jim stopped short, had a few more words, and was told that I was out on the picket with the newsboys. He then asked me to address the meeting. From that time on, Jim and I became solid close friends. That was the end of my period in the *Irish Press*. I was working for the Bar then, so I didn't mind very much. I left of my own accord, but remained on good terms with Frank Gallagher and the *Irish Press*.

At the time of the 1932 elections we had very close collaboration with Fianna Fáil in the campaign, in order to ensure that Fianna Fáil would be elected. The IRA was favourable to Fianna Fáil getting in, on the basis that this would be one way of freeing political prisoners and of ending the various emergency powers acts that were then in force, and a way of ending the systematic harassment of republicans by the police and the governmental forces. Our support was from the point of view of practical politics to get the prisoners out. Without IRA support, certainly in Dublin, Fianna Fáil would not have been elected. The election campaign in Dublin was run practically entirely by IRA officers. We were in close touch with Seán Lemass, who was a director of elections, and Eamonn Donnelly, at that time Fianna Fáil director of elections.

Immediately Fianna Fáil got into power we had very close discussions on the question of prisoners. I remember acting on a committee with Frank Aiken, at the time drawing up a list of the prisoners who should be released and these prisoners were in fact released. But apart from matters of that kind, relationships between the IRA and Fianna Fáil were strained. Also during this period, a younger generation of IRA leaders were growing up, Con Lehane, and many other younger men were going up through the ranks of the IRA, and coming to occupy positions of leadership, certainly in Dublin.

Also, after 1932 when Fianna Fáil took office, they asked the IRA, the Army Council, for cooperation in dealing with the Blueshirts. It was not for illegal action, but more in connection with what they were doing, what they intended to do, who they were, what their leadership was and what threat they posed. We did develop quite an intensive intelligence system to find out who was in the Blueshirts, what they were doing and so on. Information was then passed on to the Fianna Fáil government.

In those days we used to concentrate on big demonstrations. We had a Bodenstown demonstration, an annual event which had started at the beginning of the century. It had reached colossal proportions. I remember in the year I was running it, we had about thirty-five special trains coming from all over the country. It was a vast operation. Another year the government banned it at the last moment, forbade the railway company from running special trains, but it never made an order forbidding the bus companies. So while the trains were banned, we had fleets of buses bringing people from all over the country to Bodenstown.

I became Chief of Staff of the IRA more or less by accident, because the then Chief of Staff, Moss Twomey, had been arrested. On his arrest, the Army Council approved me. This was in June 1936. I was appointed very much in a caretaker capacity. There were various tendencies in the IRA pulling in different directions. The IRA was not doing much then beyond talking and discussing policies, whether or not it should become a political party, what its relationship with Fianna Fáil should be, what its future should be, whether they should have intensive military activities. My role was, on the whole, one of running the caretaker army council and of keeping the different elements together, and patching up the differences of opinion that existed, in the hope that ultimately it would be possible to formulate a policy which would be acceptable for the future development of the republican movement, not only for the IRA.

Concurrently with all this, the 1937 constitution was being prepared by de Valera. There was a good deal of discussion as to whether or not it would be acceptable. Naturally there were different and conflicting viewpoints on this. Some took the view that the constitution, unless it declared a Republic, did away with the oath of allegiance, and provided for the unity of the country, was worthless and should not be accepted. Others took the view that, once the constitution provided for the holding of free elections, and that candidates for the Dáil could stand freely, without having taken an oath of allegiance, that there ceased to be a situation in which it was necessary to resort to armed force.

While Saor Éire and the Republican Congress was being formed, some elements in the IRA, and particularly Seán Russell, were busy building a strong armed force wing in the republican movement, which was not concerned in any way with political developments. It rather criticised the leadership of the IRA for being too involved in politics, meaning Saor Éire and the Republican Congress. Seán Russell worked in close collaboration with Joe McGarrity in America. He was part of Clan na Gael. Russell's programme was to launch a war against Britain. This always struck me as a rather unrealistic type of operation and I did not think that the IRA was in a position to wage a war against anybody. At the time many of the arguments within the army council hinged around the capacity of the IRA to undertake any form of military action.

I remember an IRA convention when Russell made a dramatic announcement that he had arranged to purchase a whole shipload of arms that was at that very moment sailing across the Atlantic and would land arms for the whole of the IRA. This announcement was, as far as

I knew then, and as far as I know now, a complete figment of imagination. There was no such shipment of arms even seriously discussed in the United States. He may have said it to get the support of an IRA convention for some proposal. More and more I felt that Seán Russell's policy was unrealistic and irrational in many respects. I didn't particularly want to fall out with Russell, with whom I had worked for a long time in the IRA, but I felt that I couldn't really collaborate with him seriously.

I certainly took the viewpoint, that once the 1937 constitution was adopted, the whole position in the country was radically altered. We were then in the position, for the first time, of electing a parliament which did not owe allegiance to the British government, and was free to take the leadership of the country. For the first time there would be an opportunity of doing what Collins had always said, of using the treaty as a stepping stone to the republic. It was on that basis that I decided some time before 1937 that, if the constitution was enacted, we should work through it. We should accept any constitution which invested sovereignty in the people of Ireland and work through it to achieve the rest of the independence of the country. As far as the constitution was concerned, I was quite prepared to accept it, and I said so publicly on a number of occasions. I also decided that I would terminate my connection with the IRA as from then.

I remember there were a number of personalities in the IRA who played an important role. There was Jim Killeen from the midlands, adjutant general of the IRA. Jim had been a very active IRA officer during the Black and Tan period and during the civil war. He had been in Cork and Belfast, and I think was sentenced to seven years in prison in Belfast. Michael Kelly from Mayo had been arrested with him. The two of them played an important role in the IRA from their release onwards. Jim Killeen was an extremely sound thinker, and I had tremendous respect for him. Michael Kelly was also extremely able and active, and later was to become a secretary to Clann na Poblachta. Jim Killeen was a member of the Executive of Clann na Poblachta, or of the Standing Committee of Clann na Poblachta.

Also active was David Fitzgerald from Tipperary: he was very closely linked with Peadar O'Donnell, Saor Éire and with the

Republican Congress. Another man who played an important role during all this period, from the early thirties right up to the war, was Paddy McLogan. Paddy McLogan was himself a northerner, from Armagh, who was living in Portlaoise. He had a public house there. He was chairman of the army council for much of that period. He was sound, with a reasonable view usually. But it was very much a straight line view: he never saw anything to the side, one side or the other, of his target. He was rather narrow-minded in his outlook but an extremely fine person himself.

I was succeeded by Tom Barry as Chief of Staff, and Tom Barry in turn was succeeded by Michael Fitzpatrick in 1937. Seán Russell succeeded Michael Fitzpatrick as far as I remember. Russell went to Germany during the war. Frank Ryan was already there and Russell contacted Frank Ryan. I am not quite certain what negotiations or what arrangement occurred or took place in Germany between Russell and Ryan, but I think it is clearly established that they were on a submarine bound for Ireland from Germany and, in the course of a rather long journey, Seán Russell died from food poisoning in August 1940 and was buried at sea Frank Ryan was brought back to Germany, where he remained until his death in June 1944.

Throughout this period, I went back to my law studies which I had begun way back in the twenties. This had been rather shattered by events at the time. So I took up my studies again in the early thirties. I was reading for the Bar the time I was working in the *Irish Press*. Vivion de Valera was also working for the Bar with me. I know that during part of that time I was on the run, and had to do my exams on the run. This was rather amusing as Vivion de Valera's father was then in the government, and Vivion sat the same exams: we joked about this. There was a certain amount of friendship which obviated his reporting on me. But this is what ran through the whole IRA relationship with, what shall I say, the Irish establishment; there was this kind of bond of friendship which existed, for those who were working in the republican movement.

I should mention that I got a tremendous amount of help in all my law studies from Joseph O'Connor, discussing law cases and legal issues with him. He was a QC, a senior counsel and to my mind was the best criminal law advocate at the Irish Bar, certainly during my lifetime. He had defended many prisoners on the republican side and I had instructed him and worked with him on these cases, during and after the civil war. Subsequently he became a Circuit Court judge in Cork.

I remember the case, it must have been the late 1920s, of Ned O'Reilly from Tipperary who was charged with the murder of a policeman. Joe O'Connor defended that case. Then there was the case of hazy origin, of More O'Farrell. He was a landlord in Leitrim who had been murdered in February 1935 in connection with some land trouble. The IRA was linked with this, probably some dissident members of the IRA. I helped in the defence of these cases. So I had already a considerable criminal law experience. I had also become interested in constitutional law. I had read a good deal of Canadian constitutional law, and constitutional law generally. I attended law lectures in the King's Inns and in the national university, UCD, throughout that period. I had a good deal to do with Alfred O'Rahilly. Alfred had drafted a constitution and I was interested in that and had long discussions with him.

Now I would like to digress into a story about Frank Ryan. When the Spanish Civil War broke out, Frank Ryan decided to take the Republican side. He left Ireland in November 1936, was duly imprisoned and sentenced to death. But largely through the intervention of the Irish government and also through the intervention of the Vatican (Mother, who was friendly with the papal nuncio, Monsignor Robinson, had impressed upon him the importance of intervening with the Vatican) his execution was prevented. He was in very bad health, however, and conditions in the prison were harsh. Efforts were made to have him released. The Irish government, Mr de Valera's government, was very active on this. The Irish Ambassador in Madrid at the time was Leopold Kearney, to whom I have already referred. Leopold Kearney did his best with negotiations with Franco, directly I think, in regard to his release. Finally Franco said that he could not release him because there were some grave charges against him, and that it would create difficulties in his own ranks, but that he could be allowed to escape. There would be no objections to this.

Here I should also mention that at this time the war had started and that it was during the war that the escape was eventually arranged with the help of the German secret service, Leopold Kearney, and with the connivance of the Spanish government who allowed the gates to be opened at a certain time and allowed Ryan escape through the gates. He was then taken by German military services and then lived in Germany from 1940 until his death in 1944. The German government behaved very well towards him. They made a flat available and helped to keep him there. He declined to take any part in the war.

Going back to another event, Tomás MacCurtain, a son of the late Lord Mayor of Cork, MacCurtain senior who had been assassinated by the British forces in Cork in 1920, was involved in the IRA in the 1939-1940 period. He had been arrested and in and out of jail several times. I knew the family very well. I had known the father briefly when I was a youngster, doing messages from Michael Collins to him, in Cork. I knew the rest of the family very well, all the girls, one had been a law student with me, Siobhán MacCurtain. To cut a long story short, Tomás MacCurtain was involved in a shooting incident in Patrick Street, Cork, on 3 January 1940. He was arrested and charged with murder. He was finally sent for trial before a special criminal court, established under the Offences Against the State Act. I did not appear for him there. He insisted on not recognising the court and not having any legal defence. His family was anxious that I should appear for him, but Tomás was insistent that it was a waste of time and that he wouldn't be represented. Mrs MacCurtain and the family of course were upset, and kept in close touch with me. I went in and examined the legal position very carefully. I found that in view of the decision of the Supreme Court on the Burke case and on the Offences Against the State Act, I could not succeed in a *habeas corpus* application in the courts. He had been duly sentenced to death by the Special Criminal Court on 13 June 1940, and his execution was due to take place.

Various attempts had been made to secure his reprieve. A tremendous swell of public opinion had developed in the country in his favour against the execution of the son of the former Lord Mayor of Cork who had been executed by the British, and who was a hero in Cork and in the southern part of the country. Several Fianna Fáil TDs and members of the government were closely involved. The question of his reprieve came up at two or three cabinet meetings. During this time, I was in touch with Seán T. O'Kelly. He was a friend of the MacCurtain family. He was also a close friend of mine. Seán T. kept me fully informed as to the developments in connection with reprieve within the cabinet. Just a couple of days before the date of the execution was fixed, and after the reprieve had been turned down by the government, Seán T. O'Kelly sent for me and said, 'Look, they've turned down, by a majority in the cabinet, the granting of a reprieve to Tomás MacCurtain. But I think that if you could, some way or another, succeed in postponing the execution [which was then fixed to take place on 5 July], I will be able to swing things back in favour of a reprieve, get a majority of the cabinet on my side. But I need more time. It's over to you: get the execution delayed by any means you can think of.' Naturally all this was extremely confidential and whether Seán T. O'Kelly, as a government minister (Finance, 1939–45) was justified in telling me this or not, I don't know. But at least I think it was a step which we took which I think most Irish people would have approved at the time.

So the problem was over to me as to how to stop the execution. I knew that on *habeas corpus* proceedings I couldn't succeed, in the light of the Burke case and the Offences Against the State Act. Mr Justice George Gavan Duffy, then a judge of the High Court, and a most favourable judge from that point of view (he had granted me the order of *habeas corpus* in the North case and others) was a very conscientious man, and even he could not grant me an order of *habeas corpus*. Therefore I decided that I would wait until the eve of the execution. The courts sit until four o'clock. And you have until four o'clock to file notices of appeal against a decision by the High Court. I knew that if I could apply for an order of *habeas corpus* and have it refused in time for me within minutes to be able to serve notice of appeal in the office of the Registrar of the Supreme Court, that it was unlikely that they would be able to convene the same day. And therefore the Chief Justice would have to sit and make an order, postponing the execution. If a notice of appeal is lodged, it can't be ignored.

In the country generally, the execution of Tomás McCurtain had become a major issue. People were saying prayers in churches,

Pierrepoint, the British executioner and his assistant, had been brought over. He definitely had been photographed. They had measured and weighed MacCurtain. They had got new lengths of rope for the execution – all the gruesome details had been proceeding. Throughout this time, as the lawyer, the senior counsel who appeared in all these cases, I was being watched by everybody in the Law Library, and outside the Law Library. They knew that if any legal action were to be taken, I would take it. And so I was being watched most assiduously. They had, I am told, envisaged the possibility that I might come in late on the afternoon of the eve of the execution to look for an order, and leave it late so that the Supreme Court couldn't meet. They had considered that possibility and made arrangements to convene the Supreme Court that evening. The Supreme Court could sit, say at five, and dispose of the appeal that night. It would have been a difficult thing to do, for I certainly would have made it difficult for them. I would have insisted on my arguing the case fully and complaining of the way in which the case was being handled. However, be that as it may, all arrangements had been made by them to convene the Supreme Court after four o'clock, if necessary. The Registrar had been given instructions to find out where every member of the court would be, to be available, if necessary. I spent those days looking very detached, uninterested. When people spoke to me about the case, I used say 'Well, I don't think there's anything that can be done. In any case I have no instructions. There it is. He's not anxious to have someone defend him.'

At ten to four, I marched into Mr Justice Gavan Duffy's Court, and interrupted the case at hearing. Gavan Duffy guessed immediately what I was up to. I rattled out my application for an order of *habeas corpus* in about four minutes, and in one minute, Mr Justice Gavan Duffy said 'Your application is hereby refused.' My notice of appeal was ready and I went straight up to the Registrar's office and lodged it, just one minute to four.

So then they made a wild dash to get the members of the Supreme Court together. They had been keeping tabs on them the whole day. I think the Registrar of the Supreme Court then was Con Curran. He was a writer also, quite well known during that period, a literary figure in Dublin. Con said to me 'Well, you left it very late Seán, didn't you?'

1. Maud Gonne.

2. John MacBride.

3. Maud Gonne and John MacBride with their three-week old son, Seán. Taken at their home in 13 Rue de Passy, Paris.

4. Seán, aged three-months, in April 1904. The shamrocks were picked at Collville by his nurse.

5. Seán, aged eighteen-months, with his mother and sister, Iseult.

6. Seán and Brutus in the snow at Trocadero Gardens, Paris. March 1909.

7. After making his First Communion, in the garden at 13 Rue de Passy, with Barry O'Delaney and Maud Gonne. 19 March 1911.

8. The year of the Rising: Seán pictured in the Bois de Boulogne, Paris. 23 September 1916.

9. Seán's police certificate of identity, issued by Chelsea Metropolitan Police on 17 July 1918.

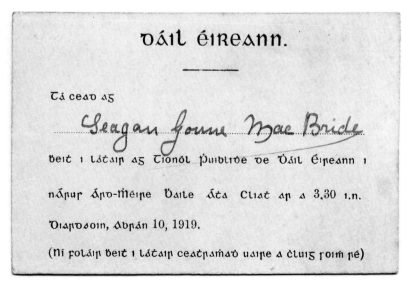

10. A Dáil pass for the sitting on 10 April 1919.

11. Seán in front of Roebuck House, 1921.

12. Seán in June 1929, taken by his wife Catalina.

13. Catalina (Kid) in June 1929.

14. Nomination day for the October 1947 by-election.

15. The counting of votes in the 1947 by-election.

16. Paddy Kinnane and Seán MacBride take their seats in the Dáil on
    5 November 1947.

17. At the St Joseph's Day Lunch at St Patrick's House, Kilmainham.
    Minister for External Affairs, Seán MacBride, serves soup to helpers
    who include Taoiseach John A. Costello and Ald. P. S. Doyle TD.

18. Lord Rugby, British Ambassador to Ireland; Clement Attlee, Prime Minister; and Seán MacBride.

19. Seán MacBride with his Ford Prefect car outside the Department for External Affairs, St Stephen's Green, Dublin.

20. Meeting of the members of the OEEC in Paris, 17 February 1949.
L-R: Osten Unden; Sweden; Joseph Bech; Luxembourg, Max Petipierre; Switzerland, Robert Schuman; France, Gustav Rasmussen; Denmark, Paul Henri Spaak; Belgium, Stafford Cripps; UK, Carlo Sforza; Italy, Neomeddin Sadak; Turkey, Averell Harriman; USA – special envoy for the Marshall Plan, Sean MacBride; Ireland, and Jose Caeiro Da Matta; Portugal.

21. Seán MacBride, Chairman of the Council of Foreign Ministers, discussing the agenda before a meeting of foreign ministers with J. C. Paris, Secretary General of the Council of Europe. On MacBride's left is F. H. Boland, Ireland's representative at the United Nations.

22. Seán MacBride and William C. Foster, US Economic Co-operation Administrator, discussing Ireland's relation with the OEEC. March 1951.

23. Seán MacBride and US Secretary of State, Dean Acheson, during MacBride's visit to the US in April 1949.

24. A photographic representation of The Book of Kells was presented to the United States Library of Congress as a gift to the people of the US from the Government of Ireland. Seán MacBride, Minister for External Affairs, made the presentation during his visit to Washington, DC in March 1951.

L-R: Luther H. Evans; Librarian of Congress, Sean Nunan; secretary of the Department of External Affairs, John Joseph Hearne; Ambassador of Ireland to the US, and Seán MacBride.

25. George Garrett, John A. Costello, unknown, Seán MacBride and
Eamon de Valera at a reception.

26. In Rome for the opening of the Holy Year in January 1950.

27. Seán MacBride.

28. Seán MacBride
delivering a public
address.

29. Seán and Kid.

30. Seán at his old home on Rue de Passy, Paris.

31. In old age.

'Yes,' I said, 'I did.' 'I was wondering how much later you would leave it.' 'Well,' I said, 'I've left it this late and there's my notice of appeal.' And Con said, 'We may have to try and get the Supreme Court together tonight.' I said, 'Isn't it a little bit late to start doing that now. It would be difficult to argue a case of this magnitude in a few hours.' 'But,' said Con, 'you only took five minutes to make your application.' The whole place had filled up when I went in.

So then they went to try and collect the judges together. One of them was Mr Justice James Murnaghan, an old judge and Curator of the National Gallery. Mr Justice Murnaghan had gone home, but had left his telephone number. When they went to the telephone to get him, he had gone to take his dog out for a walk. And Mr Justice Murnaghan did not return from the walk with his dog until seven or eight o'clock that evening.

The Supreme Court was not able to meet and the Chief Justice sat and made an order postponing the execution. The court wouldn't have been properly constituted, if one member had been absent. You couldn't deal with a capital charge case with anything less than the five judges. So I went up to Mountjoy immediately afterwards to see Tomás MacCurtain, who was furious with me. He maintained: 'It's all very well for you lawyers to amuse yourselves with your tricks, coming in and getting my execution postponed, just the night before. Now I've got to go through it all over again. I've had to say goodbye to my mother, my sisters, my girlfriend. I've had to make my peace with God, which was no easy matter. And now I've to go through this all over again now in a fortnight or three weeks' time, while you fellows are arguing, having fun arguing over my dead body.' He was very ungrateful, and remained that way for the rest of the interview!

However, I also saw Seán T. O'Kelly the next morning and said, 'Well now, I've done what you asked me to do. It's over to you. I won't be able to do it again now. There'll be an appeal and it'll be dismissed.' So Seán T. O'Kelly went to bat and finally the government, by a majority, overturned its earlier decision, and reprieved MacCurtain. The reprieve was published on 10 July 1940.

CHAPTER VIII

Clann na Poblachta

I find it very hard to place the exact point in time at which I seriously began to think about the formation of a party that would have as its purpose the bringing about of a change in government. I can concretely remember having several talks with Con Lehane, Noel Hartnett and Captain Peadar Cowan, as he was called then. Most of these talks took place in the Law Library, usually in the evening after court. I had a heavy practice and did quite a lot of work. Often after court, one or the other would come and talk to me, and Peadar and Noel in particular were always urging me to form a party, promising that if I did, they would rally round and help it. Peadar Cowan had been on the Free State side during the Civil War, and in the army. He therefore brought a completely new element into republican circles in that he was prepared to join in order to bring about change and the adoption of a more progressive policy by Irish governments. He was a good speaker, but I didn't know him very well save as a lawyer. I worked with him from time to time; he was a good solicitor. Noel Hartnett I helped quite a lot at the Bar. I gave him a hand by bringing him into cases as junior. To a certain extent I helped him to learn the trade of a practicing barrister in criminal cases. Con Lehane, of course, I knew for a long time. I worked with him quite a lot.

The three of them were very different, but they were all agreed on the need to form a new party. Con Lehane had already been involved in an attempt to form a party called Coras na Poblachta a couple of years previously. Coras na Poblachta had not succeeded, but it had done useful work in promoting the candidature of Dr Pat McCartan who had made a very good bid for the presidency. Pat McCartan also urged me to start a party and promised that he would rally round.

During this period, I was also in close contact with Donal O'Donoghue, who was running a magazine called *Republican Review* which I had been instrumental in starting. I ran the first two or three issues and then Donal O'Donoghue had taken over. In addition, I had frequent discussions with Jim Killeen and Michael Kelly. Jim Killeen had been a high ranking officer in the IRA and had been released from serving a seven-year sentence in jail in the north. He was a close friend of mine, and a man of complete integrity and honesty. In saying this I am not suggesting that the others had not complete integrity and honesty. Certainly Donal O'Donoghue was a man of tremendous rectitude and honesty.

These were roughly the people who were in contact with me about the formation of a new organisation. Finally, after resisting for some time, I eventually agreed. It was decided to launch, or rather to hold, a conference of twenty to twenty-five people that would be the nucleus upon which the new party would be founded and who would formulate a policy statement. I suppose pressure was put on me because they knew me well for a long time, through the law, through republican activities and through the IRA. Probably different reasons operated in each case. Some would have known me for a long time in the IRA, some in legal circles. Others were also very interested in my economic views. I had, for a long time, been urging reafforestation and had seen Mr de Valera several times with regard to this, but could get no proper reaction. Nothing was being done in afforestation. This led me on to taking a greater interest generally in the whole economic development of the country. I had pretty strong views on the nefarious policies that were being pursued by the government at the instance of the Central Bank. I regarded the Central Bank and the Department of Finance as being the architects of probably the most conservative and outdated economic policy that existed in Europe at that time. I had been in touch with the European movement and had followed a number of developments in the post-war period in Europe. Therefore I was closely in touch with the thinking of that period, and had given some talks to different clubs and associations, dealing with the question of developing an independent financial and monetary policy, independent from that pursued by the Bank of England. From the treaty to that period, the financial and economic policies pursued by governments were an absolute replica of those pursued by the British treasury. There was absolutely no deviation in any respect. We were investing all our savings in England at extremely low rates of interest, and starving our own economy of the capital which was necessary for its development. I had written to the papers and had made a number of speeches dealing with this. A number of my friends were also interested in these views and supported them. These are the combination of reasons which probably led a number of them to believe that I would be a suitable person to start a political party.

So we went ahead and had a conference of twenty to twenty-five people. It was in Barry's Hotel, Gardiner Place. Those whom I have mentioned already were at it. At that meeting we elaborated a draft declaration of policy which was printed and published in the papers. That was really the start of Clann na Poblachta.

The meeting which initiated Clann na Poblachta was after the death on hunger strike of Seán McCaughey on 11 May 1946. The report of the inquest was published in the papers. This came as a complete shock to the whole country; there was no appreciation that there were so many political prisoners, and that they were being so badly treated. The inquest itself was most dramatic. There had been a censorship on the press for quite a while before, but it had just been lifted. At least fifteen republicans had died at the hands of execution squads or the police or in prison; some were shot, some died in gaol and the rest were executed. Inquests were banned in some of these cases by emergency powers.

Seán McCaughey was a young Belfast man. I didn't know him well, but he used to come to ask my advice on different things; he was very upright, honest, and sincere. McCaughey had been charged in connection with the kidnapping and holding of Stephen Hayes, assault and unlawful detention, a common law offence punishable by fine or imprisonment for up to two years. Instead, the ordinary law was abrogated and he was sentenced to death in September 1941: this was commuted to penal servitude for life. He was imprisoned in Portlaoise and refused to wear prison clothes. He was kept inside prison, naked except for a blanket, without being allowed out in the fresh air, and without visits for four-and-a-half years. He was held in solitary confinement until the middle to end of 1944 without being allowed out of his cell to use the lavatory, and he was frequently subjected to body searches. He then went on hunger strike.

My recollection is that at his request I went down to visit him in Portlaoise with Con Lehane, sometime before he went on hunger strike. I also visited Tomás MacCurtain, who was serving a long term in Portlaoise prison. I satisfied myself on these occasions that they were being very badly treated and that the conditions under which they were subsisting couldn't last without permanently damaging their health. As a result, I went to see de Valera, particularly in regard to Seán McCaughey, and tried to impress upon him the damage that this was doing and that although one could understand holding people in prison, there was no need to inflict harsh treatment or not to treat them decently, once they were being held. I tried to emphasise in respect of Seán McCaughey, what a fine type he was himself, personally. I felt that de Valera, coming from a different generation, would not know him and would think that this was some irresponsible youngster, or, in any case, might disapprove of him. I think, but I'm not certain, that I went to see Gerry Boland, Minister for Justice, but with Gerry Boland I got on very badly. Gerry Boland had never forgiven me for having cross-examined him at an inquest in connection with Seán (Jack) McNeela from Mayo who had died on hunger strike. The counsel appearing for the state, had, after an adjournment, very foolishly brought in Gerry Boland, who was Minister for Justice, as a witness. This was a complete blunder, and resulted in a verdict which was adverse to the government. I cross-examined Gerry Boland rather harshly at the time, and this had got a lot of publicity. Gerry Boland made a statement afterwards, saying that this was the last damn inquest that will ever be held in this country, and made an order suppressing inquests in such cases. Jack McNeela's inquest was held on 23 April 1940; the verdict indicted the government for imposing criminal status on political prisoners. There was a separate inquest on 17 April 1940 for Tony D'Arcy from Tuam, who was one of six republican prisoners who had gone on hunger strike for political treatment.

However, to go back to Seán McCaughey: I was very upset at the time that these men should be treated in this way, in solitary confinement, without clothes, for months on end. I felt that this was bound to drive them insane in the end, that this would drive them to hunger strike, and that they would probably die. I attached quite a lot of importance to it, but got no response of any value from Mr de Valera. At the time I was fairly busy with law cases. However, one night, it must have been the night Seán McCaughey died, or at two or three o'clock in the morning, very late in any case, the phone rang. The person at the other end of the phone was Maurice Moynihan, then secretary to the cabinet or to Mr de Valera. He told me that the Taoiseach thought that I should be informed that Seán McCaughey had just died and that I might inform the family, as I was in touch with them, and also might inform his friends. The telephone call surprised me completely because normally the Taoiseach wouldn't know the condition a man was in. McCaughey had been very ill, dying for probably ten days or more, and secondly, why ring me? At the time I had no official standing. Any representations I had made on behalf of Seán McCaughey, I had made in an effort to try and prevent a tragedy, to try to soften the attitude of the government towards young men whom I believed to be complete idealists and whose motives were perfectly honest, even if one didn't agree with their actions. So I duly tried to reach his family and I reached Con Lehane. The family instructed Con Lehane to appear at the inquest and brief me to appear at the inquest. I agreed to do this. Noel Hartnett was then appointed to be my junior counsel.

We then drove down. I remember well the drive from Dublin in the morning to Portlaoise with Con Lehane and Noel Hartnett. We had probably discussed who should act as my junior, and I had probably suggested Noel Hartnett as a good junior to have. He had been a Fianna Fáil supporter; I think had been on the Executive. He was a broadcaster who worked regularly on Raidio Éireann on the staff. He had fallen out with the government for having criticised them on some aspect at a meeting. Because of that, he was dismissed from his post in Raidio

Éireann. He came to see me and I took some action, wrote to de Valera, or made some public statement criticising the attitude of the government for victimising him for having expressed political views which were not to the liking of the government. This would have been published extensively, including a long letter from Hartnett to de Valera at the time. However, be that as it may, we went down to Portlaoise for the inquest. The inquest was being held in the prison itself and there was a certain amount of delay in admitting us, with a large array of police and military, both inside and outside the prison. I forget who the coroner was, but the Department of Justice had also sent one of their senior officials, either the assistant secretary of the department or somebody else there, as an adviser to the coroner, which struck me as a most irregular proceeding. I challenged this matter at the outset.

The inquest itself was fairly dramatic. After evidence of identification of the body, the prison doctor, Dr Duane, who was a very honest man, obviously upset, was cross-examined by me. I took him through all the conditions under which Seán McCaughey had been living for the previous six months or so, the length of time he had been deprived of all his clothes, the fact that he had been in solitary confinement, merely wrapped in a blanket, and I think on a punishment diet initially. Finally, I asked the doctor, 'Have you got a dog?' Yes, he had two, he said. I then asked him, 'Would you allow your dog or dogs to be treated in the way in which this man has been treated?' The doctor turned to the coroner and asked 'Have I got to answer that question?' There was a great hugger-mugger between the official from the Department of Justice and the coroner, who gave no reply. I intervened and said, 'Yes, you have to answer the questions I ask you, and this is a perfectly legitimate question. Please give me an answer to that question.' Again there was a very long silence. Then the doctor said, 'No, I would not allow my dog to be treated in this way.' And that ended the inquest, in the midst of uproar, because for some reason, a police chief or superintendent who was present lost his nerve completely and became hysterical. He ordered the military to arrest me at the inquest before it was over! He must have gone berserk. However, I wasn't arrested.

At some stage of the inquest, Noel Hartnett was reprimanded and walked out. He created what I regarded at the time as being an unnecessary scene in order to attract attention to his role. He then left and slammed the door after him. The inquest went on and finished. We got a very mild verdict, but a verdict which criticised the government for the treatment imposed upon the prisoners, and then the body was handed over to the family and the funeral took place. The event received a considerable amount of publicity in the world press, as well as the press at home in Ireland.

Referring back to an earlier period, before the Clann was started, I was in constant contact with Mrs Berthon Waters, who was a friend of Bulmer Hobson's and who ran, with Bulmer Hobson, a series of publications called *Towards a New Ireland*. Much of it was based on what had been done by Nash and Peter Fraser in New Zealand, in the line of economic development, afforestation and all that. Bulmer Hobson was very keen on afforestation, and he and Mrs Waters ran this series of pamphlets, published by the Irish Peoples Co-Operative Society Ltd. The contributors included Séamus O'Farrell and Senator Luke Duffy, as he was afterwards, who was running the Distributive Workers Union at the time, a very able trade unionist.

They asked me to write a pamphlet, dealing with the question of civil liberties. This I did. I remember writing the pamphlet in Kinvara, spending a month or so with Roger and Patsy McHugh. It was then published by Mrs Waters in this series, called *Towards a New Ireland: Civil Liberty* (Pamphlet No. 25). In that pamphlet I reviewed the failure of the government to live up to its promises in regard to civil liberty.

From then on, events towards the formation of Clann na Poblachta went on fairly rapidly. After the conference in July 1946 we took offices in Bachelors Walk. We had financed these by collecting money here and there, by putting our hands in our pockets, by fund-raising. I remember Dr McCartan got a very large subscription for those days, of about £1,000 from Joe McGrath of the Sweepstakes with whom he was friendly. Joe McGrath had not been in office since 1924. I had also maintained good relations with Joe McGrath. He had tremendous admiration for, and was a friend of, Michael Collins and had a great sympathy for anybody who was trying to free Ireland and establish a republic. He had this kind of sentimental attachment to the movement and was also always most helpful to me in endeavouring to form a republican party.

Many teachers took an active part in the formation of Clann na Poblachta, Fionán Breathnach and others. The Association of National Teachers, which had its headquarters at Parnell Square, gave a considerable amount of support to Clann. They rallied around. There had been a national teachers strike at the time and the Teachers Club in Parnell Square was a great resort for Clann people in its early days.

There were three by-elections altogether, one in Dublin county, another in Tipperary, for which we put up Paddy Kinnane, and another in Waterford, for which we put up a teacher, Seán Feeney. We won two of the three by-elections in October 1947. This came as a surprise to the country at the time. There was a very strong swing in favour of Clann na Poblachta from then on. I got echoes from Fianna Fáil headquarters that they were worried, and that there were two different viewpoints, one was to postpone an election and the other, which de Valera favoured, was to have a general election as rapidly as possible, before we had time to organise. De Valera felt the shorter time I was given to organise, the better, because he had an exaggerated opinion of me as a good organiser.

I had refused to be chairman of the Standing Committee or the Executive of Clann na Poblachta. I had been elected leader of the party, and felt that as leader of the party I should not hold office in the Executive or in the Standing Committee, which bodies were there for the purpose of determining policy and of controlling the leader of the party if necessary. I felt, therefore, that if I was leader, chairman of the Standing Committee and chairman of the Executive, I would be in the position of complete dictator, and it would be very difficult for the party ever to get rid of me or to censor me if they wanted to. The Executive was a large body, consisting of about thirty odd members from the constituencies that met a few times a year. The Standing Committee was a much smaller body, consisting of eleven members initially, that met weekly, or sometimes bi-weekly.

Donal O'Donoghue was chairman of the Standing Committee for a very long time, right through the 1948 elections up to the wind-up of Clann. Richard (Dick) Batterbury was vice-chairman and may have been chairman for a time. The National Executive was elected by the constituencies, by the árd fheis. The supreme authority of the party was the árd fheis, an annual convention consisting of delegates from all constituencies. It then elected a National Executive which was supreme when the árd fheis wasn't sitting. The National Executive then elected a Standing Committee which was a much smaller body that used to do all the work every day and it was supreme in its decisions. The Executive always had power to reverse the decision of the Standing Committee, but for practical purposes, the Standing Committee was the body which controlled policy from day to day.

However, de Valera called a general election. He had talked about calling an election and I challenged him to call it immediately, hoping that my challenging him might put him off for some time. This didn't work. I remember for a few days issuing statements every day, asking when he was going to call an election; that it was quite obvious he had lost the confidence of the people. I felt that this would have a restraining influence on him. I would have preferred to have had another six months to organise. We had organised very quickly and rapidly, a question of improvising election machinery the whole time. The teachers were of considerable help to us during that campaign. The IRA was quiescent at the time, and while it approved of many of the things we said and did, it also considered we were not extreme enough, that we were compromisers, and that we might go the same way as Fianna Fáil. So there was no great enthusiasm on the part of the IRA for us, but they were grateful because we had focussed attention on prisoners and had succeeded in ending some of the worst abuses that were being carried out at the time by the police and by the government.

The election in February 1948 itself was interesting, quite extraordinary. I addressed roughly five meetings a day, from one end of the country to the other, beginning in the late afternoon, and finishing at about two o'clock in the morning, meeting at some places with torch-lights and so on. It was a most enthusiastic campaign. At one stage during the campaign, I thought it was going to be a landslide victory for us. We were not only going to gain a majority, but a large majority. I certainly felt like that. The role of the newspapers at the time was interesting and played an important part. The *Irish Press* was virulently, bitterly against us, in a most irresponsible way, inventing stories of all kinds, distorting news, distorting speeches. The *Independent* gave us a good deal of publicity, because they realised, perhaps, that we were going to be the death blow of Fianna Fáil and to that extent gave us quite a lot of support. The *Irish Times* pursued a liberal-unionist line of policy. It usually gave good reports of our meetings, but wrote editorials viciously attacking our policies, particularly our economic and social policy.

For example, on one or two occasions either myself or my colleagues in Clann na Poblachta had used the expression 'breaking the link with sterling'. By this we understood the reorganisation of our financial structure so as to ensure that Irish savings would be invested in Ireland and not in England. Smyllie chose to distort that into saying that we were suggesting no longer depending on sterling for currency but starting a currency of our own. This was not our policy. I did say that perhaps a stage might come when it might be desirable to do this, but that it certainly was not desirable under existing conditions. What was essential was not to follow the coat-tails of the British treasury policy as we were doing, without questioning it even. I did feel that the policy pursued by Britain and afterwards by the Free State government of investing in England at fantastically low rates of interest was wrong, our savings should have been utilised as capital for development in Ireland. I remember while I was a TD, before the 1948 government was formed, I obtained figures in reply to my parliamentary questions, which surprised everybody, including myself, as to the rate of interest which we were receiving from our investments in Britain, something like 0.85%, or 1%.

My main argument and the main theme running through all the speeches in the campaign was that Ireland is a small, impoverished, agricultural country. Britain is a large, wealthy, over-populated, industrial country. And that, nearly automatically, the policies which suited the British economy were unsuited to the Irish economy, that every single economic factor that was suitable for a highly industrial country like Britain was unsuitable to a small, impoverished, agricultural country like Ireland. While we had secured limited political freedom in 1921, we had continued to operate the same economic and financial system which had ruined the country over the centuries.

This system consisted of maintaining a large pool of unemployment in Ireland, which would provide cheap labour for two purposes. Firstly, for British industrial development and agricultural work, lower rates of wages and seasonal labour and, secondly, for the British army. In other words Ireland provided most of the British soldiers very cheaply, and by maintaining unemployment here, Britain could recruit numbers of men in Ireland for her army and for her industrial and agricultural requirements. Therefore, it suited Britain to keep depressed conditions here, to have this cheap labour pool at its disposal. It was also a labour pool that could be dispensed with and shoved back to Ireland whenever they wanted to. Moreover, British policy had been one of preventing industrial development in Ireland, so as to avoid competition with home development, in order that Ireland would remain a market for British industrial goods, which she had succeeded in doing extremely competently and well. Thirdly, Ireland should be maintained as an agricultural-producing country with low economic levels, so that it would provide food for Britain.

These were the three aims of British policy. And these were the three aims which we had to undo.

I was responsible for formulating these plans. Noel Hartnett, who was director of elections, used to complain that my speeches were too long, and that they dealt with economic matters about which nobody cared or had much interest. Would I not leave these things aside and go bald-headed for de Valera and different people, which he would do without limits. Indeed, I used to feel uncomfortable sometimes with the abuse which our speakers levelled. No, I did the long dreary speeches about economic development and all the questions about sterling and investments in England, which I think the people understood. There had been a lot of corruption in Fianna Fáil, selling licenses and so on. There had been this enquiry, which featured largely a Mr Maximo. Oliver Flanagan exposed it and there had been a part-sworn enquiry into it. I felt that, while it was desirable that these matters be exposed, they were not the long-term policy aspects which would attract support from the country: people liked you to make these attacks, but it didn't give them any confidence that you could do any better.

Be that as it may, I certainly at one stage thought that we were going to have a landslide victory. For the last ten days, however, I felt the tide turning against us, slipping back rapidly. It was a tangible thing, as if you were standing on the sand, and you feel the current pulling out the whole time from under your feet. It is very difficult to account for. Two things, I think, contributed. One, the *Irish Times* took fright; it thought we were doing too well and ran a hard campaign against us, very insidiously. While reporting our meetings still quite fairly, Smyllie never missed a day without getting a dig at us.

Secondly, there is no doubt about it that certain sections of the clergy were running a strong campaign against us. The Archbishop of Dublin, John Charles McQuaid, was blamed for some of it, but I think he stayed out of it. A lot of priests here, there, and everyplace would go about saying, 'Oh, if you elect MacBride and Clann na Poblachta, it's communism; he's going to break the link with sterling, he's going to nationalise the banks, your money won't be safe', and so on. I think this had a tremendous effect — to elect MacBride, they'll take the money from the banks and you'll have red rule and communism in the country. De Valera had cultivated some reverend mothers and I know for instance, although it sounds unbelievable, that a reverend mother in Bray told parents and everybody she spoke to quite solemnly that I was a complete atheist, and used to beat my children for going to mass on Sundays. I heard this from people to whom she had told it.

During the election campaign I also had to issue two or three writs for libel against Seán MacEntee, though I forget for what particular misdeeds. Although I issued the writs, I didn't pursue the action. I had issued the writs to make the newspapers careful about what they published.

It is very hard now to realise the bitterness of the campaign. But if one looks at the press of that period, one will get a view of the extraordinary lengths to which political journalism extended at that period; quite fantastic.

I could feel, day by day, the tide slipping back, to such an extent that at the end of the campaign I thought that I'd be lucky if I got five seats. We got eleven as it was. The number ten, frequently given, is a mistake. I know that Peadar Cowan was one of our members, but that very quickly after the election he resigned from the party. It was an exhausting campaign, fascinating. There was a desire for change, but during the last ten days I could read it on people's faces during meetings. They came there, they were sympathetic, but they were afraid. What would the consequences be if they put out de Valera? Would this man mean red rule and revolution?

Our election machinery worked well, if unevenly in some areas. I used to be rather horrified at the speeches my colleagues were making, a lot of which consisted of political abuse. That did not apply to all my colleagues, and people like Mac O'Rahilly, Donal O'Donoghue and all these always made very responsible speeches. But then, I must say, that the crowds really loved the virulent speeches of Noel Hartnett. He spoke extremely well in public. He was a very good orator.

I should mention that it was during the election campaign that Noel Harnett brought up Nöel Browne and introduced him to me as the coming young doctor who was interested in doing something for tuberculosis. I didn't know him well. I took him largely on Noel Hartnett's say-so. I realised the value of having in the party somebody who had no links with the Irish past, in the sense of IRAism, Republicanism, Fianna Fáilism or anything else. He had been introduced to me as a doctor who was interested in social issues and in medical and health services. I think the first meeting was in the Clann offices. It was arranged then that we should make an election film. It was Noel Hartnett's brainwave. This was a new departure and we would show it around the country during the election campaign. I think that I postponed any further discussion with Nöel Browne until we went over to London. We were going to make this film; we went by boat and train. I remember having a long discussion on the train from Holyhead to London with Browne and Noel Hartnett on the whole question of our policy, and trying to assess whether or not he would be a good person. He was a diffident, quiet, young man who had very good ideas with regard to health services.

One of the real evils of that period was the lack of proper hospital accommodation throughout the country, particularly the lack of hospitalisation for tubercular patients. There were huge waiting lists for every hospital, every sanatorium in the country; it might take two years before a patient could get in. During this time, patients died. It was a public scandal the way in which health services were being run and neglected, neglected, I should hasten to add, as a result of the policies of the Department of Finance. The Department of Finance would not release enough funds to build hospitals and to make accommodation available. It didn't realise that this was a completely false economy, that more and more people were becoming ill and had to be looked after, and health service pittances were being given to them. The money from the Hospitals Trust Fund, a considerable sum, instead of being used for building hospitals, was being invested in England at low rates of interest, and only the income from the money was being used to provide new hospitals.

These were all the issues which we discussed. I don't think either Noel Hartnett or Nöel Browne had really thought about where the money would come from, but I pointed out to them: well there are some very vast sums, £20 or £30 million available, which is invested in England by the Hospitals Trust. It will be a question of making that money available for a large building programme. There would have to be a crash programme for the conversion of existing buildings into sanatoria to cope with the waiting lists which existed. I said that this is something which could be done quickly, and within a very short space of time we should be able to end all the waiting lists of patients and provide decent treatment in hospitals and additional sanatorium accommodation, by using this money and by getting additional money from the government. This was the long and the short of the conversation we had.

We then did this film at a studio in London, a very juvenile attempt, but still it was the first film which had been produced for an Irish election campaign. It created quite an impact. Noel Hartnett, Nöel Browne and I were in it. It lasted about fifteen minutes, quite a short film, but it was then shown around the country.

I had deliberately avoided discussing the outcome of the election at that stage. I said, let's go out and get all the seats we can; then when the election is over we'll see what we can do. So, that was the position and certainly Browne made speeches and Hartnett made speeches that were quite reasonable. The only thing that worried me sometimes was that I felt Noel Hartnett would lose his vote by being too aggressive with his attacks on personalities.

Immediately after the elections, I was pleased, because as I've indicated, I thought we would get only five seats. I thought we had done very well. I don't think my colleagues were as conscious of the receding tide as I was. This was probably natural as I was doing five meetings a day and could sense it in addressing meetings. We met and discussed the question as to whether or not we would join the other parties in forming a government. This involved quite a lot of really serious and very reasoned and constructive discussion on the part of the Standing Committee and the Executive of Clann at the time. There was no definite immediate reaction against doing this, or in favour of doing this. It was a question of: What will we do now? What can we do?

I discussed the position with some people in Fine Gael and in the Labour Party. I discussed it first with Sir John Esmonde, who was then one of the leaders of Fine Gael and who had always shown a good deal of friendliness for republicans. He understood the republican viewpoint. I discussed it with Paddy McGilligan too, and made it clear that in any government which was formed, we should find it difficult to accept the leadership of anybody who had been very active in the civil war. Most of the people in Clann were republicans; our support came from republicans, many of whom had been voting Fianna Fáil. In particular I mentioned that we would find it very difficult to accept General Mulcahy who was regarded as one of the leading protagonists during the civil war on the other side. This was readily accepted, I found.

These discussions took place with a view to accepting a part in a coalition. I had been given a free hand from Clann to see what could be done. I had mentioned the possibility of forming an inter-party government, and discussed with Clann what would be the difficult areas. A section of Clann wanted to insist that a condition or precedent to joining a government would be the release of all political prisoners, and the repeal of the External Relations Act. I took the view that while our aim should be to secure the release of all the prisoners and to repeal the External Relations Act, I would not wish to make that a condition precedent to our joining the government. And so finally, we had a discussion as to who could lead the government. At one stage I suggested Sir John Esmonde, who apparently was not acceptable to most of the leadership or the Fine Gael party. They then suggested John A. Costello. I knew John A. Costello well from the Law Library. I had great respect for him; he was businesslike and capable. He had not really been much involved in bitter civil war politics. In addition, his son was also progressively minded and useful. So finally there was agreement on John A. Costello. I always felt that Dick Mulcahy had shown considerable judgement and generosity in a way, in never trying to push himself forward. Rather, on every occasion, he indicated that he had no desire to stand, that he would stand down in favour of national unity. His role during that period was very constructive, for which he should get credit.

My next major problem was within the Clann itself. There was general agreement that we would join with the inter-party government. We discussed how many seats we should have in the inter-party government after we had accepted in principle to join if Costello were leader. I also had discussions with Norton and the Labour Party, and had no problems there, except that Norton wanted to make quite certain that I wouldn't grab too many seats in the government, naturally enough. Then there was what was then called the National Labour Party led by Jim Everett. They were close to Fianna Fáil and were also closely linked to the Irish Transport and General Workers Union. I went to see the leaders of the ITGWU to discuss the position with them, pointing out the tremendous advance it would be if the union was represented and that this was the first time the trade union movement would take an active part in the government and this should be of tremendous help to them. This is the view which prevailed ultimately, and I think the view which made them favourable to joining the government.

My problem in Clann was who should be in the government with me? They were all agreed that I should participate as leader of Clann. We had worked it out proportionately that we were likely to get two cabinet seats. Some of my colleagues were inclined to press me that we should have three. I felt that on the grounds of numerical representation, and allowing for the fact that we had to have two branches of the Labour Party in the government and Clann na Talmhan, that two was the most we could hope for. The Labour Party would have had one, the National Party one, Clann na Talmhan one, and we would have two, so we would still be emerging as a fairly strong party. But trouble broke out as to who would be with me. At first I took the attitude that it was really up to me to decide and not for the Standing Committee. If I was the leader of the party, and entrusted to be the leader of the party in government, then it was for me to pick my own team. This the Standing Committee didn't like, obviously, and, in any case, I felt that it would be better to take them into my confidence and let them know what I had in mind. I told them what I had in mind to bring Nöel Browne into government.

I was going to look for Health to accommodate Browne. I felt that there was a job of work to be done in Health and that a young, new man and a doctor, was the best person to do it. I felt also, from the Clann point of view, that it would eradicate a lot of the criticism, suspicions that there had been, that the Clann was only a group of old IRA men, parading under a new façade and that it would build up the Clann, if among its first ministers it took a young man who was or had come from Trinity College, and that kind of conservative, unionist background. I don't think that at the time I knew that he was the son of an RIC man. I regarded him more as being part of the establishment. At the time the impression I got was that Noel Hartnett had said that Browne's father, who had been a game-keeper, had been shot and that the Chance family had brought him up and saw to it that he got a good education. This, I gather, was not true, from what I have heard since. I think he was sent to Beaumont, a Jesuit School in England, by the Chance family, who were fairly wealthy. He got TB himself at some stage and devoted himself to the eradication of tubercolosis.

There was a very strong reaction on the Executive to Nöel Browne, after I told them I was thinking of bringing him in. I was strongly warned against the dangers of doing this, that his background was unsatisfactory, that nobody knew anything about him, that he was immature, had no experience and no national tradition. The people who were strongest were Donal O'Donoghue, Dick Batterbury, Jim Killeen and Con Lehane. Hartnett was the only member of the

Executive who was in favour. I had to throw my weight heavily onto the scales to get them to agree. It was a reluctant agreement on the part of the majority of the Standing Committee. It was really a very difficult situation. Browne, of course, was not there himself, because he was not on the Standing Committee or the Executive.

CHAPTER IX

First Inter-Party government • *External Affairs*

The Lord Mayor of Dublin then invited the leaders of Fine Gael, the two Labour parties, Clann na Talmhan and Clann na Poblachta to meet in the Mansion House. We had quite a historical meeting in the Mansion House then of the leaders of the parties to decide on whether or not they would form a government, and if so, how the government would be formed. It was quite an interesting meeting from my point of view. While I had been in close touch for a long time with Jack Costello and with Paddy McGilligan at the Bar, and very occasionally with Seán MacEoin, I hadn't met many of the Fine Gael leaders since the Civil War when I met them under different circumstances. I must say it was an extremely friendly meeting, where we discussed the possibility of forming a government, and where, to everybody's amazement, I put forward a number of points, conditions upon which I would agree to enter a government.

My first condition was that a minimum of 25,000 acres of trees a year should be planted, and that money should be made available for this, whatever was required to plant these trees, without having to fight for it. Secondly, that the Hospitals Trust money and other monies that would be required for building hospitals and sanatoria would have to be made available and that nothing should stand in the way of a very rapid, active building programme. Thirdly I was concerned about old age pension and health benefits. In addition, I pointed out that the financial policy of the government should be one of promoting the repatriation of foreign investments and their conversion into investments for industrial development in Ireland. When I had outlined these, I could nearly sense a feeling of incredulity around the table, and of relief. I think that they felt I would demand immediate repeal of the External Relations Act, proclamation of a republic and so on, and that they were greatly relieved to find that I was dealing with concrete economic issues, with which they all agreed. So this was accepted enthusiastically by the Fine Gael leaders and those of the Labour parties, with considerable, visible signs of relief.

Then I immediately indicated the two posts in the government which I thought I would be interested in for my party, one was the post of Health for Dr Nöel Browne, and again a look of surprise around the table. I think they had expected Con Lehane, and Seán MacEoin came to me after the meeting and said 'Are you wise taking a young fellow like this Nöel Browne? You don't know very much about him. You'd be much better off with somebody like Con Lehane, an experienced republican and politician.' I said maybe, but that is what we have decided. I felt it was necessary to bring in somebody new and fresh to deal with this problem, to show we meant business. So that was all. I asked for Health for Browne, and indicated that I wanted External Affairs for myself.

There were a number of reasons why I wanted External Affairs. First of all I would be dealing with one of the weaknesses of the government of this time: its relationship with the British government. I felt that there would be an uneasiness, especially among the republicans, if foreign affairs were left, for instance, to General Mulcahy. He would be suspected, rightly or wrongly, of making a deal with the British the whole time. Quite apart from that, again, something which I don't think many of them understood, I had been very interested in the European movement and in the concept of sovereign international courts in regard to human rights. I had followed the drafting of the Universal Declaration of Human Rights. In the European movement we had been working towards the production of a convention on human rights for Europe. And I felt that I would be able to help in these directions. So these were my reasons, but reasons which I don't think Clann would have understood at the time because they were removed from the realm of active politics here. I think that this again produced a sigh of relief around the table of the leaders, when they heard I was interested in this kind of thing. I don't know whether anybody else might have been interested in External Affairs. McGillingan might have been, but I think I suggested myself that McGilligan be made Minister of Finance, since he had more progressive views on economic and financial matters inside Fine Gael than had the others. McGilligan had had to put up a tremendous fight in the old Cumann na nGaedheal government against the Department of Finance, which had tried to stop him from building a Shannon scheme and the ESB. I got on well with Paddy McGilligan. We were both lawyers and I had a respect for the role he had played at the Commonwealth conference which adopted the Statute of Westminster. McGilligan and Costello had both played an important part in that conference, which had been useful in loosening the bonds of the Commonwealth. He rather liked my economic and financial views. He was, unfortunately, rather ineffective as a Minister for Finance, because he was ill a good deal of the time and often allowed his officials to take decisions which he should have taken himself. But he was competent at the same time.

Getting back to the formation of the government: I know that they had agreed on MacEoin. I think they had decided that I should be Minister for Defence. I learned this afterwards, that they thought I would want to be Minister for Defence, which wouldn't have interested me at all. It was an odd way of thinking. Knowing my connection with the IRA, they thought: well, he should be in defence. Instead of that, Dr O'Higgins became Minister for Defence. He was a very nice man, who, I think, had been mapped out for the Department of Health. But I must say agreement was reached on this quickly, and I think that they were also relieved that my attitude was what they considered reasonable. I did mention in private conversation with them afterwards that I would naturally be very glad to see the External Relations Act repealed, but I realised that I hadn't got a mandate for that. This had been part of my policy only during the election and I should not try to impose policy on the other parties which was not acceptable. All the other things I had asked for were things that they had campaigned for as well, and therefore it was reasonable to ask for them. This had been an official meeting in the Lord Mayor's residence to decide on the formation of the government. A communiqué was issued from the meeting.

The night after the government was formed, MacEoin came to me and said, 'I wanted to tell you, I never appreciated anything more than your attitude, and you never mentioned a word about prisoners. I have decided tonight that they will all be released.' This is exactly what I was hoping would happen. The next day he asked me to come and see him about three or four cases, being doubtful as to whether they were political cases or not. And the order for release was signed. But the interesting thing was that I had never asked for it. I had thought it would happen. I thought it would be their reaction. If they were really genuine about cooperation, they would do this, without my having to say it. And it worked. So that helped to create a good atmosphere in the country and with them. Of course, they were criticised by some of their own right-wing people for the release of prisoners. I think there were sixty or eighty or something like that. These would mainly have been lodged under de Valera's regime, all IRA people.

I should deal with the question of the alternatives. Time after time we have been criticised since — if you hadn't gone into a coalition government, you'd have been much stronger, Clann would have been in a stronger position — and so on. This argument ignores completely what the facts of the situation were. The first thing that happens after the election when the Dáil meets is the Taoiseach has to be elected. A Taoiseach is proposed and seconded, and maybe somebody else is proposed, seconded. We would have had, within half an hour of the new Dáil meeting, to have voted either for de Valera or Richard Mulcahy. We had campaigned during the course of the election campaign, with a major poster, a very effective poster consisting of three words: PUT THEM OUT. Having campaigned for six weeks to PUT THEM OUT, we would be utterly discredited if we put them in. They were out. We had put them out. We couldn't for our very first act, vote to put them back in again. So that was one reason. If we abstained from voting, we would also be putting them in, because they would have been able to get in anyway. Supposing that we had voted for General Mulcahy, who was the leader of Fine Gael, we'd have had an awful lot to explain. Besides which, there wouldn't have been the moderating influence which we had in the government in dealing with republicans. There would have been no question of prisoners being released, and all this. The release of the prisoners was of considerable assistance, because the IRA realised that we had lived up to what they had expected of us. There was a government that had released all their prisoners, they must be given a fair chance and we mustn't embarrass them more than we can. So that really eased the path considerably. The government was duly formed and elected and we went and got our seals of office from Seán T. O'Kelly in the park. Seán T. O'Kelly was very friendly. I felt he was glad to see me as Minister for External Affairs.

Early on the morning of Good Friday, 27 March 1948, I got a phone call from Dick Mulcahy, saying he was anxious to see me as soon as possible. All the members of the government were out of town for the Easter weekend except us. I had to speak at some 1916 commemoration on Easter Sunday somewhere in the west of Ireland. He had reached Jack Costello who had asked him to deal with the matter. So I arranged to meet Dick in his Marlborough Street office at about ten or eleven on Good Friday morning. I was surprised because I couldn't think what Dick wanted to see me about. We didn't have very much to do with each other.

So I went in and we chatted. He hoped that I wouldn't be alarmed or worried by what he was going to tell me. He explained that it should have been Seán MacEoin's task because he was Minister for Justice – all this until I really was in a state of nerves. So I said, 'Well, what is it? Come on to the point.' 'Well,' he said, 'all precautions have been taken, you needn't worry. There is to be an attempt made to assassinate you.' So I laughed and said 'Oh, I don't take that very seriously. Tell me the origin of the story.' 'Well', he said, 'they have a report that there's a plot being prepared, to assassinate you, probably this weekend.' I asked who had reported this. 'The police,' he said. 'Probably the best thing is to see them and ask them yourself. I am only the intermediary. I have Chief Superintendent Carroll in the next room and Superintendent Mick Glynn. I'll call them in.'

I knew both of them. 'What's this all about?' I asked. 'It's serious,' they said, 'We have positive information that you are to be assassinated, probably this weekend. Don't worry. We'll take the necessary precautions. You needn't have the slightest fear; nothing will happen.' I asked what they knew, and they replied, 'We can't tell you the whole story.' I said, 'What do you mean you can't tell me. If I am to be assassinated, at least I should know who is to assassinate me.'

It was the British services who had informed them of this in Belfast. Apparently they had heard of some plot that was being hatched in the IRA to assassinate me. This of course made me extremely suspicious. First of all I did not have very much confidence in the efficiency or reliability of our own police force in regard to political matters. They had been trained in a political era and a political atmosphere, and I knew they resented the fact that I was in the government. They also resented the fact that I refused to have police protection. Other ministers had cars with police drivers. They had police protection. I had a state car which I used only on official government business. I kept on driving my own car around; it was a Ford Prefect. I felt that the use of a state car on one's own private business was giving bad example. There had been a lot of abuse of this in the last government. The car was there for official business, not to bring your wife to do her shopping. Indeed, some of them used to use the state car to carry pigs to the market. I remember one such occasion in County Cavan, I think it was.

Be that as it may, the police resented the fact that I was independent, and that they didn't really know what I was doing all the time. Anyway, I said, 'Did the British tell you any more? What did they tell you exactly?' Apparently they merely said that there was a plot and that they were quite certain that it had come from an absolutely reliable authority. I could keep on staying at home, but they would put a guard all around the house. It would be done as discreetly as possible. I would have an additional police officer in the car and I would have an escort. They would be as unobtrusive as possible. But I said no, I wouldn't accept this under any circumstances. I was quite capable of minding myself. I said that I was much more suspicious as to the origin of this plot, the reasons and wherefores. I would not be surprised if it had been invented by the British services in order to create dissension. I also thought, though I didn't say, that it might have been exaggerated or partly invented by the Irish detectives or secret services, in order to make themselves more important, or in order to say they were guarding me. I said I would be very glad of any advice they could give me. Mulcahy tried to press me, but I knew pretty well what was going on in the country. I knew what the IRA was doing, planning, their outlook. They may have criticised me from time to time, but on the whole they respected my viewpoint. I was worried that the British services should inform our police that such a plot existed and that our police would take it as gospel truth without any further investigation. They offered me a revolver. I agreed that if it made them happier, I'd carry one, though it wouldn't be much use and I'd rather not. Dick and I had a talk afterwards. I explained that I thought the whole story was made up and that I was worried, more worried about the cause of making up such a story at the time. Was it to frighten me off what I was doing, or to try and create dissension between the IRA and myself and the government, or to create internal divisions within the government?

Later on that evening, Carroll arrived. I had cross-examined him in law cases. On one particular occasion I remember cross-examining him very severely, and had to report himself and two other superintendents in connection with allegations made in respect of the trial of IRA men. Carroll came to see me and presented me with a small revolver, a thirty-eight automatic, in a small box with ammunition. He left a note in it, but I saw him as well. He said that one never knew, and in case of accidents it might be useful. I kept the revolver and note. Years later, I came across it, and tried to fit the bullets into it, to see if it would function properly. The ammunition didn't fit. I meant to have it checked by an arms expert. This is of course open to two other constructions: either the revolver was given to me with the knowledge that it couldn't work, or it was a piece of gross inefficiency to give me a revolver for which the ammunition didn't fit.

As soon as the Easter holidays were over, I sent a message to the British Ambassador saying I wished to see him rather urgently. I asked him what the story was about assassination plots about which the British secret service had told the police. At first he professed to know nothing. But I knew from his reaction that he did know; it wasn't a blank denial, it was rather an evasion. Lord Rugby would find it hard to lie very directly to me. But he said that these things didn't come within his province, that he was a diplomat. I asked him to find out the origins, and indeed asked each week at our lunches. Then at the end of about six or eight weeks he said that he had just got a report back and that 'It is quite true that our services did notify your services that they had had reports of some plot, originating in Belfast, to assassinate you. They wouldn't tell me any more about it than that. They said that there had been such reports and that they had received them.'

So that was the end of that. I discussed it with Jack Costello and with Seán MacEoin, who agreed with me that it was a police stunt to exaggerate their own importance, and so long as I felt that nobody was likely to assassinate me, not to worry.

I used to go to Paris very often, on short visits. I always saw Foreign Minister Georges Bidault on arrival and had a quick chat with him. He liked to think he was influencing me and I liked to pick up my gossip from him. On one occasion in June 1948 I arrived in Paris in the morning to find that the government had changed overnight. I told the embassy to ring up and say that in view of the change of government, I assumed that Bidault didn't want to see me. But Bidault insisted that he wanted to see me, his dear friend Seán, he must see me. I reluctantly went, for I didn't wish to become embroiled in the internal rows of French politics and the French parties. I arrived at the Quai d'Orsay to find Hervé Alphand waiting anxiously for me pacing up and down inside the hall. 'Thank God you've come', he said; 'we have been waiting for you. We're having terrible trouble: Bidault won't leave. He says he's not going to hand over to Schuman.'

I went in. Obviously, Bidault had had a few drinks. He threw his arms around my neck. An Irish nurse had taught him a song which he began to sing. Then he said, 'This old camel, Schuman, thinks he's going to get me out of here. He is waiting in that room to take over. I'm not going to hand over to them, double crosser.'

I tried to reason with him, but he'd get annoyed. This went on for about an hour-and-a-half. Occasionally the door opened and Hervé Alphand peeped in to see how I was getting on. At one stage I went out and told Schuman: 'Give me another hour, and I'll get him out quietly.' And I think that at about half-past eleven, I said to Bidault, '*Eh bien, on va aller manger. On va déjeuner. On va prendre un bon déjeuner ensemble, maintenant.*' And Bidault replied '*Très bonne ideé.* Where'll we go?' He and I then sailed out to have lunch and Schuman took over. I liked both of them. Bidault used to irritate the British beyond measure; he'd say to Ernie Bevin: 'Now we want to have a quiet talk, a fundamental discussion between the two of us. And I don't want any interpreters there. But our friend Seán will come, and he will interpret.' Ernie, Georges and I would disappear and lock ourselves up in an office, without any officials or interpreters. This used to drive the British Foreign Office crackers. They hated this because there would be no records. And Bidault used to do this on purpose, to irritate them. He used to say, '*Ah-ah … les Britanniques, ils n'aiment pas ça.*' But he started drinking a lot.

I should mention that during the election campaign we did campaign for the repeal of the External Relations Act, but none of the other parties in the government had. The Labour Party, or Bill Norton, had once or twice mentioned it, but one couldn't say they had campaigned for it. Therefore I felt that when we joined the government, it would be grossly unfair to try and push for the repeal of the External Relations Act, knowing all the problems it would create, certainly for Fine Gael, and also, to a certain, but lesser, extent, for the Clann na Talmhan party, because Joe Blowick was extremely conservative himself and was always terrified of anything that might possibly injure good trading relationships with our neighbouring island and our cattle trade. So I had never raised the question of repeal of the External Relations Act, and had decided not to bring it up at cabinet meetings.

A short time after we had taken over in the government, a new Argentine Ambassador or minister was appointed and called to see me. He then showed me a copy of his letters of credence, which were addressed to His Majesty, the King of England, and which referred to Ireland as if Ireland were a British colony of some sort, or certainly in terms which were not consonant with the status of an independent state.

I took the initial step of telling the Argentine minister that I thought that the government would prefer the credentials to be addressed to the President and not to the King of Great Britain. He accepted this and I informed the cabinet. We discussed it in detail and they were all very pleased that I had taken this step. They all said that it was about time we put an end to this nonsense of presenting letters of credence to Buckingham Palace. There had been a number of incidents, just before the change of government, where diplomats arrived with letters of credence addressed to His Majesty the King. The letters had been opened in Dublin and then transmitted to London. Buckingham Palace had taken exception to the fact that they had been opened, on the basis that letters addressed to His Majesty the King should be untouched and should be delivered as they were received. There had been some acrimonious correspondence to that effect.

Ambassador Bessone returned with letters of credence, duly addressed to the President of Ireland. These were accepted by me as being proper letters of credence. Arrangements were made for presentation to Mr Seán T. O'Kelly. I went to see O'Kelly and explained to him the whole situation. I told him that this was the first step towards finding a way out of the custom that had existed and also making way for our discontinuing membership of the Commonwealth. He was delighted with this and thought it was proper and fitting to mark the occasion of the first letters of credence being addressed to the President by a foreign state by giving a luncheon or a dinner. This was reported in the press, but the press missed the significance of the whole operation. They didn't report the speeches which were made at it. Normally, letters of credence were presented in the morning with inspection of the guard of honour, with top hats and God knows what, and a glass of sherry was passed about afterwards, and everyone goes off. Ambassador Bessone was the first Argentine Ambassador to Ireland. He presented his credentials on Saturday 31 July 1948 to Mr John A. Costello and had dinner that night with Seán T. O'Kelly. However, he was recalled, and left Ireland on 9 October 1949 and a successor was appointed.

So the episode of the Argentine Ambassador to Dublin was what I would regard as the first step in breaking the link with the Crown, the first step towards the repeal of the External Relations Act and towards

Ireland's departure from the Commonwealth. It must be remembered, of course, that from the time that de Valera brought in the External Relations Act, 1938 or 1939, he had been criticised very strongly, especially by Paddy McGilligan who, as a constitutional lawyer, considered this an absolutely absurd device, meaningless, which was rather *infra dig*. Indeed, if one read the External Relations Act carefully, one realised it was badly drafted, among other things, and went much further than it was intended to go. It really made the King of Britain, King of Ireland, specifically, and head of state.

I should mention that during this period I had established very good relations with Lord Rugby, the British Ambassador in Dublin. He used usually come and have a boiled egg on toast and tea at my office in Iveagh House, once a week at lunchtime. Lord Rugby rather liked his boiled egg on toast; it was a nice British type of healthy habit! Also, it gave him material for filling in his reports. I had a similar arrangement with the American Ambassador, George Garrett, who used also come and eat a boiled egg on toast with me. But for George Garrett, it was quite a painful exercise, one greatly encouraged by his wife, who thought he was eating too much. To him it was a penance, but he used manfully to do it. It was very useful. We used to have a gossip about political problems over all. He got enough material to write his reports to Washington for the week.

I had also very close relations during this period with the French Ambassador, Count Stanislaus Ostrorog. He also had boiled egg on toast with me. However, when he did, it was a question of his wanting to talk to me very much about something. I don't think he really approved of boiled egg on toast. Count Ostrorog was an extremely able diplomat who had asked to be sent to Ireland in order to get some rest. He had been very active in different posts in the world and wanted a restful post. He was a charming man, most helpful to me always. If I ever wanted to discuss any world problems, it was to him I would turn. I found his experience invaluable. He had acquired a tremendous amount of knowledge in the course of his life. He had been brought up in Istanbul and I think his family was half-Turkish. He had been in Egypt for a long time. He knew the world at the palm of his hand.

The next step with regard to the repeal of the External Relations

Act was in connection with the Citizenship Bill which was being enacted in Britain. There had been agreement between de Valera's government and the British government that a joint committee should be set up to review the citizenship laws, the nationality laws of both Great Britain and of Ireland, so that they would be consonant with each other in relation to passports, exchange of citizens, social benefits and so on. This committee had apparently been working for a long time. I heard about it and I called for the files, which I read through very carefully. Bearing in mind that I had not raised the question of repeal, I was certainly looking out for anything which might make it more difficult. I was rather horrified in reading through the reports of this joint committee, which had been working for several months, to find that many of the provisions in the new Nationality Bill would cease to operate if we left the Commonwealth and became an independent state. We were represented by Sheila Murphy, a counsellor in the Department of External Affairs. I had long discussions with Sheila, who was rather surprised to find that I wanted her to take a much stronger attitude. I gave instructions that negotiations with regard to the British Citizenship Act were to be reopened, and quite easily we were able to obtain a situation whereby if Ireland ceased to be a member of the Commonwealth, or ceased to recognise the Crown in any way, she would retain certain privileges, privileges indeed which were not even enjoyed by some Commonwealth members. The net outcome of these negotiations was that Ireland emerged from the negotiations with a British Citizenship Act, or the equivalent, which placed Ireland in a more favoured position than any member of the Commonwealth. In other words, we had additional benefits. For example, I know that we Irish people could vote in Britain on arriving, as soon as the register was made. I regarded the outcome as an extremely important step if we wanted to repeal the External Relations Act.

I did most of this work on my own. Not because I was keeping it from the government, but because I felt that most of the ministers would not be interested in it. Certainly, I discussed it with Jack Costello in detail and I am certain I discussed it with Cecil Lavery. Cecil Lavery was Attorney General, a man for whom I had great respect, a close friend of mine. I remember going to discuss it at length with Cecil, who was rather horrified at the concessions that Fianna Fáil had made during the negotiations, and who agreed with me entirely on the question of reopening them, and made some valuable suggestions at the time. It is quite likely that I didn't discuss it with the rest of the government. I may have mentioned it incidentally at a cabinet meeting. It was discussed in detail at a later stage, when the question of repeal of the Act arose, when I said, 'Well now, I've taken good care to ensure that there is nothing in the Nationality Bill that will create a problem.'

What did surprise me at the time was that the British government did accept these changes without realising the reasons for making them, the reason being that we were contemplating leaving the Commonwealth.

There was one incident of interest. Cearbhall Ó Dálaigh, who later became President, had been Attorney General in the previous de Valera government. He was very nice. Cearbhall had written an article in the *Irish Press*, reviewing these negotiations on the Nationality Act. From recollection, he had obviously had access to secret government files up to the point when I took over and had built his articles on the position as shown in these files. He was being rather critical of this new Nationality Act which would tie Ireland hand and foot to the Commonwealth. In any case, this article was, if I remember rightly, on the leader page. I have a visual memory of it still. I raised the question in the Dáil and at one stage suggested that it was highly improper for him to have made use of government files and indeed he might be liable to prosecution under the Official Secrets Act for having used material which was in confidential government files. But at the same time, getting great enjoyment for saying: whatever may have been the position when you were Attorney General, this has been remedied. Now we have a Nationality Act which permits us to the leave the Commonwealth if we want to.

Let me hasten to explain that I always had excellent relations with Cearbhall Ó Dálaigh, and that I merely used this as a threat, to make sure that in future the files would not be used. Cearbhall at that time did not realise that I had changed the political course of the negotiations.

So I would regard the rectification of the nationality position, which de Valera's government had agreed to with the British, as being the second major step in preparing for repeal of the External Relations Act. It was a very important step. It is always difficult to reopen a nationality issue between two countries once it is adopted; vested interests grow, and property rights and all kinds of other things flow from it.

The third step was an invitation which was sent by the British Prime Minister, Mr Attlee, on 14 October 1948 to Mr Costello, inviting Mr Costello and the government to be represented at a conference of Commonwealth ministers which was to take place shortly. The invitation was discussed first of all by the Taoiseach and myself, and then at a cabinet meeting. I was given the task of drafting a reply. On my advice, it was decided that Mr Costello would not attend; that if anybody went, I should go as Minister for External Affairs. But the decision was not to go because we did not regard ourselves as being part of the British Commonwealth, that since the adoption of the constitution we had ceased to be members of the Commonwealth and that therefore we would not go as a member of the Commonwealth. However, we would be prepared to go to discussions, if the British government and the Prime Minister were prepared to discuss the ending of the partition of the country. We would welcome the occasion of discussing this and of reaching an agreement for securing the future unification of the country.

We used to, at my lunches with Lord Rugby, talk very frankly about these various things. I think he told me that the letter had created quite a flutter in the dovecots in Whitehall and they didn't know what to do. What did we mean by it? I said we meant exactly what we said: that we would like to go and meet our colleagues of the Commonwealth, provided we could discuss partition and the ending of partition. We saw no purpose in attending, and it would irritate our public opinion more than ever if we went to discuss Irish affairs in London, unless there was some purpose to be gained affecting the unity of the country.

The Commonwealth then was rather different to the Commonwealth of later years. The British, for some reason, used to have a club within the Commonwealth, to whom they entrusted various major questions. On questions relating to Ireland, they excluded countries such as India and South Africa, so the Commonwealth meeting would consist only of

New Zealand, Australia, Canada, Britain and Ireland, a very reduced Commonwealth.

I should mention that I maintained close contact with the Canadians, with Lester Pearson, Minister for Foreign Affairs, whom I knew. I also knew Herbert Evatt, Minister for External Affairs of Australia, for whom I had tremendous respect, although he was criticised a good lot in Australia afterwards. He was a High Court judge, and he resigned this position, with its security and all that, to take up a post in the government, which very few judges are ever prepared to do — to step down from the security on the Bench, from pomp and ceremony to the everyday work of politics. He also played a very active role in the formation of the United Nations.

I also had relationships outside that, with India and with South Africa. These I had developed previously and when I became Foreign Minister. I was lucky in the case of India, that I knew Pandit Nehru from the time when he was struggling for the independence of India. He had even been here and stayed with me in Ireland. I also knew Krishna Menon, later Indian Ambassador here and a very controversial figure. I knew Nehru's sister particularly well. She had been engaged in the feminist movement and she knew Mother. She was a very fine person. So I had very good links with Nehru and the Indian government. I saw him many times after I became minister. I immediately made a bee-line and I met him in Paris two or three times. I also arranged for him to come over here. The Freedom of the City of Dublin was conferred on him and he was received in Dáil Éireann and so on. This was part of my policy. I arranged this as I felt that relationships with India were very important. With Nehru I discussed at length the question of our leaving the Commonwealth. He was incensed that India had not been invited to this meeting and that India had not been informed of the correspondence that had passed between the British government and the Irish government. So naturally, I furnished him with a copy of the correspondence. I felt that as a member of the Commonwealth, India was entitled to a copy of the correspondence.

Nehru was at the time adopting a constitution, which was largely based on the Irish constitution of 1937. Many of the chapters of the constitution are identical. We discussed various aspects. Some articles he did not understand, he wasn't very keen on.

I met his daughter, Indira, a young woman at the time, who became Prime Minister and was later assassinated.

In Paris, there was a meeting of the United Nations at which the Universal Declaration of Human Rights was adopted. Nehru argued that, in the case of India, there would be many advantages in remaining part of the Commonwealth. India would need technical assistance from the British, and the British civil service had done a reasonably good job in the building up of the civil administration, something which they were anxious to maintain. He also felt that India was so big and so far away that they could discount British influence. In the case of Ireland, I pointed out, and he accepted, the position was quite different. We were too close to Britain and too small. If we were in the Commonwealth, we would be swallowed up by Britain the whole time.

Nehru did realise that Ireland was in a different position, whereby on account of her size and proximity to Britain, she would be dominated in everyday life. In the end, while Nehru himself probably favoured our remaining in the Commonwealth, largely because he thought we would be a useful ally, he came around to the point of view that we were quite justified in leaving.

In the case of South Africa, my relationship was entirely different. My relationship with South Africa stemmed largely from the fact that Father and Mother had been instrumental in organising an Irish Brigade which fought on the Boer side in the Transvaal war.

The Minister for Foreign Affairs at that period was Eric Louw, who was a fierce Afrikaans. He had been pro-German during the war and I think had been arrested by the British because he was suspected of this, and suspected of furnishing information to Germany. Eric Louw had written a book on Ireland, on the IRA and on my father. Accordingly there was a kind of relationship which made him very friendly towards us. He also asked me why it was that South Africa had not been invited to any of these discussions. I also supplied him with copies of correspondence since I felt that he too was a member of the Commonwealth and entitled to a copy of the correspondence. Many years later I met Eric Louw in completely different circumstances when I was on a mission for Amnesty International, trying to get people out of jail.

So the Commonwealth was really limited, for all practical intents and purposes, to the countries that I mentioned: Australia, Canada, New Zealand, Britain and Ireland. All the others were excluded. Officially they should have been included in every Commonwealth decision. But they worked out some strange formula, for they were of course attacked by the Indians and by the South Africans for ostracising their governments, but they wrote a typical British letter saying, well, we considered that because you were so far away, and the interests of Ireland and South Africa and India were so unrelated to each other, you would not be interested in participating. To which, I think they got tart replies saying that it was up to South Africa and India to decide whether to go or not.

As far as Australia was concerned, I was nearly in constant touch with Herbert Evatt. He used to telephone me – he was in Paris a lot of the time, or he was in London – and I would go and meet him or have a telephone conversation, very frequently during that period. Less frequently Canada, though I met Lester Pearson two or three times in connection with it. I also met Arnold Smith, who was a secretary to Lester Pearson and a subsequent secretary to the British Commonwealth. The only one of these countries which I didn't know, and which I anticipated would be hostile, was New Zealand. I had tremendous admiration for the New Zealand Prime Minister, Peter Fraser. He was a very able man and had done a considerable amount of work on the economic development of New Zealand and afforestation. He had played a large part in the inspiration of Mrs Waters, Bulmer Hobson and me in that series of pamphlets *Towards a New Ireland*. I was familiar with his work and with his philosophy.

Here, I might digress to bring in a story which was very gratifying. There was a Commonwealth conference called at Chequers composed of Britain, Australia, Canada, ourselves and New Zealand. The only person around the table whom I had never met was Peter Fraser. I knew what he stood for and what his philosophy was. Strangely enough, we just happened to sit side by side. There was a moment of delay while they were looking for papers and organising who would preside and so on. Peter Fraser leaned over to me and said 'How's your beloved mother?' I said 'She's very well. Do you know her?' and he answered 'Oh indeed I do, very well. I used to attend her meetings when she was organising meetings in Glasgow against recruiting for the British Army to fight in the Transvaal war. I had great admiration for her.' So I felt that I wasn't so lonely after all there. And at some other interval, he leaned over and said 'How are James Connolly's children doing? James Connolly was a great friend of mine.' This was a complete surprise to me. I didn't know that he had any Irish links or interest. In the end it turned out that he was very strongly pro-Irish and, helped us throughout the whole negotiations. The purpose of the negotiations, from the British point of view, was 'to persuade our good friends the Irish' to remain in the Commonwealth and not to rock the boat. I said we were perfectly prepared to discuss all this, provided we could also discuss partition. This was at the meeting in Chequers on 17 October 1948. Atlee made an opening statement referring to our good friends, the Irish, that they didn't want to lose them from the Commonwealth, the traditional links and so on. I replied, pointing out that, unfortunately, the traditional links that welded the United Kingdom with the other members of the Commonwealth were somewhat different to those that existed between Ireland and Great Britain. In our long history, the link with Great Britain had been one of oppression and one in which the name of His Majesty the King was used to evict people from their houses and to dispossess people of their lands, and that therefore there was no traditional link of friendship. If anything, the link which existed was one which would lead to unfriendliness. And therefore, traditional links counted for very little with us, but that we would be prepared to remain in association with the Commonwealth on condition that the unnatural partition of the country could be remedied and could be ended.

Immediately I had finished, Attlee said, 'We can't discuss this. We can't discuss the partition of Ireland.' Herbert Evatt asked, 'Why can we not discuss the partition of Ireland? Why can we not discuss anything we like with our Irish friends? We are free countries here.' Lester Pearson said, 'I don't see how, Mr Prime Minister, you can stop us from discussing anything we think should be discussed.' And then Peter Fraser weighted in, to the horror of the British round the table who thought that he was a good Union Jack country man. And he came out and he said, 'I'm not going to stay here for five minutes if I'm not going to be allowed discuss the unnatural partition of Ireland with our Irish friends here; they're perfectly right in asking us to discuss it. This was an outrageous thing to do in the country. And we should remedy it now.' This went on for some time and it was on that note that the conference ended.

There was a previous incident in which Philip Noel-Baker who later became a great friend of mine, was involved. He was Commonwealth Foreign Secretary at the time. But here comes the interesting sidelight, which is somewhat typical of British methods when they are in a corner. At the beginning of the conference the British told us that there were lots of press men around the place looking for news and interviews and they said, 'Could we all make an agreement that we will not give any interviews to any newspaper men, except a joint communiqué that we will agree on.' So I said: Yes, that's fine. And Herbert Evatt, who was probably more experienced than I was on such matters, said, 'Yes, but I want to see the communiqué that is going to be issued first. I know how these things are manoeuvred. And so we'll make an agreement now that nothing will be said to the papers, but that we'll draft a communiqué ourselves here. This matter of trying to bully our Irish friends here into preventing them from trying to establish a republic is a matter which concerns the Irish population in my country, and I want to be very careful with regard to what is issued.' So the conference went sour for the British, completely, the whole way through.

I think that the drafting of the press release took longer than the actual conference itself. The issues at the conferences were quite simple and clear-cut. We were not prepared to discuss staying in the Commonwealth, unless the British were prepared, together with the Commonwealth ministers, to discuss the reunification of Ireland. The British were not prepared to accept this, and therefore there was nothing further to talk about.

During the drafting of the communiqué, I spent most of my time in discussions with the Canadian Prime Minister, Monsieur St Laurent. Evatt was very much involved in the drafting of the communiqué, so was Peter Fraser of New Zealand. Finally the communiqué was read over, copies were typed, alterations were made and we all parted company and returned to London. I am not certain if I went straight back to the airport to get the next flight to Dublin.

I suppose it was nine or ten at night when we got back to Dublin. A short time after I was home, I started to get messages from the Department of External Affairs and from John Dulanty in London saying that all kinds of very garbled and unfriendly statements were appearing in the British press and that there had been an informed commentary on the conference, given out to the British newspapers. Apparently some kind of press conference was organised in the Commonwealth Office in London that evening at which some statements were given out as to the conference. From recollection, I think some of them implied that the British government might have to resort to economic sanctions against Ireland unless Ireland took a more reasonable attitude to the Commonwealth. The following day, Herbert Evatt and Peter Fraser were on the phone early, complaining bitterly at the press and particularly complaining at the fact that this was being put out by British government sources.

Later I was contacted by a journalist friend of mine who was in London at the time, representing an American newspaper. He rang me up and was outraged at the way in which this had been handled. From him, I got a detailed account of a press briefing which was held in the Commonwealth Relations Office, at which a handout was made available, giving a completely different account to that which was issued in the agreed communiqué. To my surprise, Philip Noel-Baker, who was present, answered some questions posed by a newspaper man. This shocked me very considerably, because I was a friend of Noel-Baker, and I was surprised that he had agreed to such tactics. Statements were issued, but the damage was done. Herbert Evatt and Peter Fraser were very indignant and were on the phone to me from London two or three times, suggesting various courses of action and telling me what they had told the British concerning the breach of faith committed in regard to the agreed press statement.

The conference had proved to be completely abortive as far as Anglo-Irish relations were concerned. The British had not yielded an inch, and we had not yielded an inch. We had, on the other hand, succeeded very clearly in alienating the Commonwealth countries from them in regard to Ireland. Australia, Canada and New Zealand had all agreed that there was no reason against the partition of Ireland being discussed at a Commonwealth meeting, and that they would welcome this opportunity of undoing what appeared to be a wrong done in 1922. However, the British wouldn't hear a word of this.

Sometime after, I had a phone call from Herbert Evatt in Paris. He was then President of the General Assembly which was meeting at the Palais de Chaillot, near the Trocadero Gardens, to adopt the Universal Declaration of Human Rights. He told me that the British were going to propose a further conference in order to try and patch things up. At that stage, relations had been fairly strained and for my part, I had made some disparaging remarks about British methods. In order to play up to our sense of national pride and to show friendliness, they were going to suggest to me that they would like the conference to be held in Dublin. Evatt urged me on no account to agree to this. He said, 'This is a dodge. I'm presiding in Paris. I cannot leave. Neither can Peter Fraser. It's doubtful whether Mike Pearson would be able to come, so you'd find yourself with a conference consisting of the British and yourselves.'

I had hardly put the telephone down when I got a message to say that Lord Rugby had called and was anxious to see me. Lord Rugby came in, his usual charming self, and said that the Prime Minister was extremely worried at developments and felt that one more effort should be made to try and solve the tension that existed between Ireland and Britain. They felt that it would be very useful if we could discuss the position. In order to make things easier, realising the adverse publicity that might result from my going to London too frequently, they were suggesting that the conference should take place in Dublin and it was a question of discussing dates. I thanked him very profusely of course. I said that naturally I would be very glad to meet the Prime Minister and the Commonwealth ministers as well, but that it should be clear that, as far as we were concerned, unless we could have a discussion on achieving the reunification of Ireland, further talks would be abortive.

Then, as an afterthought, I said, 'By the way, before we decide on the date, I think we better ascertain the convenience of the other ministers. Would it not be a good plan if I rang up Herbert Evatt immediately, to find out whether he would be able to come?' Rugby didn't seem very anxious for this, but I put a phone call through to Evatt and told him I had just been approached by the British, who were anxious that there should be another meeting to discuss whether any solution could be reached, that Lord Rugby was present in the room with me, but before fixing a date or site I had thought we had better ring him up. Upon hearing this, Evatt roared with laughter. I don't think Rugby could hear him. He said, 'I told you so. On no account could I come to a conference in Dublin on these dates. I'll be tied up in Paris. But *I* invite you as President of the General Assembly, to hold the next conference in Paris at the Palais de Chaillot and I will make all the necessary arrangements.' So I conveyed this to Rugby, who said that he would have to get fresh instructions, that he didn't know whether his Prime Minister would be willing to go to Paris or not, to meet under UN auspices. I pointed out that if the Commonwealth ministers were all in Paris, it would be ridiculous to suggest that they come to Dublin. Lord Rugby, I must say, was very crestfallen at these developments.

So it was agreed that we would meet in Paris. Evatt and Pearson were there, as well as St Laurent, the Canadian Prime Minister. The conference started badly. The British wanted to meet at their embassy. Evatt wanted the conference to be held at the United Nations on neutral ground. With me at the conference was Cecil Lavery. Freddy Boland and Val Iremonger were also there.

Then the British, with a great splash and flourish, invited us all to dinner at the Hotel Meurice on the Place Vendome. It was a big hotel and this was a disastrous dinner.

The chief British delegate was Jowitt, the Labour Lord Chancellor. He was rather blustery and considered himself quite liberal but he was really was an out and out Tory at heart. He had the misfortune of making a speech at the dinner, about the Irish having such long memories. How much better the world would be if the Irish didn't have such long memories. Whereupon Cecil Lavery got up and said how dare they talk about people with long memories, when the leader of the Irish delegation was Seán MacBride, whose father had been executed by them and who had been imprisoned by them, and who had seen various towns in Ireland being burned by them. It didn't require a very long memory to remember these things.

The next morning, 15 November 1948, we met in the Palais de Chaillot. We would have been provided with the necessary facilities by the United Nations. The Lord Chancellor was presiding. He had a prepared speech. Philip Noel-Baker was present throughout this whole conference in Paris. We were a bit late, with everybody settling down. The ministers were at the table, with their civil servants lined up behind them in rows. The Lord Chancellor started to make his opening statement which he was reading out. Suddenly I became conscious, and everybody else became conscious, of noise going on in the room. Looking around I identified the noise and found that it was Peter Fraser, who had a cast in his eye. Peter was leaning over the table with a handful of coins, French money, that he was spreading out on the table, and he was calling his secretary saying, 'Mr McIntosh, please come here. Take some of that money, whatever you want. Go outside this building, there are newspaper kiosks there, and buy all the papers you can find and bring them back here. I want to find out whether our good friends the British have again poisoned the wells, while we are meeting here as friends.'

So Mr McIntosh, his secretary, who I believe was subsequently promoted from being a junior secretary to one of New Zealand's senior posts, Ambassador in Rome, sheepishly took the money and proceeded to go out. I think he was stopped at the door. And Herbert Evatt said, 'Now that our good friend, the Prime Minister of New Zealand, has raised this question, I think, Mr Lord Chancellor, we had better have this out. We met as good friends in Chequers. We didn't reach agreement, but we discussed Anglo-Irish relations in a friendly fashion. We agreed that nothing would be said to the press. We spent a long time in preparing an agreed communiqué. We had it typed, we read it over. We corrected everything to ensure that it was perfect. It was of great concern to me because one third of the population of Australia is Irish and of course all these things have their political repercussions. And we all left feeling happy, secure that we could rely on the confidence which everybody had displayed, and that there would be no leaks to the press. Next morning, I woke up to find that some British officials had given a press conference and had released poisoned accounts of what had taken place at Chequers and I want an explanation for this.'

It should be remembered that by this time the Lord Chancellor had begun, and had got through, I suppose, the first twenty lines of his written speech. He then said, 'Oh Mr Evatt, the Prime Minister of Australia must remember that in Britain we have a free press, thank God. We do not exercise any censorship and we cannot control what the press publishes.' But Evatt said, 'As far as I heard, there was a press conference. Is that so, or not?'

At this stage I intervened. I said that I hadn't intended making an issue of this but now that it had been raised, I felt that it was only proper that I should tell the ministers of the Commonwealth what the truth was. 'There had been agreement in Chequers. There had been a communiqué. But that while we were on our way back from Chequers, a press conference was called at the Commonwealth Office in London. A written handout, of which this was a copy (an original, actually of the stencilled copy), had been prepared by the Commonwealth Office and distributed, and Mr Philip Noel-Baker had been present.'

Philip Noel-Baker was looking very uneasy. It should be remembered that the Lord Chancellor had denied that anything like that took place beforehand. Noel-Baker said, 'Well, I am afraid that this is so. I wasn't aware at the time that this undertaking had been given by the Prime Minister, that there would be no press releases, but only the agreed communiqué.' Upon which, there was loud laughter from Evatt. 'You didn't know. What was the press communiqué about, unless it was an agreed one?' Acrimonious discussion then developed and the meeting ended. It was quite an extraordinary meeting because it never started. Lord Jowitt never finished his speech. There was no discussion as to the merits of the situation.

The British, I remember, produced a copy of the Republic of Ireland Bill, and said this is what they are going to elect in Ireland now. And I replied, 'Yes, this is the Bill. We've told you we are going to leave the Commonwealth and establish a Republic. We have no apologies to make for it.'

CHAPTER X

External Relations Act • *Colleagues*

The next development, chronologically, towards the repeal of the External Relations Act was the visit of the Taoiseach to Canada. The Taoiseach was very keen on Canada; he knew Mackenzie King well, and a number of Canadian ministers. Jack Costello was essentially a lawyer, pleased at having an opportunity to address the Canadian Bar Association. He felt that, as a lawyer, he had to give a good performance. He spent a lot of time preparing his speech and he consulted me with regard to portions of it, which gave a clear indication of our intentions. I think Paddy Lynch, then his private secretary, had probably prepared the first draft. It was a very good speech, my only criticism being that it was too long and the audience might not listen to it. This was the only occasion upon which any speech made by the Taoiseach, or indeed by any other member of the government, was circulated to the cabinet for their views, and was discussed at a cabinet meeting.

I suppose that I was in the driver's seat for a lot of this but I was very careful never to put Fine Gael or the rest of the government in a position where I would be exerting pressure on them. I felt I was not entitled to do that; they hadn't a mandate and they should do it only of their own free will. The more time went on, the more they realised themselves that the retention of the External Relations Act was ridiculous. De Valera had said himself in the Dáil on 6 August 1948: 'Repeal it if you like, I won't raise any objection.' I made a speech a short time before this, introducing my estimates on 20 July and made it clear that the External Relations Act would go. Then Bill Norton made a similar speech, though I'm not sure that Bill Norton didn't make a speech before mine. The *Sunday Independent* published a full spread on its front page on 5 September mentioning that both Norton and I had made speeches a short time before, which meant that the government had decided to repeal the External Relations Act and that the Taoiseach's speech in Canada was a confirmation of this. This received considerable publicity.

The Taoiseach made the speech on 1 September 1948, but, as far as I remember, the actual speech passed by the press in Canada, unnoticed. At a press conference a couple of days later in Ottawa on 7 September, one of the journalists, maybe from Reuters, had read the speech and it suddenly dawned on him what this meant, and he asked, 'Does this mean you are going to repeal the External Relations Act and leave the British Commonwealth?' Jack Costello said, 'Yes, of course it does.'

All these events were merely steps in a process to create an atmosphere in which this was regarded as accepted and inevitable. It is absolutely nonsensical to suggest, as was suggested for years, by Fianna Fáil politicians, the *Irish Press* and *Irish Times*, that Mr Costello had made the speech in a fit of bad temper because some insulting remark had been made at a banquet which the Governor General was giving, and that this was merely an intemperate reaction of the Taoiseach to an irritating incident. This is complete nonsense, because the speech was typed, circulated, corrected, amended, retyped, recirculated and roneo-copied before the Taoiseach left for Canada, and so could have nothing to do with an incident which took place in Ottawa.

My attitude as a lawyer was that the whole position created by the External Relations Act was unpalatable. It was unclear what the status of the country was. Why did we introduce the king into our constitution when the king had been carefully eliminated. It just made no sense. Costello, to his credit, always had a very sound national outlook, nothing like the IRA or republicanism, but he told me one story which explained his attitude at that period. He was telling me about some election meeting that he had been at outside Haddington Road Chapel. It was a rainy day and he was to address a meeting after mass there. This was not the 1948 campaign, but an earlier election. He was sheltering in a shed. There were two youngsters talking outside the shed and one said, 'There's going to be a Free State meeting.' 'What's a Free State meeting?' asked the other boy: 'Oh, the pro-English people who want to sell out the country to Britain.'

Jack was listening to this from behind the door: he said it made a deep impression on him. That was the image which Cumann na nGaedheal had succeeded in creating for itself. He felt that it was essential to change that image. That small incident affected him for the rest of his career. He had the frankness to tell me all this.

I remember one incident at a cabinet meeting when I remarked, 'I think the time has come when we really have to say straight out that we are not members of the Commonwealth.' James Dillon turned around to me saying, 'Well, Seán, I have been waiting for this for a long time and I was wondering whether you would say it, or whether I would have to propose the Repeal of the External Relations Act instead of you. I didn't want to do it because I felt it was your job.' This had quite an effect around the cabinet table, because James Dillon was regarded as a most empire-minded minister. The Fine Gael ministers took a deep breath as if to say that settles that. And Norton immediately said, 'Well, James, you're a great man to say things out straight. That's what we've all been thinking.' From there it went on. Seán MacEoin was always very enthusiastic about repealing it. He felt it was an insult to our republican tradition.

There was never any doubt in anybody's mind, and there was never any opposition. Joe Blowick was a bit concerned. He used to lean over to me at cabinet meetings saying, 'Seán, if we repeal this Act, do you think we will have any trouble about selling our cattle in England'? And I would reassure him, and he would lean over again saying, 'You don't think the British government would declare an economic war against our cattle?' I reassured him again, and he used to say, 'Well that's all right.' He used to explain that he didn't know much about these things, 'but I know that anything that would damage our cattle trade would do us a lot of damage, politically, in the west.'

Throughout all this period, there was always a proviso at the back of my mind that if the British were prepared to discuss partition, accept and bring about reunification of the country, we would postpone any action on the Repeal of the External Relations Act. This was certainly what I led the British to understand, time after time during negotiations. There were several really detailed discussions in regard to the whole situation between myself and Attlee. I remember one evening spending four or five hours with him in Downing Street, late into the night in a small attic, which he had as a flat upstairs. Mrs Attlee was also present there. We had tea and we had a discussion in great depth on the whole question of Anglo-Irish relations. I pointed out that the Crown was no asset in this regard. I thought that Anglo-Irish relations would normally be friendly if it wasn't for introducing the Crown and partition. The Crown never meant anything to the Irish people. It was an instrument of oppression. The Crown was over all the courthouses; if anybody was prosecuted for anything at all, it was in the name of the king, evictions were all carried out in the name of the king. The Crown formed no useful bond.

I delivered a lecture at the Royal Institute for International Affairs, Chatham House on 24 February 1949 in which I set out these matters and the whole position with regard to partition.

The southern unionists were fairly quiet at the time. In the Dáil we had one representative called Sheldon, he was quite friendly, we got on well. He would have preferred if the External Relations Act were not repealed, but I don't think it worried him very much, though it made the position awkward. Throughout this period I also had contacts with the Belfast people, with Cahir Healy, nationalist MP McAteer and people like that who were pro-Fianna Fáil. They didn't know quite what to make of our government. They were surprised to find it was so good. We ran a very extensive campaign on partition and published a considerable amount of material with the quiescence of the Fine Gael members of government. All these things were circulated. I also met Lord Brookborough and Major Topping, who became a judge but who was then an extreme right-wing unionist. With him on one occasion was Mr Douglas, who was then secretary of the Unionist Party. Afterwards, when the British passed the Ireland Act, we held a meeting and set up the Mansion House Committee, consisting of the Taoiseach, Mr Costello; the leader of the Opposition, Mr de Valera; the leader of the Labour Party; and myself. We held a big joint public meeting in

O'Connell Street which was probably the only occasion upon which de Valera, Fine Gael, Labour and republican representatives spoke from the same platform.

My contacts with the British were directly with Attlee, whom I rather liked and respected. He was an honest man, but I think he let himself be overborne by his civil servants on Irish questions, and also by the Unionist Party. I remember on one occasion Attlee said, 'Well, I'll go as far as I can go, but we must get Churchill to go along. I can't take a separate line. I can't divide the country on the Irish question. I want you to meet Churchill and see how well you can get on with him.' So Attlee organised quite a formal dinner and put me on his right, with Churchill on my right. The Lord Chancellor and possibly Philip Noel-Baker were there. I was the only Irish person present. Attlee had made great preparations for this dinner, thinking it was very important that I should or would talk Churchill into some form of agreement. However, the dinner didn't go as planned. While Churchill sat next to me, we barely exchanged politeness about the weather, and there were long silences. The soup course arrived. Churchill turned to me saying, 'I believe your father was in South Africa?' 'Yes.' 'Well,' said Churchhill, 'we were on different sides.' He himself had been in South Africa and had been taken prisoner. I have never quite established whether the Irish Brigade had a hand in holding him for a time or taking him prisoner. But this apparently rankled very much in Churchill's mind. And so the next course went through with practically no conversation, except for passing the salt or the pepper.

Then I timidly said that it was an awful pity that Ireland was divided as it was and that it would be a great help if the country could be united, that the treaty was a mistake. Churchill said, 'Oh, yes, I'm very fond of Ireland. I love Ireland dearly, but I can't do anything against my friends in Ireland. I cannot let down my friends in Ireland. So I can see no solution.' So the dinner was pretty abortive from this point of view. Attlee, on my other side, was listening to all this and two or three times he tried to re-establish conversation, but that never worked.

I became very friendly with Churchill later and often had dinner with him under other circumstances. Again, as a refrain, whenever we touched on Irish matters, Churchill would say, 'Don't ask me to let down my friends. I can't do it.' It always struck me that he had quite an interest in Ireland. It struck me also that he realised that the treaty had been a disaster and the splitting of Ireland a disaster. I argued later on with him a good deal in Strasbourg. I had long sittings with him then. He said quite frankly then that the partition of Ireland was a terrible mistake; it should never have happened. He didn't know how it came about, he thought that Collins should have resisted.

Philip Noel-Baker came over to Ireland and stayed in Old Head. This was probably before the Ireland Act. And Attlee came over. During those long talks in Downing Street I probably said, 'Well, come to Ireland.' He reacted favourably to that and so did his wife. He said, 'Would it be safe? Would it be all right?' I said it would be ideal. So he came to Ireland with his wife, his daughter and his dog. I greeted him, we had a reception for them in Dublin and then we went down to the west and stayed in Newport. Some Anglo-Irish ascendancy people had a big house in Newport – Newport House – a good fishing place. Attlee was staying there and I stayed across the bay with J. C. Garvey, an old solicitor who used to brief me. He lived in grand style in an old house at Murrisk Abbey which used to be a castle. And he had an excellent cook. It was a lovely house, dating from the twelfth or thirteenth century. J. C. was a good friend of mine and Attlee came over and had lunch and dinners there. One of the great attractions of J. C.'s was that he had a private oyster bed outside his front door. He used to go out with a bucket and bring oysters onto the lawn. We had oysters and champagne at eleven o'clock in the morning, with Attlee and his wife and daughter. It was very enjoyable and we had beautiful weather. His visit would probably have been in the summer of 1948.

The police were rather worried and great safety measures were discreetly taken. The police were moderate. I used to drive my own car — I didn't drive in a state car when I could avoid it. Attlee and I used to go off together in my Ford Prefect. We had long talks and drives. This used to upset the police considerably because I had let them know that I would rather they wouldn't follow us too closely and that we wanted to drive on our own.

Attlee had many talks with people in the countryside and got on very well with them. He was a nice, simple man who was genuinely interested in Ireland. He had been a captain in the British Army after World War I. He frequently described to me, how as captain, when Terence MacSwiney died on hunger strike, he went to the funeral in Southwark Cathedral. Though he wasn't a Catholic, he participated in the mass and followed the hearse. This created consternation at the time. He had tremendous admiration for Terence MacSwiney and also for Pearse's writings. We also discussed Casement several times.

Attlee genuinely wanted to do something, but I think he allowed himself be overborne on the one hand by Churchill and the Tory party, and on the other hand by his permanent officials. I think they disapproved of the close, rather informal links which Attlee and I had built up together. I was in the position whereby I could go to London, and just ring up and see him some time that day. We had an extremely good personal relationship, until the introduction of the Ireland Bill. Then I was very direct with him and told him that I thought it was a tremendous mistake and that he should not allow the Conservative Party to dictate the policy of a Labour government on Ireland.

Philip Noel-Baker had returned from the Oldhead Hotel and was staying with Lord Rugby when the Taoiseach made his speech in Ottawa. Rugby arrived in to me on the morning of the press uproar about the repeal of the External Relations in a terrible state and said, 'This is terrible, why didn't you warn me of this before?' Rugby was upset, because he said it made him look a fool, with his minister staying with him, waking up and reading this in the papers, instead of having been informed by his ambassador that this was taking place. I have often wondered about this since, and I think that, genuinely, Rugby had missed all the signs. The British Embassy had not been doing its homework the way it should have been, neither reading the speeches made in the Dáil, nor the various comments, nor had they read Jack Costello's speech in Canada. If they had, they would have known what was coming. Rugby gave me the impression that it was a complete surprise to him and it was a bombshell to Philip Noel-Baker, who was in a terrible state. I went to see Philip that day to soothe him down and pointed out that it was no surprise. I told him that we had been saying this the whole time, and that they should have known it from our attitude at Commonwealth meetings.

That period was very interesting insofar as the press, the British Embassy and the Commonwealth Relations Office were apparently asleep. They didn't appreciate the decision that had been taken by the Irish government and didn't seem to put two and two together when these announcements were being made. This had all happened without our having to mislead them in any way, or without being as frank as one should be with them. Indeed, I think that during the boiled egg on toast 'Rugby' lunches, I discussed on and off the inevitability of the repeal of the External Relations Act. This was my usual approach, that it was inevitable and only a question of time, and there is no question of our remaining in the Commonwealth unless we can reunify Ireland. Remaining in the Commonwealth was a device which was accepted in the belief that there was a possibility that we could reunify the country. Now, twenty-six years afterwards, it was quite obvious that this hadn't brought about reunification.

I would answer any critics of repealing the Act in exactly the same way. Maintaining a link with the British crown served no useful purpose. It was a militant in our relations. At first it was thought to be justified on the basis that it would help to bring about reunification. Partition was there and I don't think it mattered two hoots what you called the country, whether you called it a dominion, a colony or a republic. The people who were running the administration in Belfast had a vested interest in keeping it so and the non-Catholic population had been induced to create a situation in which they would have a privileged position, financially, economically and otherwise. Any reunification of the country meant an end to this privileged position which enabled them to treat the Catholic and national population as second- or third-class citizens.

We ran a campaign on the publicity side which was successful in making the partition issue known. It's rather like Namibia, which I have compared it with in my own mind. When I took over as Commissioner for Namibia, I think that most people didn't know where Namibia was, or what the problem was. When I took over the Department of External Affairs, I think that there was abroad no knowledge of partition, what was involved or what effect it had on the country. We then published a series of pamphlets, leaflets and some books on the economics of partition. All that had quite an impact on world opinion at that time. The Irish American influence lobby also became quite strong.

It is difficult to recapture the organisation and feeling of the Department of External Affairs at that time. Most of the officials in the department were strongly Fianna Fáil. Joe Walshe, for instance, who had been secretary of the department before Freddy Boland. He was Ambassador in the Vatican. Fianna Fáil had been in office for sixteen years and had pretty well implanted its people into the department. Of course they would all take the anti-partition line policy. There was complete consternation in the department when they realised we were going to repeal the External Relations Act. Not because they thought it was a bad thing to do, but because by so doing we were exposing Fianna Fáil policy. This could have been done any time, but we were doing it and showing that it could be done without any repercussion.

When I took over in the Department of External Affairs, I gathered that for the first week some of the girls spent their time weeping at the disaster that this meant. However, afterwards, to give them their due, my own civil service staff worked loyally and cooperatively for me when they realised that we were earnest about partition and trying to secure the independence of the country.

The person I had most to do with in the first period in the department was Freddy Boland. Freddy, I always thought, belonged very much to the establishment and was horrified at the thought that I was going to repeal the External Relations Act, horrified at the partition campaign. He agreed, but only to a certain extent, with my criticism of the Department of Finance and the Central Bank. Freddy and I spent long evenings together discussing such problems. He was much more conservative than I was, much more to the right. But he was sufficiently well informed internationally to know that the policies which the Department of Finance was pursuing were suicidal from our point of view. We had a common viewpoint on this and collaborated quite freely. I made him Ambassador to London.

Then as a replacement I took Seán Nunan in 1950. Seán had been a great Fianna Fáil supporter. He was in line for promotion. There was a certain rhythm of promotion and development in the Department of External Affairs. People remained, for example, three years in the department and three years out. I tried to establish this. Unfortunately the staff was too small to do this as effectively as one would wish. But I felt that at the time Seán deserved promotion, that he was a sincere man and that he would be loyal to me as well, on partition issues and matters of that kind. He wasn't a ball of fire, but he was doing his best. I don't think he had enough experience of European affairs. I didn't mind that, because I was up to my neck in European affairs at the time – Council of Europe, the Organisation for European Economic Cooperation (OEEC) – and I didn't really require the departmental secretary to do a lot in connection with that. I wanted him to look after partition and the American side of affairs. He came to America on a lecture with me and was very useful there. He knew a lot of congressmen from his old experience. De Valera had, for some time, tried to run a rival campaign and I think that it was helpful to have Seán Nunan working as secretary to the department at that time, counteracting this.

Conor Cruise O'Brien was in the department then; a good pen, he was one of the intelligent people, very able and ambitious, but I felt that I couldn't trust him. He wrote a lot of anti-partition literature. Many of the pamphlets that were used extensively were produced by him, using all the arguments which he later decried. I found it difficult to feel confidence in his judgement because I felt, on the one hand, that he was not always responsible in his attitude and, on the other hand, he had an intriguing mentality. He intrigued quite heavily in the department from time to time. He wrote articles attacking me under false names in *The Leader* and other newspapers. Conor used to inspire journalists in writing critical articles. I think at some stage himself and Noel Hartnett combined together to criticise me publicly. His official line would have been that of a civil servant doing as his minister said, but very often he tried to escape that. I remember on one occasion he had drafted a document which I had asked for and he had slipped in his own views, views which I regarded at the time as being too Marxist for a government statement. I remember having a talk and I said, 'Look, you know what the government's views are, you know what my views are. Please try and comply with those views instead of trying to insert your own. It only means that I have to cut them out, change, and rewrite portions. This causes trouble to you and me.' I think he was a second secretary then. I had a fair amount of contact with him. From my point of view he was untrustworthy and unreliable.

My private secretary was Val Iremonger, who got on very well with Conor. Val was a writer, a poet and had a certain amount of sympathy with Cruise O'Brien. Val Iremonger was capable, nice and very pleasant to work with. I must have been an extremely difficult boss for him.

We had Michael MacWhite in Rome, who was Minister to the Quirinal, to the Italian government. And we had Joe Walshe who had been former secretary to the department and was Ambassador to the Vatican. The two of them reported assiduously on each other's activities. They couldn't stand the sight of each other. Joe Walshe was Fianna Fáil, and Michael MacWhite was Cumann na nGaedheal. So relations there were not particularly happy, but they counterbalanced one another.

I had a lot of trouble getting the kind of people I wanted into the department; every obstacle was put in my way by Finance. I had Labhrás Ó Nualláin, who was dealing with partition issues and who wrote a book; he did his work well. In addition to Labhrás, I had Frank Gallagher. Frank Gallagher had been the editor of the *Irish Press* and I used him to write a number of articles and pamphlets in connection with partition. He was quite happy to work on partition. As far as I remember, he also worked with Conor Cruise O'Brien on a number of these pamphlets and articles. In the light of Cruise O'Brien's subsequent attitude in regard to partition, it is rather amusing to note that he was one of the people writing all this material on partition at the time, with Frank Gallagher. There was the Anti-Partition League in Britain, which I had close relations with and it was in close contact with our embassy in London the whole time.

Another person I found extremely able and very helpful always was Denis Devlin. I think I made him Ambassador to Rome in 1950, but he died afterwards. I also succeeded in getting Tim O'Driscoll, then in the Department of Industry and Commerce to come over to my department in order to handle OEEC matters.

Someone from whom I got a lot of really valuable help, particularly on the economic side and on anything involving detailed research, was Con Cremin. Con was absolutely excellent. I had a very high opinion of his work. If anything, he was too detailed often in the work he did, but it was always well done. He was in the department when I came in. He was an assistant secretary. I think I made him Ambassador to Paris which was regarded as promotion at the time.

Early on, when I got into External Affairs, I realised that I needed an economist, preferably one who was very familiar with our whole agricultural situation. I tried to find somebody within the department who was competent in that field. I didn't find anybody, so I decided that I would try to recruit from outside. I came down very quickly to Louis Smith, whom I knew to be a good economist and familiar with agricultural problems in the country and who had had some international experience already at that time. So I decided to try and recruit Louis Smith. I had to battle with several barriers which were erected all about me by my own department and the Department of Finance, to prevent me from recruiting an outsider to fill this role. I was given all kinds of arguments as to why somebody else could easily do it. The Department of Agriculture or the Department of Finance could furnish somebody. But I decided I wanted my own economic and agricultural adviser. I discussed the matter with Louis, who very kindly accepted to take on the post, and I succeeded through cabinet order in getting him appointed. He then commenced as agricultural and economic adviser in connection with OEEC and problems of that kind. But after he had been working for a month or six weeks, I received a notice saying his services has been dispensed with because he had failed to pass an Irish exam. Irish was being used by the officials in order to prevent people from coming into the department. The Department of External Affairs was regarded very much as being part of the preserve of the civil service and they didn't like the idea of outsiders coming in.

I also had quite a lot of problems later on when I wanted to appoint Mrs Josephine MacNeill as our Minister to The Hague. She wasn't in the civil service. She was a woman and there had never been a woman appointed before. And it was unusual to appoint somebody who wasn't in the civil service. I had to battle that one through and, again, I had to get a cabinet decision to make the appointment. Mrs MacNeill was the widow of James MacNeill who had been a former Governor General. She was very good, intelligent and she proved to be one of our best foreign diplomats afterwards. She was appointed in February 1950. She held several other posts afterwards, until she retired. Josephine MacNeill was generally reckoned to be a most successful diplomat.

My own department didn't really give me trouble. I had very few difficulties and I understood them well. I could see that the people who had worked for Fianna Fáil for sixteen years naturally had an attachment to de Valera and to his policies. It was a radical change to find the department standing on its own legs and it was quite something to get them used to it. They used to run to the Taoiseach's department for everything. I didn't get rid of anybody, but I did reorganise the department. Because of the growth of the economic side and the Council of Europe side, I asked for more staff, particularly in connection with the economic development programme and Marshall Aid. After a lot of battles they sent me twelve clerks from the Land Commission. When I looked at them, it was quite obvious that they had spent their lives behind tall desks with quill pens. They were utterly useless for the kind of work I needed them for.

I wanted to recruit people from outside, to recruit people from the universities, and I got tremendous opposition from the Department of Finance and even from the officials. External Affairs wasn't really a department, a separate ministry in the proper sense of the word because de Valera had been the Minister for External Affairs during his term of office. There had been no independent minister since Paddy McGilligan had been there. At that stage it was very much an embryo department that hadn't acquired its own sea legs so to speak.

Finance resented very much the role that I was playing. I welcomed and represented Ireland within the OEEC, which was an economic organisation. I was representing Ireland at the Council of Europe. They felt that they should have been playing an active role in economic cooperation. I was having increasingly more of a say in the economic and industrial development of the country. I was gradually succeeding in changing its direction. It was not easy to do, because my colleagues had absorbed the doctrines which were now unsuitable and outdated. Seán MacEoin was the best on these issues; he had done a good deal of reading on economics and had an independent viewpoint. James Dillon was good in his own way, but James always looked to Britain as being the mother country. At least he had an open mind, was intelligent and did some thinking on his own. Paddy McGilligan was very good on this; he had realised from the struggles which he had with Finance, when he was trying to build up the Shannon scheme, that these policies were completely suicidal from the point of view of Ireland.

I deliberately, and with I think the full connivance of Paddy, kept all that work in my department, because I felt that we needed a new approach, that the Threadneedle Street and Treasury approach would dominate if the Department of Finance were running it. From that point of view, they regarded me as a complete enemy. I remember on one occasion the decision to plant 25,000 acres a year of forestry had been made and announced by me. Freddy Boland arrived into the office, chuckling. He said that he had met Jimmy McElligott on the way into the office in Stephen's Green, and that McElligott had stopped, saying, 'I can't believe it! This minister of yours is running the country into debt with all these trees he wants to plant. It's going to wreck the country and cause inflation. I can't believe it. I read it in the papers.'

In the past few of our politicians, with the possible exception of Arthur Griffith, knew anything about economics; certainly Mr de Valera didn't, neither did Mr Cosgrave nor Mr Blythe. They were all politicians by accident; they were not economists by profession. My view was that as long as we continued to rely only on the British market, that we would get lower prices. We had everything to gain from becoming independent of the stranglehold of the British economy. This was not being anti-British, as I was often accused of being at this period. I was not particularly anti-British. On the contrary, in many respects I rather admired the British for some of the things they did. I was always very critical of them in their dealings with Ireland. I thought that they had been not only unjust, but short-sighted, as well as being brutal. But axiomatically, it stands to reason that a basic rule is that whatever financial or economic policy suits a big industrialised, largely populated country such as Britain, their policies have to be different, and usually diametrically opposed to the policies of a small under-developed country with a higher rate of emigration.

In Finance were Joe Brennan, Governor of the Central Bank, and Jimmy McElligott, secretary. Between them, they had run the financial policies of the country since the treaty. Their policy had been nefarious and had prevented the development of the country. In cabinet I had several battles about them with the government and with the Taoiseach in particular. At one stage, I had to make a formal plea to have the secretary to the Department of Finance removed because of some conversations he had had behind my back with the American Ambassador, who subsequently told me about these conversations. I wasn't successful. The Fine Gael members of the government were conservative on the whole in their approach. In addition to that, most of them knew Jimmy McElligott and Joe Brennan very well from the old days, and I think that they considered that this would create too much of an upheaval, if suddenly the secretary of the Department of Finance was removed.

CHAPTER XI

Council of Europe • Personalities
Convention on Human Rights

During my period in office I concentrated a lot of my efforts in building up the Council of Europe towards the unification of Europe, a bold ambitious concept of which I was then, and still am, in favour. Ireland, for the first time really, took part in European affairs from the time I came in. I had been involved in the European movement and I was very enthusiastic. I had been in the Pan-European Union, formed by Coudenhove Kalergi, a Hungarian count who had developed this notion of a united Europe. I had a lot of contact with him and helped him with extending the movement and I had been a member of the European Round Table.

After the war American economists realised quickly that Europe had ceased to be a viable unit, and in what was I thought a very constructive gesture, set up Marshall Aid. General Marshall, Secretary of State in America, had announced his plan on 5 June 1947, and there had already been one preliminary meeting. The Organisation for European Economic Cooperation was started largely because of Americ, and its task was to divide this huge cake of American money among different European countries. I was given the important task of building up the organisation on the one hand and also of supervising and assisting in the division of Marshall Aid money – quite a difficult assignment. I paid a lot of attention to this and worked very hard. I got on well with all the European ministers and became Vice-President of the OEEC. Co-Vice President was Karl Gruber, foreign minister of Austria. Paul-Henri

Spaak became president. We worked closely together and I got on well with him. He dealt more with the political aspects of the OEEC while I was concerned with the administrative side and with settling the many and varied issues which arose in regard to the division of the monies. I was probably given this task because I had good relations with all the other ministers, but probably also by reason of the fact that the amount in Marshall Aid for Ireland was going to be very small and everybody knew this. I was regarded as being independent therefore, and had many close consultations with the foreign and finance ministers of the individual countries. The OEEC included Canada, the United States and Portugal, but not Spain.

I regarded both the OEEC and the Council of Europe as extremely valuable ways of doing away with any division of Ireland. Obviously if Europe was being built as one economic entity, then Ireland as part of Europe would have to be built as one economic entity. Indeed, in the Council of Europe it might have been possible to secure an overall Irish representation, which would have included north and south except for British objections. The British have travelled a long way since those days. I remember well the first meetings I attended for the OEEC and the Council of Europe; the opposition there was to describing Ireland as the Republic of Ireland. For some reason they always wanted to call the country Éire. They wouldn't admit that there could be an Irish Republic. They also referred to us as Éire. They tried to avoid using Ireland to describe the state or the Republic of Ireland, which was anathema to them. On repeated occasions I had to pull them up on this.

All this brought me into close relations with Stafford Cripps, Chancellor of the Exchequer. Stafford was an odd person. Initially we all spent a lot of time working out the statutes, the regulations, its policies and what the OEEC would do. Finally we met in Paris on 14 April 1948 to review and sign it. My plane arrived late and the meeting had already started when I arrived, but everyone was in utter gloom. 'Thank goodness you have come,' said Schuman privately to me. '*He* won't agree to the name of the organisation. He agreed to the statute but won't agree to the name and we can't find out why.' I got on very well with the French, I spoke French and they liked this. They had certain sympathies for Ireland also. So they then explained more formally, 'Well, we have agreed on the statute, but Sir Stafford won't agree to the name.' I read the name out, Organisation for European Economic Cooperation, OEEC. Cripps laughed and said, 'Well, you'll understand why I can't agree to *that*.' 'No, I don't,' I replied. 'Oh, my dear boy, you must understand.' We adjourned, and he and I went outside to another room. 'You don't understand why I can't agree to this?' he said. I repeated that I couldn't. So he repeated OEEC. I said, 'I swear to you Stafford, I don't know what you're talking about.' Finally he said 'EC. Earthen Closet! In different parts of England, EC is the same as WC. Earthen Closet. We can't possibly agree to this!' So I spent probably half an hour talking him out of this. There was more trouble rejoining our colleagues — Stafford didn't want them to know why he objected. Finally, however, I had to tell some of them. They split their sides laughing. But this held us up for two hours I am sure.

Stafford Cripps was a nice man in many ways. Churchill described him as a sheep: 'There goes a sheep, in lion's clothing' in the House of Commons. One thing that always left me speechless, was an occasion on which at the Council of Ministers of the OEEC, at a public session, he got up and said that he had heard that there were a lot of rumours that the pound was going to be devalued. He then proceeded to declare that he wished to 'avail of the occasion to assure you that these rumours are completely unfounded. There is no question of devaluing sterling. I can give you my personal assurance.' We all knew he was lying. Forty eight hours later, on 18 September 1949, sterling was devalued.

This is significant in regard to our own internal or administrative system. I had heard from the French finance minister, René Mayer (a friend of mine who was also involved later on in the Executive of the International Commission of Jurists) and Georges Bidault that they had private indications from their own information services that the pound was to be devalued. This was about six weeks before the devaluation. This rumour came from impeccable sources. I had also got a hint of it from the Swiss foreign minister, Monsieur Petitpierre, who wasn't in the Council of Europe, but whom I knew from outside. When I returned home I conveyed this to the Taoiseach, the Department of Finance and the Governor of the Central Bank. I told them how I had received reports which I regarded as absolutely reliable that the pound was about to be devalued and we should begin, straight off, to take some precautionary measures. In other words we should get rid of some of the sterling we had, if we could, and convert it into dollars. No, was the answer; there was no possibility of this. I raised it at a cabinet meeting in June 1949. I felt so keenly about it, I wrote a letter to the Minister of Finance; again, complete denial that there was any possibility of this. And no action was taken. For six weeks we knew, I knew, that the pound was going to be devalued and several precautionary measures could have been taken that would have saved this country millions, but they were not taken. This was because the Irish Department of Finance and the Central Bank relied entirely on the assurances which they received from the British Treasury to the effect that the pound was not going to be devalued. I knew during this period there were regular meetings between Treasury and Finance officials. Again, I could never find out what went on. It struck me that this collaboration was too close to be healthy. I wrote to the Taoiseach, saying that I thought this was really irresponsible behaviour. Then the crash came, the pound was being devalued. I had raised it at the cabinet meetings, time after time.

Often Paddy McGilligan wasn't well and used to be laid up. During these periods the officials could do what they liked. It was hard to ever get Paddy to go dead against his officials, except in regard to some particular specific thing. On this they assured him that they were quite certain the pound wouldn't be devalued.

To illustrate a small incident. I think that it was on a Saturday that the pound was devalued. I was on to the Taoiseach, who tried to call a cabinet meeting immediately and asked me to arrange this. We held a cabinet meeting at Iveagh House. This in itself was a complete departure, since it was the only cabinet meeting ever held in Iveagh House. The secretary of the Department of Finance and the Governor of the Central Bank were in attendance. I showed my irritation in no uncertain terms at the fact that they had ignored the warnings that had been given. Now it was too late to take any measures, beyond those which one takes after devaluation. But we could have taken steps beforehand which would have saved a lot of money.

The discussion went on for a long time in our office. I organised to have tea brought in and all that. Joe Blowick, the Clann na Talmhan man, was present. He was the man who was always afraid that something might happen to the 'cattle trade with Britain'. He came and whispered in my ear over my shoulders, 'Would you mind very much if I went off to the pictures. I like going to the pictures on a Saturday. And I don't understand much about these things like currency and sterling. Only, if I do go away, will you see that nothing happens to the cattle trade with this devaluation business?' So I told Joe that he could go off to the pictures and Joe trundled off to the pictures while the cabinet meeting continued.

One strange thing about all this period is that Nöel Browne was very seldom at a cabinet meeting. (He was at this one, however.) I remonstrated with him on several occasions about this. There was always a pretty hefty agenda, something concerning each department and always something concerning health was on the agenda. Nöel wouldn't turn up, but his secretary or officials would bring me down a file at a cabinet meeting, saying, if this comes up, this is the file. It wasn't a very satisfactory way of doing things, because I wasn't very conversant in the matter and didn't have time to read the file. In any case, I had enough things on my own plate to look after.

I was seldom out of Dublin at that period for more than two or three days. I always tried to make it my business to be present at cabinet meetings. The impression was that I was out of the country the whole time because each time there was usually some reference or a photograph. I can't remember missing cabinet meetings.

The people who mattered most in the cabinet were, in my view, the Taoiseach, who presided; James Dillon, an active and efficient Minister for Agriculture, who usually had views on most topics. These views were always amusing and interesting, and reasonably sound. I had known James from school. Paddy McGilligan, who was quite good always. Dr Tom O'Higgins, who was a very good Minister for Defence, used to join in the general discussions with a solid viewpoint. William Norton was an active cabinet member. Dick Mulcahy seldom intervened in discussions except for his own department, Education. Dan Morrissey, Minister for Industry and Commerce, would take a greater part, though I don't think Dan Morrissey's views were necessarily always as useful as Dr Tom O'Higgins. MacEoin took part, a common sense viewpoint usually. Norton was certainly most vocal from the Labour side. And Joe Blowick very seldom intervened in anything.

Incidentally, I don't remember any controversy in the cabinet on the army. I urged that it was necessary for us to have as efficient an army as possible. I felt that the army had been neglected. The army should never be regarded as part of the police force for internal use, but as a real defence force. I remember another incident which rather amused me. After the Ireland Act, when the partition issue was getting very hot, I decided that we should have information concerning the military issue in the north, how strong the British army was, what their positions was. I either had a word with the army chief of staff or with Tom O'Higgins. Colonel Dan Bryan of Military Intelligence was sent to see me. He arrived, with a military air, clicking his heels and saluting. He sat down and I proceeded to ask him some questions as to the strength of the British forces in the north. He didn't know, nor where there were stations. He had virtually no information at all. He had obviously not given any thought to that aspect, or pretended to me that he had not given it any thought. I was quite aghast at the complete lack of information which he had about the British forces in Northern Ireland. Some army people were against policy in regard to Northern Ireland; he had been for the Free State, brought up in that tradition, and perhaps resented this. But I was rather aghast to find that our military people didn't know the strength or the disposition of British forces in the north. I think he probably would have told me if he had known, because he was quite sheepish about it in the end, and he said that he hadn't realised what I wanted to discuss with him or he would have obtained more information about it. I saw him a second time and he had very little more information on it. He gave me the impression of being far more interested in what divisions the Russians had on the Polish border, the German border, than what the strength of the British forces was in our own country. He seemed to be much more interested in Cold War politics than he was in the condition of the North of Ireland.

O'Higgins was efficient, attending to all the ministerial functions of the Minister of Defence: promotions, equipment, armament, pay and all that kind of thing. While it didn't cross my mind to take military action with regard to the north, I felt we should be in a position to take it if a really serious situation developed; for instance, if there were pogroms. I think a section of the army would have supported this. The Taoiseach had a healthy outlook that our national duty was to try and bring about the reunification of the country. Of course he wouldn't like the idea of the army intervening in politics at all.

In my suggestions for maintaining an effective army in the country, it was mainly on the basis of effective neutrality, and the possibility of having to deal, some time or another, with what has since been referred to as the doomsday situation. A situation could develop in which we would have to defend the Catholic population in the north from being massacred. Also, there was the possibility of a war situation developing, that we would need to have an army. Undoubtedly our army had been very useful in ensuring our neutrality during the last war. To those who held that my activities regarding partition and publicity helped to create a 'war' situation which wouldn't have been there otherwise, I pointed out that the situation was there the whole time, during de Valera's governments, right up to 1948. I think I am right in saying that the 1948-51 period was the only period in our history since the treaty in which there were no IRA activities in the country, north or south, and during which there was nobody in prison. This is the only three-year period since 1922 of which this can be said.

However, returning to Europe. I was always friendly with the Icelanders. I made a lot of fuss about them, because they were an island, friendly, and had achieved their independence. Iceland was a new state; they had been a Danish colony. They liked Ireland because they felt that Ireland had a kind of similar tradition. However, my rather close friendship with the Icelanders in the European movement rather irritated the Danes, who felt they should be their main consultants. But because Denmark had been their overlords for a long time, the Icelanders wanted to get away from this. Alphabetically, Iceland and Ireland were next to each other and when it came to be the turn of the Icelanders to preside at the Council of Ministers meetings at the Council of Europe, they said that they would prefer if Ireland took their turn. I had the task, therefore, of presiding out of turn over the Council of Ministers for longer than I would have otherwise, and sometimes at rather crucial times. The Icelanders explained that they wanted me to do this because I was more fluent and had more experience. They had only one ambassador in the world – in Paris. He was a brother of the foreign minister. One nice touch, I should mention, for which I was always grateful to them, was that when I was defeated at the end of the inter-party government, the Icelandic government invited me to visit, and asked me to give some lectures on Ireland in the University of Reykjavik. I felt that this was a thoughtful gesture on their part, a kind of personal sign of sympathy. I did this, and I enjoyed visiting Iceland very much.

On one occasion we had had terse discussions at a meeting of foreign and finance ministers in Paris, at which Stafford Cripps had been attacking Averell Harriman – special representative of the United States to the OEEC – right, left and centre. He had refused to attend meetings with him. As the Icelandic foreign minister, Beneditksson, and I were leaving the building we saw Stafford Cripps looking wildly about for his car. We pulled up immediately and said, 'Stafford, can we give you a lift?' 'Yes,' said Stafford. 'The embassy car is missing. I am lost'. Stafford opened up immediately and said: 'This terrible man Averell Harriman. We shouldn't meet him. I have refused to go to his cocktail parties.' I asked what was wrong with Averell Harriman. 'Don't you know? He tried to have an affair with Randolph Churchill's wife during the war. This was a most foul thing. I can't have anything to do with a man like that.'

I had to explain this diatribe against Harriman in French to the Icelander, who didn't know what was happening.

There was a terrible tragedy later on. Beneditksson died. He was burned alive in a summer house, the whole family was burned.

I became friendly with Averell Harriman. He had, I think, been named by President Truman to liaise with Europe in the reconstruction programme, and we worked closely together. I formed a high opinion of his abilities. Harriman had been the US ambassador to London, maybe during the war. Stafford Cripps' violent personal dislike of him – which he carried to extremes by refusing to attend Harriman's dinners and cocktail parties – made relationships very difficult.

This brings me to a story of that period. Robert Schuman was conscious of this enmity and realised it was having a harmful effect regarding Marshall Aid and economic cooperation. So one day Schuman said: 'I have decided that I'll try and organise a small dinner. We can't go on like this. I'd like you to sit between myself and Cripps and act as interpreter. I don't want to make it formal and have interpreters there. You can interpret.' Schuman, rather amusingly, warned me, saying, 'Now be very careful not to say anything, none of your anti-British jokes or cracks about Anglo-Irish relations with Cripps at this dinner. Don't do anything to irritate him. We want to get him into really good humour.' The dinner was duly held in the private dining room in the Quai d'Orsay which the foreign minister had at his disposal. It was sumptuously organised, waiters, everything laid on. We dressed up. Cripps, however, arrived in a kind of knickerbocker tweed trousers, deliberately, I think.

Everybody was being charming. We had all got the same injunction from Schuman to be as nice as possible to Cripps and butter him up so that by the end of the dinner he would open up and talk of his relationship with Averell Harriman. So the dinner started off, hors d'oeuvres or oysters, then soup. At the soup stage, I noticed, along with Hervé Alphand, secretary of the French Foreign Office (an old friend of mine, we had been at school together in Paris and he had an Irish grandfather) that Cripps wasn't eating. He hadn't touched his soup, or eaten anything. Alphand asked him could he get him something else and Cripps said, hoity toity, 'No. Of course, I am a vegetarian.' We had all known that he was a vegetarian, but nobody had thought of it. Cripps was standing up straight, saying: 'I don't approve of eating flesh of any kind.' Then he was offered an omelette: 'I don't eat eggs.' He was offered fish: 'I don't eat fish.' Then he was asked by Hervé Alphand, what could be got for him, what would he like to eat. 'I would like some carrots, some raw, shredded carrots. Raw carrots just shredded. That will suffice completely,' said Cripps, in a prickly tone of voice. Hervé disappeared and came back pale. He said there were no raw carrots left in the kitchen. 'Any carrots there were have been cooked. But we have sent out a police car to try and find some.' He whispered all this to me. By this time the whole dinner was held up; nobody was eating. Cripps wouldn't eat, and in deference to Cripps, no one else ate. We talked to each other, smoked a cigarette and that kind of thing. But there was a long delay before the raw carrots were produced. Schuman felt guilty. He had remembered every detail except that Cripps was a vegetarian. Hervé Alphand should have seen to it. I should have known about it and thought of it. But because it wasn't my responsibility, I wasn't thinking about it. Even the conversation was sticky.

There was a lull and Schuman said in French, 'Would you ever ask Stafford what his hobbies are?' Schuman thought he was very British talking about hobbies. 'I knit,' said Stafford. I turned around and said, '*Il tricote.*' Schuman looked at me with wild eyes, you're not inventing that, '*Vous n'inventez pa ça?*' '*Non, non, il tricote.*' Poor Schuman exclaimed: 'I don't believe it. He doesn't drink. He doesn't eat meat. He doesn't eat fish. He doesn't eat eggs. He wants raw carrots, and *il tricote.*' It was even more difficult then, while I tried to engage Stafford in conversation about knitting. 'Yes, I learned it at my mother's knees,' said he. It had always intrigued him; he very often spent his Sunday evenings, sitting with his wife, knitting, while she was reading. I explained all this to Schuman, who was becoming more and more convinced that Cripps was not a responsible, serious man for the position he held. He didn't say this but I could see it all running though his head: no wonder we are having all these troubles.

Finally, the carrots arrived and dinner continued. But the atmosphere was ruined and we couldn't discuss anything. I have often wondered since, and even at the time, whether Cripps hadn't deliberately done all this. Cripps knew perfectly well that he was invited to this dinner to soften him up. He may have deliberately tried to arrive in tweed clothes with strange golfing trousers and created this scene about his food, in order to prevent any talks. Cripps had, at one stage, been ambassador to Moscow.

Ernie Bevin wasn't there on this occasion. But Ernie would always shrug his shoulders saying, 'Ah, Stafford. Nobody pays any attention to him, but a very sincere man'. And undoubtedly he was a very sincere man.

I was engaged in the active promotion of trade treaties with different countries. During my three years in External Affairs, there were quite a substantial number of treaties entered. This was a move towards internationalising our trade. I felt that this was important, because for so long as our trade depended entirely on one market, we would never get good prices and would be limited to the British market.

In addition to that, on a completely different level, I also initiated negotiations with the United States government in regard to the formal Treaty of Friendship Commerce and Navigation between Ireland and the USA. This was a standard treaty which governs relations between any two states, in regard to consular matters, representation and the establishment rights of citizens in both countries. For instance, it was under this treaty that Irish doctors were permitted to take up practice in the United States, subject to passing an examination (ECFMG). But that treaty was quite far-reaching and important, and we took the best part of a year to negotiate it. I got a tremendous amount of help from George Garrett, who was the American ambassador here, and who was most helpful and cooperative. The only matter I failed in was to get the equivalent of law degrees recognised, and the State Department provided the explanation: 'Look we can't do that. There are too many lawyers in Congress and they will oppose ratification of the treaty if we allow Irish lawyers to come and practice in the United States. They would feel that Irish lawyers would probably scoop the pool, and they will oppose this tooth and nail. Therefore, please don't insist on this, or we'll never get the treaty through.' I thought it was rather interesting to find how, very often, things are prevented through professional interests in a parliament. But that was a major treaty and a major achievement.

I was interested in Europe. I travelled around the Continent, knew it fairly well and felt that European culture was important. But apart from that, I had reasoned to myself that Europe seemed to be the storm centre for wars. Therefore it was essential to bring about a closer understanding in Europe to try and avoid wars. Another reason which I developed early on was that, by membership of the Council of Europe or any European organisation, we could begin to solve some of our own internal problems and some of the difficulties we had with Britain; in other words, to use external bodies to solve internal problems. For example, if we could construct a customs free zone in

Europe, which included Britain, Northern Ireland and the twenty-six countries, then obviously we were removing some of the obstacles to partition. In that way we were doing away with frontiers. Likewise, if we were to establish European passports, we were doing away with the political barriers which existed between countries. I think this was a very realistic concept and in fact it was taken up by Europe. I wasn't the initiator of such policy in Europe. A lot of people had been advocating it long before me, like Count Coudenhove Kalergi. The European movement had been founded very soon after the war, somewhat influenced by America. A lot of Americans had the idea of forming a United States of Europe at the time. Since then, I have seen reports, and I think that they are probably true, that the European movement was heavily financed in its initial years by the CIA and by the American government as an instrument of their policy to bring about a closer degree of political, military and economic unity in Europe itself, a form of European alliance that would link with the Americans. At the military level, I always had very strong objections. I felt that we shouldn't build a united Europe on a military alliance and, voiced that view repeatedly. Hence, when the Statute of the Council of Europe was finally adopted, and I had quite an active part in drafting it, there was a clause in the Statute of the Council of Europe precluding the Council of Europe from entering into any military alliance.

On the American side, I remember that the person involved, certainly at the first conference which I attended in Hamburg, was General Bill Donovan. He was always suspected of being linked with the American State Department and American Intelligence (CIA was not in existence then). Other people involved in Europe included Paul-Henri Spaak, Robert Schuman, Georges Bidault and several Belgians, mainly at a non-governmental level. Certainly the European movement did quite a lot of initial work, pointing out that now that Europe was dismantling the colonial empires, Europe would have to achieve close economic cooperation between the states in order to remain viable. Until World War II, the economy of Europe was built upon colonial exploitation: Britain, France, Belgium Germany, Holland and Italy had colonies. To put it very briefly and probably as an over-simplification, they had built their wealth on obtaining cheap raw materials from slave labour in their colonial areas and reselling to them the same materials converted into consumer goods. Therefore the colonial empires provided the market for goods produced by the European home countries, and at the same time provided cheap raw materials and cheap labour. World War II marked the final demolition of colonialism, which was already on the decline in the days of the League of Nations. Anybody who thought fairly keenly at the time about it realised that Europe was ceasing to be a workable economic unit, because the source of its wealth, the colonial empires, were gone. Europe would have to reorganise and readjust its economic policies so as to render itself viable without the colonial empires.

The British wouldn't admit this. They felt they could get over it by concentrating on building up the Commonwealth and the Empire, and that they could replace colonial trade by trade with Commonwealth countries. They seemed to suffer from myopia in this regard. It also led to Britain's refusal to join the European Economic Community for a long time. She felt she could go it alone, but this proved to be very fallacious, because Commonwealth countries were themselves building up their own industrial potential. Canada, Australia, in fact all the Commonwealth countries, were beginning, not only to become self-sufficient, but to export and compete with Britain in markets throughout the world.

I was also interested in another aspect of the European movement which subsequently proved to be very important. A number of us, principally I think some French members, Pierre Henri Teitgen and Robert Schuman, conceived the idea that we could have a European Convention for the Protection of Human Rights and Fundamental Freedoms. I was very enthusiastic about this. I felt that one could never rely on domestic courts and tribunals in times of crisis to act objectively. I felt that the last war probably would never have occurred if there had been a judicial body, a forum, before which complaints could have been brought as to what was happening in Germany, as to the arrest of Jews, their prosecution and extermination. But these matters were kept more or less suppressed and for some extraordinary reason the world press didn't take it up. A few newspapers did, but there was doubt as to whether these things were or were not taking place. I don't think that this suppression was due to a government not wishing to go to war or a reluctance to be forced into that position. I think that there was a genuine lack of information. The Hitler regime was able to do things secretly and cover it up with a tremendous fanfare of trumpets and speechmaking, parades and all that, while at the same time they were able to arrest people behind the scenes and put them into gas chambers. I felt that we should try and establish mechanisms to prevent this from happening again. The Universal Declaration of 1948 was a tremendous step forward, but it was still only a declaration of intention.

We had begun working on the Statute for the Council of Europe some time in 1948. It was completely new. I was one of the founding members. There were also Count Sforza from Italy, Ernie Bevin from Britain, Osten Unden from Sweden, the Norwegian foreign minister Halvard Lange. Also there was the Danish foreign minister, Gustav Rasmussen, Luxembourg's Joseph Bech, who was a very close friend of mine, with whom I got on very well. The foreign minister of Belgium rotated some times between Spaak and Van Zeeland; both poles apart politically, but both Europeans. The idea of the Council of Europe was probably seen as the first step towards a united Europe, politically and economically, but not militarily. This was not only understood but written into the Statute, desired by all and accepted unanimously. The Germans, of course, were not admitted at that stage; they were kept out of it. It was quite some time before Germany was admitted. I had discussed this several times with the French, the British and the Scandinavians. The British were not in favour, whereas the French were quite enthusiastic. Schuman was very anxious that the Germans would be invited, but it would have been politically inconvenient for him to propose it, and he asked me if I would propose the admission of Germany to the Council of Europe. Because I felt that Germany should be brought in, I finally proposed it, and there was rather a long and acrimonious discussion about it. Finally, I think it was adopted, but without enthusiasm. This was after the war, and the person most bitterly opposed to Germany's admission was Count Sforza, who said, 'Oh, if we had Germany in, we would have the Council of Europe dominated by a whole lot of Herr Doktors.' It proved to be quite an effective argument. And Ernie Bevin would say, 'We can't have these Huns in here. We can't forget what they have done to our people and to our countries. It's all very well for you from Ireland proposing that they should be admitted, but you were neutral. You didn't have to suffer what we had to suffer from the Huns.' Sweden kept remarkably silent about this. Unden was very conservative, very unlike the Sweden of today. He was a lawyer and a socialist, able but conservative. I had endless problems with Unden in regard to the European Convention on Human Rights because he felt that this involved a negation of Swedish sovereignty and he wanted to maintain national sovereignty above everything else. He didn't want anything that even could be described as supra-national. So there were all these different difficulties.

Another bone of contention during the course of the formation of the Council of Europe was the power that would be given to the Consultative Assembly, the Committee of Ministers, and ultimately the Court of Human Rights. Most of the governments, particularly the Swedish and the British, were against giving any functions or powers at all to the Assembly. The Assembly was to be purely consultative: it would meet and listen to reports from the Council of Ministers. It would have little or no powers beyond making recommendations. I felt that it was ridiculous to think that an assembly of this kind should be brought together, consisting of senior parliamentarians from all over Europe and being told as it were: now, you have no powers, you have just come here to listen and we'll be glad to receive your advice, but don't go too far.

After the first meeting it was obvious that the Assembly was not going to accept this position. A demand was made that a representative of the Council of Ministers should appear before the Assembly to give an account, a statement of policy, and to reply to questions that might be asked. The British were very opposed to this and felt it should be rejected. We had strong debates on this that went on for two days in Strasbourg, when, I think the Assembly was meeting. The demands from the Assembly were very insistent and clear-cut, and publicised extensively. Finally, at the last moment just before the meeting of the Assembly that afternoon, the Committee of Ministers decided that I would appear and represent the European governments at the Assembly and address them. I was the first European minister to appear on behalf of the Council of Ministers at this Assembly of the Council of Europe. I was Chairman of the Committee of Ministers at the time.

Another of my hopes in regard to the Council of Europe and the Consultative Assembly was that it would enable the different Irish political parties to meet and collaborate. There still remained a tremendous amount of hostility in the Dáil. Several times I proposed setting up a foreign affairs committee, representative of the government and the opposition, but this was always rejected. There was no enthusiasm for this either in the government parties or the opposition. I felt that the delegation to the Council of Europe would have to consist proportionately of members of the opposition and of the government parties. This was provided for in the Statute of the Council of Europe. Accordingly, this would bring them closer together and have a unifying effect on the Irish parties. So I went to see de Valera and urged him to come himself to the Council of Europe. He was rather taken aback by this, and I think thought there was some catch in it, but finally he came in 1949. I made it my business to see that he was treated with great deference and made available all the services that could be made available to him, cars and so on. So it was useful from that point of view. For the first time, the members of the different parties in the Dáil were meeting in a different atmosphere and were being brought together to consider aspects of political issues that they didn't consider at home. It also helped to inform our own politicians as to political and economic issues in other countries, and as to how they were run. It gave them a much broader outlook than they had. It broke, to a certain extent, the insularity, first of all of Ireland itself, and then of Ireland and Britain as one philosophical area.

As I've mentioned, a number of us had conceived the idea of having an effective Convention on Human Rights which was not merely declaratory, as was the Universal Declaration. Although not one of the fundamental ideas proposed as a basis for setting up the Council, it was now part of it. We realised that it would take a long time before the United Nations would finally adopt covenants which would convert the Declaration of Human Rights into effective international law, and would provide a mechanism for the enforcement of the Convention on Human Rights. So we had conceived the idea that we should start doing this in Europe, on a regional basis. The French were very anxious that this be done. France, Belgium, Luxembourg and Ireland were the main protagonists in favour, the British were lukewarm, the Danes and Norwegians were alright, though certainly the Swedes were holding back a good deal.

We had endless meetings, each representative had to report back to his government and obtain sanction before going ahead. I was in the happy position that the government in Dublin was busy with other things. I made reports to them, but I always felt that they were not particularly interested. They felt that it was a good thing. They liked the idea of being more interested and more European. It was a new direction of policy and they were pleased that I was engaged in this, rather than in too much anti-British propaganda. They felt that this would be a good occupation for me. But to give them their due, they did like the idea of playing an active part in Europe, a European concept and a European tradition. I had many long talks with the Taoiseach always on these occasions. He was very keen on it. I think he had implicit confidence in what I was doing.

I should bring in an incident which always interested me. It was an incident which enabled the European Convention on Human Rights to be adopted and to make headway despite the opposition which was there. Ernie Bevin at that time was British Foreign Secretary. I knew him from before. I had been consulted, as a lawyer, by the trade unions in Ireland, and also by some trade unions in England, particularly in connection with one special case. The Fianna Fáil government, with Lemass at its head, had tried to force all unions involved in transport and in CIE to join the Irish Transport and General Workers Union. It had also then tried to pass a trade union act which would have the effect of wiping out the smaller unions, and *inter alia*, the NUR, the National Union of Railwaymen, which was a British union, established in Ireland as well. I was retained and acted for the trade unions in this, and for the NUR. It came to the courts and I succeeded in getting the act declared unconstitutional. It was one of the most important constitutional decisions which we had made since the state was set up. I certainly put in a lot of work. This was before the 1948 government was formed.

It was in that context that I had met Bevin, and quite a few of the

British trade union leaders. I was on very friendly terms with them, because I was fighting to a certain extent the battles of the smaller unions against the state-sponsored unions. However, Ernie Bevin was bitterly against Winston Churchill. He just hated Churchill and on several occasions at the Council of Europe meetings with the foreign ministers, when I was in the chair, Ernie would launch attacks on Churchill. I had to intervene on more than one occasion to say, 'Well, Mr Bevin, we're not really discussing Winston Churchill here. He is one of your distinguished politicians, and I quite well understand your feelings about him; possibly I would share them, but really we are not here to discuss these things.' Churchill by this time was one of the key people in Europe. After the war, when he had been defeated in the election, he wrapped the flag of Europe round his middle, and campaigned for a united Europe. This had antagonised Bevin against Europe. I was having a lot of difficulties because Bevin wouldn't go far enough, partly because his officials were so conservative and were holding him back. But in addition he had this animosity against Churchill, and the concept of a united Europe was a Churchillian plot. So I had to battle against this a good deal.

On one occasion, I remember there was quite an incident. I had to finally rule Bevin out of order at a meeting of the Council of Ministers, by hammering the table saying, 'Mr Bevin, you are out of order. I have told you that we are not here to discuss Winston Churchill.' Of course, Winston Churchill was behaving most provocatively at the time. He was also in Strasbourg and holding public meetings with huge crowds, as 'the man who won the war'.

However, be that as it may, I decided I would try to convert Bevin to a Convention on Human Rights. I had mentioned it a good few times but he had always been against it, saying it was no use, and so on. So one night I invited Ernie to come and have dinner with me at the Irish Legation, as it was then, in Paris. We had a very good dinner and it was arranged that afterwards, Ernie and I would be left alone together to talk. So we talked at great length into the small hours of the morning. I told him that I understood his irritation with Churchill, 'But the fact that Churchill advocates a united Europe is no reason for opposing a united Europe. I think that you should be more European than Churchill. That is the best way of meeting the situation. Europe has ceased to be viable. I think that people accept the idea that there has to be European cooperation. What people would be most interested in would be a Convention for the Protection of Human Rights and Fundamental Freedoms, to ensure that never again would we drift into a position where millions of people would be put into a gas chamber, unbeknownst to the rest of the world, and nobody would do anything against this. Instead of agitating about Churchill, why don't you take the lead in urging the adoption of a Convention for the Protection of Human Rights within Europe? In that way you would probably weaken Churchill and enhance your own position.' The night ended up with Ernie Bevin being really interested in the idea of supporting a European Convention for the Protection of Human Rights and Fundamental Freedoms.

The end of that night was marked by Ernie Bevin saying, 'Well, I'd like to discuss that with you again. Can you come and see me in the morning at the Embassy?' Ernie left his hat behind him in the Legation and so the next morning I brought his hat over to the British Embassy where we resumed our conversations. I had already a draft of the kind of objectives that we should aim at having. I gave him this and we discussed it. He was very enthusiastic about the idea and he made a speech either in Strasbourg or in the House of Commons a few days later saying that, 'It was essential that Europe should take the lead to ensure that never again could human rights be violated in Europe. There must be judicial machinery, there must be a rule of law to protect individuals, and fundamental liberties.'

That was the turning point. Once I had Britain supporting the Convention on Human Rights, they all became much stronger on it. Sforza became very strong. Italy had a rather weak, shilly-shallying position at the time, suffering from a guilt complex because of the war. When they saw France and Britain petitioning for a Convention on Human Rights, they jumped on the bandwagon.

The Swedes were the most difficult. It sounds very strange now, because they are the best human rights country in Europe, or in the world. Unden was very conservative. It was completely against his concept of Swedish constitutional law, that there should be a supra-national court that could tell Sweden 'You are not to do this.' Finally I had to spend a lot of time with Unden to try and persuade him. We were staying in Strasbourg in the Nouvel Hotel, which was rather old-fashioned. Unden had the room over mine. I often arranged that I would go up after dinner. He would get into bed, because he was tired, and I used to discuss various bits and pieces of the European Convention on Human Rights with him to get his accord.

The negotiations for the Convention for Human Rights, which was signed on 4 November 1950, were long and protracted. I was dissatisfied with the idea that the right of initial recourse to the Commission on Human Rights, or to the Court should depend upon an optional clause. It is only on that basis that the Swedes accepted, and some of the other countries, including, I think, the British. The British were prepared to go a certain distance and were really quite afraid of the European Convention. It was an innovation. And of course, in truth, though this had never been said publicly, once the British ratified the European Convention on Human Rights, they in fact accepted a written constitution, which they never had before. Because it is a written constitution, they have to abide by it. And the decisions of the Commission and of the Court can override the home courts. So, to that extent, they had waived sovereignty.

My disagreement in regard to the European Convention went so far that right up to the last moment I had considered not signing it. The Convention was adopted in Rome, and on rereading the Convention on the way over, I really felt very strongly against some portions of it. There were also lots of omissions from the Convention. I have forgotten what the actual issues were, but I was able to get some additions put into the Convention at the final meeting in Rome before signing. Even when I signed it, in the public statement which I made, I indicated that I had had grave doubts as to whether or not I should sign it, as I didn't think it went far enough. I explained why, but went on to say that, nevertheless, I had decided to sign it as a step forward.

Schuman was always anxious that the centre of the Council of Europe should be in Strasbourg, for he came from that part of the country. He felt it would be difficult to propose this, for the French would say the Council should be in Paris, the Belgians that it should be in Brussels, and so on. It was agreed between us that I would propose Strasbourg, and that is how Strasbourg became the seat of the Council of Europe. This has often been criticised, but by and large it wasn't a bad choice. Strasbourg has one main advantage over other places in that when people come to Strasbourg to attend conferences, they have nothing else to do, and they attend their meetings fairly regularly. When there are meetings in Paris or Brussels, there are many other counter-attractions that deflect their attention from the real task. Strasbourg had that advantage, though it has been criticised often as being rather inaccessible.

The Council of Europe has been of colossal use in regard to human rights. It has been a bit of a failure in regard to other things. It has done a good deal of useful work on the standardisation of legal systems. But it is in decline now. Governments don't care about human rights. They'd like to see the Council of Europe buried and done away with in this kind of atmosphere of the moment; they want NATO, military alliances and political alliances, not a mechanism for the protection of human rights. With regard to the building of the Council of Europe headquarters, we started on it very soon and it was built in record time. Indeed, I think that I laid the foundation stone, and opened it, as President of the Council of Ministers, with Churchill.

It is extraordinary the way in which things leak out the grapevine in international organisations. Churchill had heard that at a Council of Ministers I had ruled Ernie Bevin out of order for attacking him and was very grateful to me. He felt that I was a great protagonist. He came over one day saying he had heard this and was 'terribly grateful' to me and 'would love' if I would go and have lunch with him. We had lunch several times together. He had a house, either of his own or belonging to the Conservative Party, in Strasbourg. I don't know who was financing it. But always, when I turned to Ireland he would say 'Ah, don't ask me to let down my friends. I would love to see Ireland unified, a pity to divide Ireland.' His friends were Brookeborough and Lord Craigavon.

CHAPTER XII

Partition Policy • News Agency
Difficult Times

In regard to partition, the following was roughly my policy. First of all, we had to make the issues clear. To that end, I considered it important that we should have broadcasts in Ireland and throughout the world, and we should also issue pamphlets on religious and political discrimination, as well as on the violation of human rights. I felt it was also necessary to explain what the electoral position was and, accordingly, I instructed our missions abroad to make these facts known. This was phase one of the policy.

The second phase was to work towards European economic and political unity, in the hope that, in that broader context, the country would become unified gradually within a united Europe.

Thirdly, my policy was to enter into discussions and work directly with the British in regard to partition. Attlee and Rugby both made the point to me that one of the obstacles to ending partition was that Britain needed for her defence, not bases in Ireland, but the potential of the Belfast shipyards. These were essential in the event of a war. These were very extensive shipyards, capable of quick production, and they were farther removed from Europe than the shipyards in England. I accepted the general basis of the argument, but pointed out that we could easily come to some arrangements whereby the shipyards would be vested in a company that was British-owned but operated by license from an Irish government. They said that the shipyards in peacetime were always in debt; it was necessary to subsidise them in order that they would be available in wartime. I felt that this was a matter which could easily be undertaken by the British government. Of course we couldn't undertake to finance the shipyards, as a possible war service, but that we would have no objection to the British government doing so. We would encourage anything which would further the development of the shipyards, increase production and modernise them; this would also benefit Ireland. We discussed the kind of company which might be formed. I suggested it should be a company in which the British should have the major shareholding, and with which the Irish government would also be involved, so that there would be a joint interest in keeping the shipyard going.

I was interested in this point because it had never been made before. It seemed to be the newest approach from the military point of view to the question of the unification of Ireland. Until then it had been argued that naval facilities and bases would be required by Britain in the Six Counties. This is of interest, because it shows the consistent opposition of what I would call the military and naval establishment to the reunification of Ireland. Lord Rugby in Dublin and Clement Attlee in London would be in favour of ending partition provided they could mollify the Tories.

Sir Gilbert Laithwaite, with whom I had very few relations, replaced Rugby in 1949. He was always boasting of being very pro-Irish in a typical British diplomatic way which always spelled bad relations. I much preferred Rugby, who was a good, rip-roaring Tory. You knew where you were with him, and he was an intelligent man. Laithwaite professed to be sympathetic to the Irish, professed to understand them and their grievances. He was related to somebody or other in Ireland, but relations were never as good with him. Relations with Lord Rugby were good. We liked each other and got on very well.

I also concentrated a good deal on building up public opinion abroad, particularly in the United States, on partition. I have always been impressed by the importance of the Irish American vote and political influence in the United States. We had never won the war militarily against Britain. On the other hand, Britain could never wage war in the way her military people advised, by reason of the fact that she could not afford to antagonise the Irish American vote in the

United States. The importance of this following upon 1916 and subsequently has been overlooked completely in the course of writing our history. The United States Senate gave a very positive and definite direction to President Wilson that he was to raise the question of self-determination for Ireland as one of the major issues at the Versailles peace conference in 1919. He did not do this, largely as a result of British influence, and the Senate as a result refused to ratify the Versailles Treaty and refused to join the League of Nations.

I was conscious of the tremendous potential that lay there and felt it should be developed, so I visited America two or three times for discussions with various people. I addressed a joint meeting of the Senate and the House of Representatives in Washington on one occasion.

Indeed, Liam Cosgrave, then parliamentary secretary to the Taoiseach, made a speech attacking me in regard to an interview which I had given on an American TV programme called *Meet the Press*. I had compared what Britain was doing in the north with what the Russians were doing in some areas of the world. This created an awkward situation: a junior parliamentary secretary launching an attack on the Minister for Foreign Affairs. Jack Costello explained to me that this had been done without prior consultation and he was very upset when he read the speech at the time.

Some time after the inception of the Council of Europe, the idea of forming a North Atlantic Alliance was developed. The British and indeed the Americans should have known what my reply was likely to be. Be that as it may, a letter was sent through the American ambassador inviting us to participate in a meeting to discuss the formation of the North Atlantic Alliance. I sent a strong reply to this and I also used a number of links I had with the State Department to make our views known in no uncertain terms. The terms of the reply were published as a White Paper. We discussed it of course at government level and everybody agreed that we shouldn't join.

My own reasons could be classified under two or three different headings. First of all I regarded NATO as being a rather dangerous military alliance that might well involve Europe in another war at more or less the wish of the United States. I could quite well see the American anti-communist view pushing NATO into a cold war first, and then into an active war. Secondly, as I said in my reply to the United States government, it was completely illogical for us to enter into a military alliance with Britain while a part of our country was still being occupied by British forces. We would be condoning and accepting the British occupation of Northern Ireland by entering into a military alliance with Britain. On another aspect: if ever we had to defend Ireland in a war of aggression, we could only defend it as one entity; we could not organise the defence of a small island like Ireland under two different military controls or governments.

I can't think of any good reason why Ireland should join NATO, then or now. NATO is a dangerous military alliance and I have noticed that there is a great deal of hesitancy among many of the NATO countries. I am very glad that we didn't join and that we didn't spend vast sums of money on quite unnecessary armament. In addition, if we had joined NATO, with the British occupation of Northern Ireland we would have had practically a civil war the whole time. The IRA would have found this a reason for attacking our defence forces because they had become part of a British alliance.

Following upon my reply to the invitation to join NATO, there were a few indirect threats of economic pressure made against us. They came from the State Department and the British Foreign Office. I let it be known that if any pressure were attempted or exerted against us, we would have to denounce this very publicly at the Council of Europe. We had a good deal of influence through the Council of Europe particularly and through the OEEC. So that was an end to our participation in NATO. Nobody has every suggested seriously since that we should join it.

I was helped a great deal during this period by George Garrett, who was friendly and who knew perfectly well what our attitude was to joining NATO. Marshall was anxious to exercise pressure against us. Garrett explained this to me, and shortly afterwards I visited America, largely to talk to Marshall. Some of the junior officials in the State Department, those dealing with Irish affairs, did hint to me on a number of occasions that of course America might have to withhold any financial assistance to Ireland, indeed exert economic pressure against Ireland, if we didn't join NATO. I reacted very strongly to this.

At one stage I met President Truman. One of the problems in America is to discover where the centre of power lies at any given moment on any given situation. I had been in the States, meeting Congressmen Fogarty and others, giving some talks around that time, after the refusal to join NATO. A cruise was being organised on the Potomac on the Presidential yacht, at which the Deputy Assistant Secretary of State attended and several congressmen. In the course of that cruise we discussed the whole situation in detail. They had asked Truman to see me; they were surprised to find that we hadn't met. I wasn't particularly bothered about it; I was leaving shortly afterwards for Dublin. I think the Browne issues were beginning to create problems. Just a few hours before leaving, I got phone messages from the White House and from Senator Mansfield, asking me to postpone my departure because President Truman wished to see me. This was a complete reversal of attitudes, which no doubt had been brought about by Irish-American congressmen and senators, who probably communicated their reaction to his failure to meet me.

So I had a long, polite, interview with Truman. We discussed Ireland's attitude in regard to NATO, and in regard to partition. I remember asking the American government to give us more support in our efforts to try and end partition, and Truman being rather non-committal, but at the same time being slightly encouraging. This because he felt he had to do something to appease the Irish Americans.

With regard to reaction at home to my policy vis-à-vis NATO, Fianna Fáil remained silent. There were hints that, though we were not joining NATO, I had entered into some secret military agreement with the Americans and with the British. Completely false! A few right-wing outriders in the country started writing letters to the papers, saying that it was scandalous that we didn't join NATO, and support our allies and so on. Fine Gael remained quiescent. It was policy; we had discussed it at cabinet, and we agreed on it.

One of the reasons why Clann was started was to try to get away from the Civil War past and concentrate on the economic development of the country on a rational basis. I thought we should have tried to avoid having the whole situation always bedevilled by civil war issues on the one hand, or by completely ill-informed or uninformed views on the other hand. In order to do this, I was anxious to get a variety of people from different backgrounds into Clann na Poblachta. I knew we could count on the support of people in the IRA or traditional republicans like the Brughas, Donal O'Donoghue, Con Lehane, Dick Batterbury and Michael Fitzpatrick. Accordingly I was glad when Noel Hartnett and Peadar Cowan approached me in regard to participating actively in the formation of a party and working in Clann. They represented completely different and new angles

Likewise, I was glad when Noel Hartnett, during the period of the by-elections, or between the by-elections and the general election of 1948, first brought Nöel Browne to me as a young, progressive, independent-minded Trinity graduate (aged 33 in 1948). Browne had not taken any active part or interest in national, or civil war issues before. So I welcomed him from that point of view. Noel Hartnett, in addition, was a very good election organiser. He had worked in Fianna Fáil and knew the Fianna Fáil mechanisms in detail for elections and the way in which they were run. So to that extent he was also useful. To be quite frank, the only thing that worried me about him even then was that he was egocentric. Noel often used to bring back to his own experience in any discussion we used to have, his own part in certain events. It must have been a short time after the government was formed, he approached me and said that he hoped when it came to naming members of the Senate, I would not do as Fianna Fáil had done in the past and pass him by. He hoped that I would put him in the Senate. I immediately explained to him that I didn't think this was possible. I felt that if we named our director of elections as senator, this would be used against us. People would say these people are no better than Fianna Fáil or Fine Gael: they are nominating their party henchmen to jobs. We had two seats in the Senate allocated to us. I felt I should approach the question of senators on the basis of merit. After giving the matter a good deal of thought, I came to the conclusion that there were two people who should be in the Senate: one was Denis Ireland from Belfast, a writer and experienced journalist. He also had a sound fundamental grasp of economics, certainly as far as Ireland was concerned. I felt it was ridiculous that our whole parliament should not include any representative from the North, not even a senator. The other person I nominated was Dr Patrick McCartan, one of the elder statesmen of the republican movement. He also came from the North – Tyrone. In addition to that he had run as presidential candidate and had obtained a very substantial poll. On these grounds, I regarded him as a suitable and proper person for the Senate, the type of person one would expect to find in an upper house. So I made up my mind firmly that these were the two senators we should have.

When I announced this at the Standing Committee of Clann, I was met with a barrage of opposition, led by Noel. Some days after the meeting he told me he felt I had let him down, just as de Valera had let him down by not putting him into the Senate. From that moment on, I realised that I was going to have a good deal of hostility from Noel Hartnett and a good many problems. Shortly before that, I had had a very stiff battle with the Standing Committee, in regard to the appointment of Nöel Browne as a Co-Minister. Then I had the full support of Noel Hartnett, who was a very close friend of Nöel Browne. Indeed I felt at times that Hartnett's strong enthusiasm for Browne caused a certain reaction amongst the other members of the Standing Committee, who didn't have very much confidence in Hartnett. Throughout, I was always in some difficulty on these issues. I felt that very often opposition to a certain viewpoint on the Standing Committee, or the Executive of Clann might spring from a hangover of past political differences from the Civil War, or of even more recent times. There was a tendency for the old members of Clann to regard Hartnett as being a newcomer, and not to treat him in the same way as they would treat old republicans. Noel Hartnett had never been in the IRA, nor had he ever been active in the republican movement. Now that shouldn't have militated against him, because he was probably too young to have been in the IRA, but there was this type of clannishness among older republicans, indeed about which Nöel Browne later complained, publicly. There was a certain amount in it, but it was this type of clannishness which you get with people of different generations in any event.

As far as Nöel Browne was concerned, he was a complete newcomer, and had no pretensions of knowing what the word Sinn Féin or republican even meant. He had never been interested in them. He had been in Trinity and had moved and lived another life in another strata of the community. He was interested in improving the position of health services in the country, of that I have no doubt; I have always accepted this. But he was a different type of animal, if you like, to the rest of us. We had all gone through the republican movement in one form or another. Noel Hartnett had gone through it in a sense with Fianna Fáil and had acquired a republican tradition. I had to protect Nöel Browne from the old-timers and also to a certain extent protect Noel Hartnett. This sounds ridiculous for Hartnett was well able to protect himself.

During the by-elections leading up to the 1948 general election, our strongest supporters were the teachers, the INTO. These were not necessarily republicans. By and large the teachers formed a background to our organisation throughout the country and they probably were better educated than many others at the time. They realised that many of the ideas we were propounding made sense. Apart from that, they had grievances against the government; there had been a strike and we had backed them, so there was this kind of bond between us. In addition, they may have been a little more outward-looking than many of the others. They had contact with international teachers organisations and probably saw what was being done abroad.

So there was an uneasy situation in the Clann Executive always as far as Nöel Browne and Noel Hartnett were concerned. But it didn't worry me very much. I felt that we could overcome it. I think all my colleagues on the Standing Committee realised that we had to lean backwards a little bit to make Browne and Hartnett feel at home on the Standing Committee. Also I should mention Peadar Cowan, who was in the same boat. Peadar Cowan was regarded as purely a Free State army officer by some of my republican colleagues, who were rather alarmed to have him involved in Clann under any circumstances. I had this rather difficult trio to preside over, as well as the republicans, who were very good. The fact that they were republicans probably meant they had greater interest in the future of the country. They had been working at it, they had been involved and interested. They also differed very much in type and quality, which was useful for a political party. We had Con Lehane, with a Dubliner's and an IRA man's viewpoint. We had men like Vincent Shields, an old-timer from Tyrone, Donal O'Donoghue, an active republican, with a philosophical outlook and approach to problems. Dick Batterbury, rather an extraordinary man. Dick had been the OC of one of the Dublin Battalions, I think 4th of the Dublin Brigade. He had also been offered the Chair of English in University College Dublin, but had turned it down. He was a very able man, quiet and unassuming. He always kept in the background, unceasingly working. During an election campaign he would spend his days just distributing handbills; he used to enjoy doing that. But he didn't like telephones, a new invention. He usually used to walk from place to place in Dublin, rather than go in a motor car. I often reprimanded him on this matter, pointing out that, apart from imposing hardship on himself, he was wasting valuable time which he could use otherwise.

However, it was not a bad Executive. Nor was it a bad Standing Committee, representing all the different elements. They worked reasonably well. I was conscious that Noel Hartnett felt dissatisfied because he hadn't been elected to the Dáil. He stood in Dun Laoghaire-Rathdown, but missed being elected by a short time. Not unjustly, he felt he had missed out because he was director of elections and had to spend too much time ensuring that I and others would be elected. I think Noel was rightly conscious of this and probably suffered a little bit of a grievance that somebody should have looked after his constituency. To some extent he was justified in that.

It was at that time I conceived the idea of a news agency – my idea was to put Noel Hartnett in charge. It was quite a simple idea. We were, as far as I know, then one of the only countries in Europe without a news agency of our own. This would be an agency to relay reports from this country and to feed us with information. Our entire sources for news or information were British or American – Reuters was the dominating news agency in Ireland and Britain and had been set up with the help of the British government in order to ensure that the British viewpoint would be put across the world. This was done very successfully. The same happened with the Press Association in England,

Associated Press in America and United Press International; they all had received either direct or indirect subventions from their respective governments, in the sense of selling their news services to them. I felt it was essential, if we were going to assert our own independence, if we were serious about reunification, that we should have our own news services and be in a position to send out our own reports.

Fianna Fáil, which should have been first to welcome this, ran a really dishonest campaign against a news agency and succeeded in getting a number of journalists to back them up, pretending it would put journalists out of work, it would mean we were to have a state-owned press service, thereby exercising a form of censorship. This was all nonsense. It might apply to any news agency in the world. Every country which was independent had a news agency of its own and we were the exception. There was no reason why it should be biased. We could ensure this by seeing that the board of control of the news agency would be independent. Ireland's handicap in not having a news agency was demonstrated very clearly at the time when the IRA bombing campaign started in England. The then government under Jack Lynch promptly proceeded to try and set up a news service, and hurriedly recruited a great many people, sending them out to different corners of the globe to get them to try to put across the Irish government's viewpoint. These people were ill equipped and ill trained. In many cases they had no experience of this kind of work, and were also regarded as being merely agents who were sent out for propaganda purposes.

I had no illusions as to the financial viability of the news agency. I knew certainly that we would not make a success at least for five or six years after its inception. I knew we would have to spend a good deal of money to get it established. Afterwards it might become self-sufficient if it provided a good service, if it could sell its service outside the country and if the Irish papers would themselves buy its service. It did get off the ground, it was working and was beginning to become effective when the change of government took place and it was finally killed.

Relations with Browne were quite normal, certainly during the first few months of the inter-party government. I used to see him fairly frequently. He and I were both busy in our respective ministries. I was

217

away often. My one fear at the beginning, when he took over, was that he would be over-influenced by the civil service in the department, who were rather conservative, I thought, and under the influence of the medical profession. It is fear which was ill-founded, for I discovered that Nöel Browne was fully conscious of this. This was a great relief to me and gave me much more confidence. He had received a considerable amount of assistance from all the other members of the government. He was new to political life, and they went out of their way to help him. In particular I remember Tom O'Higgins, who was himself a doctor and familiar with Irish Medical Association politics, really collaborated with Browne to assist him and give any help that he could.

Browne took this help well. I was rather amused to find that very often he would discuss matters with Fine Gael ministers in great detail, more than he would with me. With this I was rather pleased. I felt that it was a sure sign that there was a healthy spirit of collaboration in the government itself. The only person who showed signs of anxiety from time to time about Nöel Browne's activities was Bill Norton, leader of the Labour Party. He told me he thought Browne was inexperienced and somewhat irresponsible. Norton was Tánaiste and Minister for Social Welfare. What worried Norton were the statements which Browne made at cabinet or in discussions concerning trade unions, showing an abysmal ignorance on Browne's part of the various problems relating to trade unions. On more than one occasion Norton said that he thought I had made a mistake in not bringing a more experienced person, such as Con Lehane, into the cabinet.

However, there were no major problems as far as I was concerned until Browne was complaining that his hospital-building scheme was being held up by the unavailability of skilled building labour, carpenters, et al. He was anxious to start a campaign to bring some of them back from England. He felt that this would also be a good public relations exercise – advertising and making speeches asking people to come back. Everybody in the cabinet was very enthusiastic about this. I felt that he was not experienced enough to run a campaign of that kind and that there were some pitfalls about it. It was very bad to bring people home on the basis that there would be immediate employment, unless they were in fact able to get immediate and continuous employment.

However, he was encouraged to do this. Then one day in the Dáil he told me rather aggressively, 'Your officials are trying to prevent me from doing this; they're not cooperating. They all consider themselves diplomats. They're not concerned with the plight of the people.' This struck me as odd. He had said they refused to help him, so I said, 'We'll have a talk about this and see what we can do.' I had two or three talks with him and with people in the Department of External Affairs. It transpired, though I'm rather vague on this, that the cause of the trouble was that he wanted to make a broadcast appeal, and the officials of External Affairs said it would have to be done in arrangement with Radio Éireann and the Minister for Posts and Telegraphs.

Browne was childishly inexperienced as far as government was concerned in many respects. This is not to say he was not intelligent. Until he came into the Dáil and was made minister, he had no idea what the functions of a minister were – but he learned quickly. So he made remarks about my officials. Finally I noticed that he was being more aggressive with me in casual conversations, suggesting that of course I didn't care what happened to him and his department. These I just shrugged off. Nöel very often did not attend cabinet meetings; this became an increasing tendency. He had been ill for some weeks, probably a few months. He had been at home. I used to get news of him from Hartnett. Nöel apparently complained while he was ill that I wasn't doing enough to help him. I didn't pay much attention to all this; he was probably overworked. All this may have been preying on his mind.

He also had been seeing a good deal of Oliver J. Flanagan. On one occasion – I learned this afterwards – Browne asked Oliver had I been to see him in hospital. Oliver said no, that I was probably too busy or away, and Browne said 'Oh no, no. MacBride doesn't like you; he wouldn't go to see you.' Flanagan didn't know why I should dislike him and was told, 'I know he doesn't like you because at one stage it was suggested that you should be made a parliamentary secretary and he opposed it at a cabinet meeting.' This rather shocked me. I don't remember whether it was true or not. It is quite possible that I may have said we ought to get somebody more experienced than Oliver, who himself was fairly new at the time.

I was extremely busy at the time in my own department. The

Council of Europe was building up. I had serious hopes of being able to build up pressure on the White House from Congress. I had hopes that I might be able to get something tangible done in regard to partition.

One day in the Dáil, I said to Nöel, 'Let's go out and have dinner. We can discuss various things. Come on, we'll have a good dinner in the Russell. I'll leave word so, if a Division rings , we can be called back in good time.' So we went off to have dinner in the Russell. I hadn't really been worried so far by Browne very much. I thought he had been acting oddly, but it hadn't really worried me. I may have been at fault. I should have taken a lot of these signs to heart and done something about them earlier. But I didn't think the frictions that were happening were sufficiently big to worry about.

However, we sat down and had dinner at the Russell Hotel. Browne immediately opened up by saying that he felt he ought to tell me that he had lost complete confidence in me and that his intentions were to bring down the government. It was probably the most extraordinary conversation that ever took place between two government ministers, or between the leader of a political party and his principal assistant. I now realised how serious the position was. Finally the question was the extent to which he really meant the things he had said. But this certainly disclosed an extremely serious position in which he had made very definite threats that unless I agreed to certain conditions, which involved the change of the personnel of the Standing Committee and which also involved giving Noel Hartnett a good deal more power and responsibility, he would bring down the government. I was so impressed by all this that when I got home that night, I decided to write down the gist of the conversation, which I duly did and transmitted it to Donal O'Donoghue, Chairman of the Clann na Poblachta Standing Committee.

After dinner we went back to the Dáil. The conversation continued in a desultory way, but it was all on very polite terms. I wrote to Donal the following day transmitting the notes I had made of the conversation I had had with Browne, explaining that I felt this was a serious position, and I didn't feel able to handle it. I wanted some help. From that time on, there were several attempts made by Donal O'Donoghue and other members of the Standing Committee, as well as by the chairman and members of the Executive, to talk things out with Browne, either by himself or with me. All these attempts proved abortive. Browne was becoming more and more impossible and difficult to deal with.

His relations with other members of the government remained quite normal. I did get some echoes, which I have never been able to verify, that did worry me a good deal. I heard that he had met some IRA people in the west of Ireland. He had had discussions and said that he would arrange to have them provided with arms. That certainly shook me for there was no question of armed intervention by the IRA at the time. I didn't have any direct relationship with the IRA, but the IRA understood what the government was trying to do and were not trying to create difficulties or indulge in armed activities. The impression I had was that they would refrain from creating any difficulties. The idea that Browne, who didn't know the first thing about the IRA, should engage in conversations with some people purporting to be the IRA (they might or might not have been) concerning arms certainly worried me. I heard it from some Clann people, but I can't say I ever got it confirmed.

Another issue that worried me a good deal was his complete lack of responsibility in his dealings relating to the Mother and Child Scheme. He had a lot of confidence in Noel Hartnett and certainly consulted Hartnett about everything. Hartnett had told him on one occasion in my presence, and certainly it was one of his basic beliefs, that in order to succeed in Irish politics you had to pick a row with the Irish hierarchy. Browne did say to me on two or three occasions at the beginning of the Mother and Child Scheme, 'If I can really pick a row with the Irish hierarchy, I'll be made.' Browne had rather a childish, immature way of hearing a thing, getting a suggestion, acting on it without knowing very much or without being responsible in doing it. So I am quite certain that from the beginning of the Mother and Child proposals, he had in mind this idea of picking a row with the hierarchy. He came to me one day, very pleased with himself and said, 'See now, I've been photographed with the Protestant Archbishop of Dublin. This will irritate the Archbishop of Dublin.' I said, 'Yes, and I think it is rather unwise of you to do it.' Afterwards he said I had criticised him for getting photographed with the Protestant Archbishop of Dublin.

But this was all part of a systematic effort on his part to pick a row with the bishops. He had definitely decided to bring down the government, and also to try and bring down Clann na Poblachta. He probably would try and start a party of his own with Noel Hartnett. On the basis of discussions we had had, I felt satisfied with this. There were other incidents which worried me. One was an anonymous circular letter sent out to the medical professions in February 1951, to newspapers, all kinds of people about the IMA and the Mother and Child Scheme. It contained lots of statements which Browne couldn't really stand over, either in language or form. He repudiated having had anything to do with it. In point of fact he had written it, or caused it to be written. He had tried to have it distributed through the Clann office. It had been stencilled in the Department of Health. It was a rather virulent circular, quite impossible for any minister to have stood over. Browne realised this and in a long discussion one day he said, 'I can't stand over this. I must repudiate it. It would be disastrous if it were found out that I had had anything to do with it.' The whole thing struck me as completely irresponsible; he didn't realise that this would obviously leak out. There were several other incidents of the same kind.

Finally I came to the conclusion that he would wreck the government completely and probably also wreck Clann. Throughout all this, I consulted the Standing Committee and Executive. All this was discussed in detail. Browne was present during these meetings but he made a habit of walking out whenever somebody said something which he didn't like. It was under these circumstances that I finally came to write a letter to Browne requesting his submission of resignation on 10 April 1951. I could no longer take responsibility for him. I was hoping that I would be able to bring Browne back to his senses. It was a difficult balance to maintain, to decide to what extent I had to be considerate of a colleague, whom I thought was overwrought and inexperienced. I also felt a duty to the government to prevent any kind of open dissension from arising, to prevent the collapse. This worried me day after day. That is why I finally wrote to the Taoiseach, telling him I was going to write him this letter, and the Taoiseach said that possibly we should hold off, we might be able to do something. I said no; I had come to the conclusion that there was nothing more I could do to retrieve the situation.

I was in favour of the Mother and Child Scheme. I saw no virtue in making it completely free to everybody. I had reached a compromise which I think would have been acceptable, and certainly acceptable to the government, whereby there would be free medical services for all families in receipt of an income of less than £1,000 a year. This would really have covered all the requirements of that situation. It would have overcome objections, and made the scheme more easily workable, financially and operationally. It would have been accepted by everybody.

I am sure a formula could have been found to get over the specific rejection providing for the education of mothers and their children up to the age of sixteen. The hierarchy behaved extremely stupidly and irresponsibly in regard to the Scheme; some of their statements were quite indefensible. I was caught between the devil and the deep sea. I was placed in the position of having to stand over the attitude of the hierarchy in some respects, and the attitude of Browne in other respects. Amid the controversy that raged at that time, it was practically impossible to secure a reasonable hearing from either side.

A number of things went wrong. Browne made no attempt to try and placate the hierarchy or the Irish Medical Association. I am certain that attempts could have been made to placate the bishops, and with a bit of tact, this could have been achieved. The IMA would have been more difficult. I had no brief at all for the IMA which was concerned only with its own financial gain. Attempts could have been made to get some IMA elements on his side. Browne, however, said his objective was to pick a quarrel with the hierarchy, as he had been advised to do by Hartnett. He was extremely successful in doing this and doing it in a way which got him a lot of public sympathy.

It is very hard to know what Browne thought, because his reaction was so peculiar. Whenever it suited him to say he didn't understand something, he said he didn't understand. I often felt he understood perfectly well. Another minister could have got this through, I have no doubt, with handling and skill.

To be fair, the Taoiseach would not have allowed the hierarchy to intervene in government matters as such. Jack would probably have had talks with individual bishops, to try and find settlements. With Browne this was impossible. This was bad handling on Browne's part. Browne should have made sure that his own government were going to stand by him. He should have consulted them, brought them along, and not tried to play tricks, as he did. I have no doubt that Hartnett had a continued influence on Browne. I believe Hartnett's purpose at that stage was to bring down the government and also to bring down Clann. Hartnett had resigned from the Standing Committee and from Clann in a letter of 8 February 1951.

One of the striking things about Browne's position in the government was his failure to attend cabinet meetings. I compiled a list of meetings he attended and those he did not. It gives quite a picture. An important minister wouldn't turn up at cabinet meetings! I asked him several times, why? He used to say, 'They're no use, a waste of time, cabinet meetings.' Or he would say he had forgotten. I would say, 'Does your secretary not remind you?' 'Ah yes,' he'd say, 'but it's not very important.' Certainly in getting the building programme underway, he was able to break through a lot of the red tape which was very necessary. Possibly it was his success on that, and the praise which we all gave him, that went to his head.

I always considered the IMA to be a profit-motivated organisation controlled by doctors who regarded social improvements as possibly endangering their own financial privilege in the medical field. They much preferred to have a system whereby they would have a number of beds reserved for them in the hospitals, for which they could collect large treatment fees. I did feel there were many doctors who were well motivated, but they didn't get themselves into key positions in the IMA.

My relationships with the hierarchy were few and far between. I deliberately avoided getting too closely involved concerning any matters regarding political developments in the country. As far as political issues were involved, they were my responsibility. My attitude always was that the viewpoint of the hierarchy should be taken into account in the same way as the Protestant hierarchy or the Jewish rabbinical council. In Ireland, a Catholic country, the hierarchy had a special position of privilege as the visible heads of the Church. Noel Hartnett was quite right – somebody who faces up to the hierarchy and embattles with them usually has the support of a large section of public opinion in the country.

The hierarchy did not really have the political confidence of the people. When they spoke on religious or moral issues, they would be listened to. But there was always an *arrière-pensée* at the back of peoples' minds: is there a political motive for this? In relation to the Mother and Child Scheme, I don't think the viewpoint of the hierarchy would have cut much ice in the country. Browne was very clever in making it an issue. The idea of a Mother and Child Scheme is appealing. Conditions were different. Regarding mothers and children, facilities were inadequate, so anything which provided for improvement, and was to be free, had tremendous appeal politically in the country.

Browne manoeuvred himself in an extremely capable fashion into becoming a martyr. He was ably guided by Noel Hartnett in all this. He was quite a clever political animal, in spite of his lack of experience. Let me say this as a hindsight commentary. He was extremely clever in fashioning an issue in which he could have really swept the country. He was disastrously inept in his handling of the issue which he had so well fashioned. I think that if he had been clever, he could certainly have built up a big party for himself, and ultimately have become possibly the head of a government. But because of his irresponsible way of handling it, and because of the childishly crude methods which he used from time to time, he destroyed the strength of the issue which he had fashioned.

I had relations of varying degrees with some of the hierarchy, for instance Dr Dignan, Bishop of Clonfert, for whom I had tremendous respect and with whom I worked on the building of a hospital in Ballinasloe. He was the only progressive bishop at that time. I always had fairly friendly contacts with the Dr Kyne from Mullingar. I had talks with him from time to time on social revolution and the need for a more progressive attitude on the part of the Church and the part of the State, and so on. I also had relations with the Archbishop of Dublin, John Charles. My relations with him were cold, but became friendlier as time went on. We used to talk about a number of matters. He was a Francophile too and was very interested in the attitudes of the French

Church. These were the kind of rather non-political discussions which we used have. It was interesting; he was well informed. I represented Ireland at the opening of Holy Year in Rome in January 1950, for purely diplomatic reasons, the same as thirty or forty other Catholic countries did throughout the world. It was natural that the government should be represented at the major Catholic celebration in Rome. My recollection is that I travelled together with several other ministers, on a plane from Paris to Rome.

I knew Dr Walsh, Archbishop of Tuam. He was a nice old man, a friend. I can't say that there was ever any pressure exerted on me. The Taoiseach might have been a little bit more deferential to the bishops than I was. I had been excommunicated twice. The first time it was a rather vague kind of excommunication. A declaration was made by some bishops against the IRA, saying that any person who was actively in the IRA was breaking the law of God. And then we were excommunicated – bell, book and candle. This led to a feeling that the hierarchy may have their views, but they are not necessarily acceptable when it comes to politics.

On the question of afforestation, I got very interested, particularly at the time of the Currency Commission and in connection with the work I was doing with Mrs Berthon Waters, Bulmer Hobson and Peadar O'Loughlin. As far as trees were concerned, our support came from varying quarters, from people involved in forestry, and some professional foresters like Hugh Fitzpatrick. Others who had been studying Irish economics were interested in forestry and there was also general support from those who liked the countryside.

Afforestation had been one of our principal planks on the Clann na Poblachta platform in the pre-1948 situation. It was one of the conditions I had made before participating in the government, that we would place no financial limits on afforestation. Later on I was to arrange that, under the Marshall Aid plan for economic recovery, we would plant a minimum of 20,000 acres a year in the country. This was done with a considerable amount of difficulty, not from my colleagues in the government, but from the civil service, particularly the Department of Lands and the Department of Finance. Finance, as usual, opposed any investment projects. Forests were an investment project. I could never understand their basis for objection, as investment in forestry was far sounder than investment in foreign securities, which they favoured. It was also a form of public work which provided much greater labour content. On a given expenditure, many more people are employed in planting trees than in building roads. In order to back these moves, we formed an association called 'Trees for Ireland'. It undertook the task of promoting a favourable public climate for afforestation throughout Ireland. It has done quite a lot of useful work, quietly, on that front.

I was also very much involved in the development of waterways. I felt that they had been badly neglected. There was a tendency to want to shut down the Grand Canal completely so we started a campaign against this. Throughout the war the canal had been one of our main arteries, enabling us to feed Dublin. There was also a tendency in favour of building bridges over the Shannon which would prevent any large boats from passing up and down the Shannon. I felt that this was also a retrograde step. We started a campaign for the development of the Shannon. I was able to arrange with Bill Norton in the second inter-party government (though I wasn't a member of it) to open up the Shannon for tourist purposes, and to that end we arranged to have a service of pleasure boats set up from Killaloe to Carrick-on-Shannon. These were operated by CIE in order to get the Shannon better known and to develop it. This had a tremendous impact on the development of the Shannon, which is now one of the principal tourist attractions of the country. There are several thousand boats on the Shannon now. I was always interested in boats. I absolutely love the Shannon; it is a beautiful place. I knew it well, and had a boat there since the 1930s, a very old boat called the *Lady Di*. We finally founded the Inland Waterways Association in 1953. Harry Rice from Athlone was a tremendous help in all this; indeed, he was really the prime mover. As far as the inland waterways were concerned, support came from a very different segment. First of all it came from people who enjoyed boats, sailing, who enjoyed the environmental aspects of the Shannon, the canal and so on. It also came from those who realised that there was an economic future in the development of the waterways.

I fought an unsuccessful battle to protect our railways, which started during the administration of the second inter-party government. I discovered a memorandum that had been leaked, pointing out that our railway system was wholly uneconomic, that we should not keep it, that it should be scrapped. I raised this very sharply at the time, with Norton in particular. This I think had been done unbeknownst to Norton. I was able to obtain some assurances from the government that this would not be acted upon.

Civil servants tended to be anti-railway and pro-road transport. That never appealed to me very much in that I felt that the estimates on which they based the economics of road transport disregarded the cost of road-making and road maintenance. They were based purely and simply on the cost of the lorries and the labour employed. If a comparison were to be made, it would have to be based on the cost of roads and road transport matched against maintaining the permanent track on a railway line. There had been an anti-railway bias and finally it was decided to set up an investigation. A good report was prepared by an English railway executive, which provided the solution which I believe should have been adopted then. The government didn't adopt it; it was shelved. In brief, this engineer, whose name I think was Milne, proposed that roads and railway tracks should be treated equally and financed by government. The railway lines could then be hired out to railway companies or to a state railway company. The basic course of maintenance of tracks and roads should be done by the government itself. Thereafter there should be free competition between road and rail. This was successfully buried by government and the civil service.

A change of government then took place and promptly the suburban lines were scrapped with indecent haste. I have never seen a government operation or concern acting as rapidly as they did in dismantling the railway line from Harcourt Street to Bray. This was a piece of gross political indecency in my view. Of course Todd Andrews was following government policy, they knew very little about railways.

INDEX